CARS, TRAINS, SHIPS & PLANES

SMITHSONIAN INSTITUTION

Established in 1846, the Smithsonian Institution—the world's largest museum and research complex—includes 19 museums and galleries and the National Zoological Park. The total number of artefacts, works of art, and specimens in the Smithsonian's collection is estimated at 137 million, the bulk of which is contained in the National Museum of Natural History, which holds more than 126 million specimens and objects. The Smithsonian is a renowned research centre, dedicated to public education, national service, and scholarship in the arts, sciences, and history.

ABOUT THE AUTHOR

Clive Gifford is the winner of the Royal Society Young People's Book Prize and the School Library Association Information Book Award. He has written more than 150 books including **Wow! Science**, **Car Crazy**, and **Super Trucks**.

SMITHSONIAN

CARS, TRAINS, SHIPS & PLANES

A visual encyclopedia of every vehicle

WRITTEN BY **CLIVE GIFFORD**

DK India

Project Editor Sneha Sunder Benjamin
Project Art Editor Vaibhav Rastogi
Editor Medha Gupta
Art Editor Rakesh Khundongbam
Assistant Editor Isha Sharma
Assistant Art Editors Anusri Saha, Riti Sodhi
Jacket Designer Dhirendra Singh
Jacket Managing Editor Saloni Singh
DTP Designer Jaypal Chauhan
Senior DTP Designers Harish Aggarwal, Neeraj Bhatia
Picture Researcher Aditya Katyal
Managing Editor Rohan Sinha
Managing Art Editor Sudakshina Basu
Pre-production Manager Balwant Singh
Production Manager Pankaj Sharma

DK UK

Senior Editor Francesca Baines
Senior Art Editor Rachael Grady
US Editor Allison Singer
Jacket Designer Mark Cavanagh
Jacket Assistant Claire Gell
Managing Editor Linda Esposito
Managing Art Editor Philip Letsu
Pre-production Controllers Nikoleta Parasaki, Gillian Reid
Production Controller Srijana Gurung
Design Development Manager Sophia MTT
Publisher Andrew Macintyre
Art Director Karen Self
Associate Publishing Director Liz Wheeler
Publishing Director Jonathan Metcalf

First American Edition, 2015
Published in the United States by DK Publishing
345 Hudson Street, New York, New York 10014

Copyright © 2015 Dorling Kindersley Limited
A Penguin Random House Company

17 18 19 10 9 8 7 6 5 4 3
005–192634–September/2015

Published in Great Britain by Dorling Kindersley Limited.

A catalog record for this book is available from the Library of Congress.

ISBN 978-1-4654-3805-8

DK books are available at special discounts when purchased in bulk for sales promotions, premiums, fund-raising, or educational use. For details, contact: DK Publishing Special Markets, 345 Hudson Street, New York, New York 10014 or SpecialSales@dk.com

Printed in China

A WORLD OF IDEAS:
SEE ALL THERE IS TO KNOW

www.dk.com

CONTENTS

Water 152

Air 196

KTM 350 SX-F

Peel P50

New Holland T6.140

Foreword

Welcome to the world of fast cars and even faster planes, of mighty ships, awesome motorcycles, and heavy hauling trucks and trains. All these and many more machines that move people, goods, and materials can be found in this big book of transportation.

I have had a fascination with transportation for as long as I can remember. My father flew gliders and worked for an early airline company that offered many people their first taste of air travel. I remember him taking me to an air show when I was eleven to see an array of amazing aircraft—from massive jet bombers to nimble aerobatic biplanes. I found them astonishing, just as I did the giant trucks and two Ferrari supercars in the air show's parking lot. I was hooked and have remained excited by all forms of transportation ever since.

This book is packed with vehicles, craft, and vessels that have enabled people to travel farther, faster, and with greater ease—from the slickest street bike to the most powerful diesel train. Many have played their part in changing people's lives, and how and where they work and live. Before the development of modern cars, trains, ships, and planes, few people traveled outside

DHR Class B

De Dion-Bouton Type O

Bücker Bü133C Jungmeister

Montgolfier Hot-air Balloon

of their own neighborhood and even fewer traveled long distances overseas. Today, coast-to-coast journeys that once took weeks take hours, while you can cross the planet in less than a day on a giant jet airliner. Shipping now connects all parts of the globe, enabling you to buy food grown on the other side of the world and many other goods, too. Advances in transportation have helped people explore and settle new lands, make exciting discoveries about our world, and even blast off, leaving the planet altogether to explore the marvels of space.

Clive Gifford

Throughout this book you will find scale boxes that show the sizes of types of transportation compared to either a child or a school bus.

 Child = 4 ft 9 in (1.45 m) tall

 School bus = 36 ft (11 m) long

Unicycle

Sea-Doo® Spark™

John Deere 650K XLT

On the road

The first automobile was a steam-powered cart that set off in 1769 at a top speed of 2.5 mph (4 km/h). Over the years, many clever inventions have helped shape modern motor vehicles. Today, more than one billion travel along the world's roads.

1769 French inventor Nicolas-Joseph Cugnot builds the first working automobile.

1868 The first traffic lights are installed in London. Not long afterward, they explode!

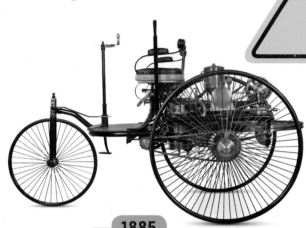

1927
The Napier-Campbell *Blue Bird* sets a land-speed record of 195 mph (314 km/h).

Blue Bird

1876
German engineer Nikolaus Otto builds the first internal combustion engine.

1885
The Benz Motorwagen, the first wheeled vehicle powered by an internal combustion engine, takes to the road.

1850

1900

1894
In Germany, Hildebrand and Wolfmüller build the Motorrad, the first production motorcycle.

1880
Several inventors develop so-called "safety bicycles" driven by a pedal and chain mechanism.

1908
The Ford Model T goes on sale in the USA. It becomes the first car to be mass-produced on an assembly line.

1871
The High Wheeler, the first bicycle with big front wheels to boost speed, is designed.

1916 The first fully working armored tank, the Mark 1, goes into battle in France in World War I.

Ford Model T

1979 Bigfoot, the first monster truck, is developed in the USA by Bob Chandler for off-road adventures.

2013 British company FlashPark invents a talking parking ticket.

1938

The Volkswagen Type 1, or Beetle, rolls off the production line in Germany. Over the years, a further 21.5 million are built.

1997

Thrust SSC sets a world land-speed record of 763 mph (1,228 km/h), faster than the speed of sound.

1950

The world's first Formula 1 World Championship is won by Italy's Giuseppe Farina in an Alfa Romeo 159.

1980

The world's longest recorded traffic jam of 105 miles (170 km) blocks roads in France.

1950

2000

1946

In Italy, Vespa produces its first scooter, sparking a fashion craze from the 1950s onward.

1981

Stumpjumper, the first mass-produced mountain bicycle, goes on sale in the USA.

2005

A Bugatti Veyron sets the record for the world's fastest production car, clocking 253 mph (407 km/h).

1940

The Jeep is first introduced as a general purpose light truck.

Jeep

Bugatti Veyron

1949 Sierra Sam becomes the first fully formed crash test dummy, used to test the safety features of cars.

9

Along the tracks

Steam locomotives were known as "iron horses" when they started a transportation revolution in the early 1800s, speeding up the movement of people and goods all over the world. Today, diesel and electric locomotives have taken over from steam.

1829

The first modern steam locomotive, the *Rocket*, built by Robert Stephenson, sets new speed records.

1830 The first intercity steam passenger service, the Liverpool and Manchester Railway, begins.

1913
Grand Central Terminal opens in New York. The station has the most number of tracks— 67 in all.

1881

The first electric streetcar service begins in Germany.

1770

Scottish inventor James Watt invents the compound steam engine, versions of which will power early locomotives.

1869

The first Transcontinental Railroad across the USA is completed—a total of 1,907 miles (3,069 km) of tracks.

1800

1850

1900

1804

The *Pen-y-Darren* locomotive is built by British inventor Richard Trevithick, for work in mines.

1863

The first underground city railroad, the Metropolitan Line, opens in London.

1914

Throughout World War I, railroads prove invaluable for moving troops and supplies.

1906
The Simplon Tunnel, connecting Italy and Switzerland under the Alps, opens. It is the world's longest railroad tunnel.

Pen-y-Darren locomotive

10

Golden Eagle Trans-Siberian Express

1916

The world's longest railroad line, the Trans-Siberian Railway across Russia, is completed. It runs for 5,772 miles (9,289 km).

1937

German inventor Hermann Kemper develops magnetic levitation (maglev) as a force for moving trains.

1960

French Railways introduce the world's first 125 mph (200 km/h) service—the Le Capitole.

1964

The world's first bullet train, Shinkansen, connects Tokyo to other cities of Japan.

1994
The high-speed Channel Tunnel Eurostar service begins from London to Paris.

1984

In the UK, the first commercial maglev transportation system opens, connecting Birmingham International Airport and nearby terminals.

2012

Tokyo metro carries 3.29 billion passengers in a year, making it the busiest metro system in the world.

1950

2000

1955

Initial trials of the English Electric *Deltic*—the most powerful diesel locomotive in the world—take place.

1975

In the UK, the Inter-City HST becomes the fastest diesel-powered train in the world.

2007

An experimental French TGV sets the world record for the fastest electric train, with a speed of 357 mph (574 km/h).

2015

First passenger-carrying test run of Japan's new maglev train system. Trains reach speeds of 373 mph (600 km/h).

1938

The *Mallard* sets the world record for the fastest-ever steam locomotive, at a speed of more than 125 mph (200 km/h).

1988 The world's longest underwater railroad tunnel, the Seikan Tunnel, 33.5 miles (53.9 km) long, is built to connect two Japanese islands.

Across the water

Humans have been traveling by water for so long that it is impossible to know exactly when the first boats were built. Some have changed little over the centuries, but today there are also hi-tech speedboats, mighty tankers, and giant cruise liners on the waters of the world.

Santa Maria

1768
Captain James Cook sets off from England to explore the South Pacific. His voyage takes three years and covers more than 30,000 miles (48,000 km).

1492
Explorer Christopher Columbus sails west from Spain in the *Santa Maria*. He crosses the Atlantic Ocean and lands in the Bahamas.

1661
The first recorded yacht race takes place, between the English King Charles II and his brother James, on the Thames River in London.

1500

1600

1700

1510
The English ship *Mary Rose* is one of the first to be built with gunports, holes for cannons to fire through.

1620
The *Mayflower* leaves Plymouth, England, taking 102 pilgrims to settle in the New World (America).

Mayflower

1716
In the early 1700s, the waters of the Caribbean were at their most dangerous, as pirates plundered Spanish treasure ships.

1519
Portuguese navigator Ferdinand Magellan sets out with a fleet of five ships. Just one would make it back in 1522, having completed the first voyage around the world.

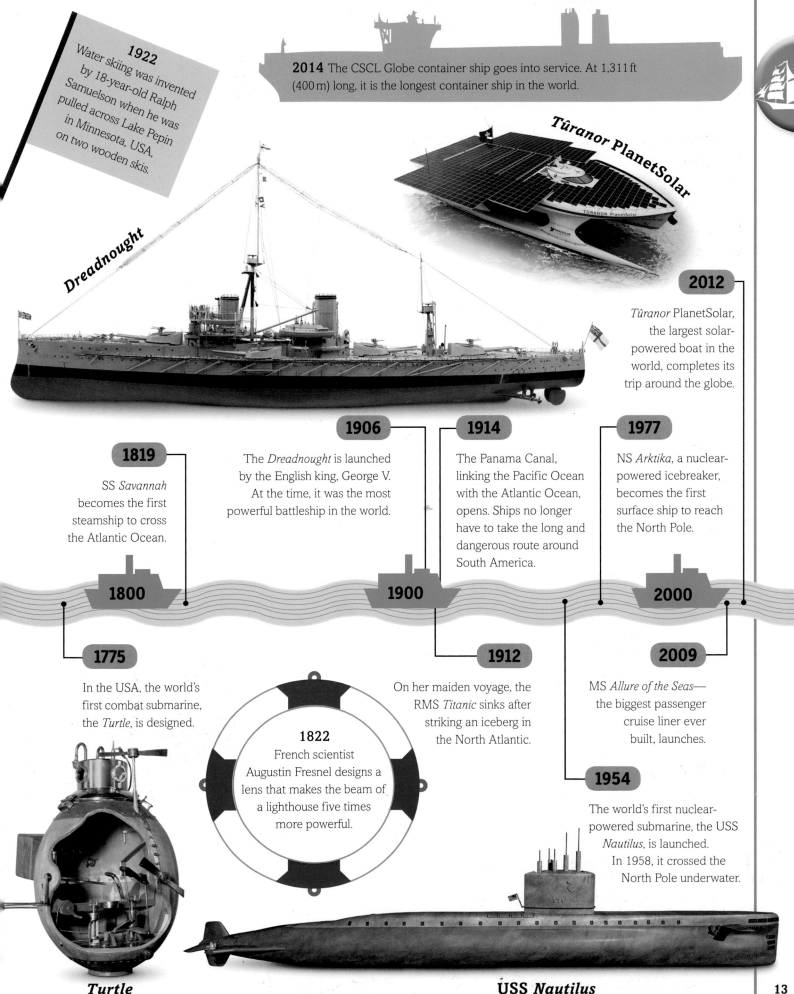

1922 Water skiing was invented by 18-year-old Ralph Samuelson when he was pulled across Lake Pepin in Minnesota, USA, on two wooden skis.

2014 The CSCL Globe container ship goes into service. At 1,311 ft (400 m) long, it is the longest container ship in the world.

Tûranor PlanetSolar

Dreadnought

2012
Tûranor PlanetSolar, the largest solar-powered boat in the world, completes its trip around the globe.

1819
SS *Savannah* becomes the first steamship to cross the Atlantic Ocean.

1906
The *Dreadnought* is launched by the English king, George V. At the time, it was the most powerful battleship in the world.

1914
The Panama Canal, linking the Pacific Ocean with the Atlantic Ocean, opens. Ships no longer have to take the long and dangerous route around South America.

1977
NS *Arktika*, a nuclear-powered icebreaker, becomes the first surface ship to reach the North Pole.

1800

1900

2000

1775
In the USA, the world's first combat submarine, the *Turtle*, is designed.

1822
French scientist Augustin Fresnel designs a lens that makes the beam of a lighthouse five times more powerful.

1912
On her maiden voyage, the RMS *Titanic* sinks after striking an iceberg in the North Atlantic.

2009
MS *Allure of the Seas*— the biggest passenger cruise liner ever built, launches.

1954
The world's first nuclear-powered submarine, the USS *Nautilus*, is launched. In 1958, it crossed the North Pole underwater.

Turtle

USS Nautilus

Up in the air

Powered flight took off in 1903 when American brothers Wilbur and Orville Wright attached an engine to a glider and traveled through air for 12 seconds. This short flight blazed the trail for supersonic jets, giant airliners, and even spacecraft.

1913 Russian Pyotr Nesterov becomes the first pilot to fly a loop-the-loop.

1785 Frenchman Jean-Pierre Blanchard and American John Jeffries fly across the English Channel in a balloon.

1783

In Paris, France, the Montgolfier brothers' hot-air balloon makes the world's first manned flight, lasting 25 minutes.

1900 The first rigid airship, the Zeppelin LZ1, makes its maiden voyage in Germany.

1903

The Wright brothers' first powered flying machine, the *Wright Flyer*, takes off in the USA.

1850

1900

1907

The first flight of a rotary-wing aircraft, forerunner of the helicopter, is piloted by French engineer Paul Cornu.

1896

American inventor Samuel Pierpont Langley flies his steam-powered model aircraft, the *Aerodrome*.

1891

German "Flying man" Otto Lilienthal makes the first of more than 2,000 flights in a series of fixed-wing gliders.

1852

Frenchman Jules Henri Giffard's steam-powered airship makes its first flight, proving controlled flight is possible.

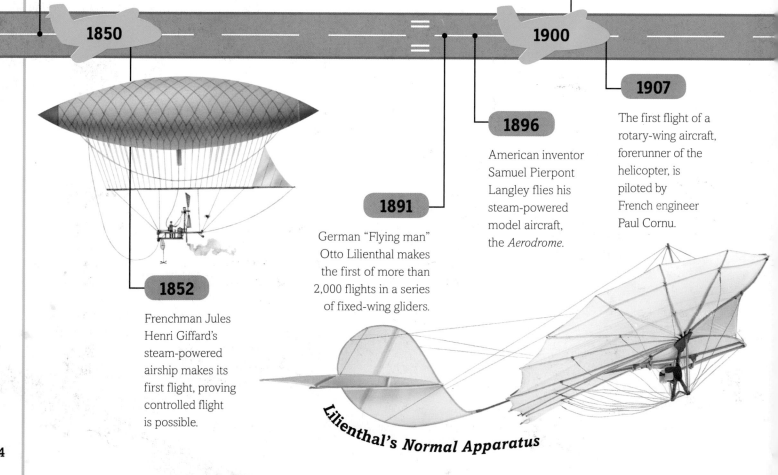

Lilienthal's Normal Apparatus

1930 A nurse by profession, Ellen Church becomes the first flight attendant.

Space Shuttle Columbia

1969

In the UK, the Hawker Siddeley Harrier becomes the first vertical-take-off-and-landing (VTOL) military jet in service.

1969

The US Apollo 11 spacecraft takes off for the moon. Two of its astronauts become the first humans to walk on the lunar surface.

1981

Space Shuttle *Columbia* lifts off from Cape Canaveral, Florida, for its first space mission. The Space Shuttle program continues until 2011.

1938

The American Boeing 307 Stratoliner, the first airliner with a pressurized cabin, helps make flying a pleasant experience for passengers.

1950

1952

In the UK, the first commercial jet airliner, the de Havilland Comet, enters service.

British airways

2000

1961

Russian cosmonaut Yuri Gagarin becomes the first man in space. He orbits the Earth for 108 minutes onboard his Vostok 1 spacecraft.

1927

American Charles Lindbergh makes the first nonstop flight across North Atlantic in his Ryan NYP *Spirit of St Louis*, a distance of more than 3,600 miles (5,800 km).

1976

The UK/French supersonic airliner the Concorde enters passenger service.

2014

After a 10-year journey, the European Space Agency spacecraft *Rosetta* reaches a comet and lands a probe on its surface.

1949 A B-50 Superfortress makes the first nonstop flight around the world. It is refueled in midair four times!

LAND

Animal power

*Handler, called **musher**, gives commands to dogs*

Husky sled Arctic region

Roman chariots pulled by **four horses** could race at speeds of 30 mph (50 km/h).

Wooden, spoked wheel

Chariot Rome 200 BCE

Leather harness

Canvas cover stretched over iron hoops to provide protection against weather

Reins are attached to the harness at the mouth

Liverpool gig UK 1800s

Straight backrest

Chuck wagon USA 1866

Conestoga wagon USA 18th and 19th century

Distinctive glass lanterns

The Glass Coach is used for the **weddings** of the British royal family.

The Glass Coach UK 1881

For thousands of years, people have harnessed the power of large animals to transport them and their goods. Oxen, dogs, horses, mules, and reindeer have all been used to pull sleds or haul wagons and, in some parts of the world, still do.

As early as 3000 BCE, animals were used to pull the first chariots into battle in the Middle East and Asia. Later, the Romans turned **chariot** racing into a sport, using lightweight designs in which the driver rode from a small platform over the wheel axle. Wagons got bigger when pioneers set

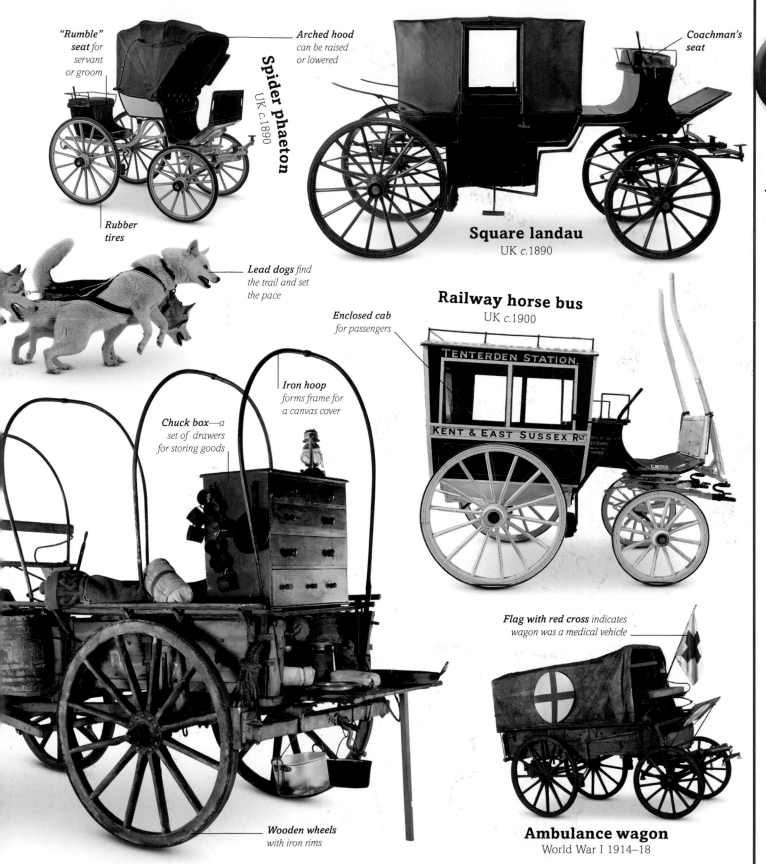

"Rumble" seat for servant or groom

Arched hood can be raised or lowered

Spider phaeton
UK c.1890

Rubber tires

Coachman's seat

Square landau
UK c.1890

Lead dogs find the trail and set the pace

Railway horse bus
UK c.1900

Enclosed cab for passengers

TENTERDEN STATION.

KENT & EAST SUSSEX R{ LY}

Iron hoop forms frame for a canvas cover

Chuck box—a set of drawers for storing goods

Flag with red cross indicates wagon was a medical vehicle

Wooden wheels with iron rims

Ambulance wagon
World War I 1914–18

off across North America in the 18th and 19th centuries. The four-wheeled, covered **Conestoga wagon** could carry five tons of food, tools, and belongings, and was usually pulled by oxen. Not long after, fully working kitchens on wheels, called **chuck wagons**, could be seen following cowboys

as they herded cattle across the country. In the towns, small, lightweight carriages such as the **Liverpool gig** or the **Spider phaeton** carried up to two people on short journeys, while bigger carriages, such as the **Square landau** could transport four people in greater comfort.

CAMEL CARAVAN

Out of the way, there's a convoy coming through! It's made up of camels carrying salt—Ethiopia's white gold, mined from the Danakil Depression. Highly prized, both to flavor food and preserve it, salt is levered out of the giant salt flats at Danakil in slabs. These slabs are then cut into blocks and lashed onto the backs of the camels, the ultimate desert pack animal.

Caravans (convoys) of pack animals—from camels, horses, and mules, to yaks, llamas, and even elephants—have been used throughout history to transport food, materials, and goods for trade. Camels are famed for their ability to withstand heat and a lack of water, making them perfect for cargo-carrying trips across hot deserts. This route across Ethiopia, from Danakil to the trading center of Mekele, involves a 60-mile (100-km) trek across one of the hottest places on Earth, with temperatures soaring past 122°F (50°C). Salt caravans have crossed the Sahara for more than 2,000 years. In the past, thousands of animals made up the camel trains, but today 20 to 30 are more common.

Bicycle

Bicycles are a fun and efficient way of getting around. A cyclist can travel around four to five times faster than a walker, using the same amount of energy. Although designs vary, most bicycles share common key parts. A chain, powered by a chainwheel and driven by pedals and cranks, transmits power to the rear wheel, which turns and drives the bicycle forward.

Saddle ❯ The bicycle's seat can be solid or padded for comfort. It is attached to a seat post, which slides into the frame's seat tube.

Seat post

Rear brake cable

Seat tube

Rear brake

Wheel and tire ❯ These support the weight of the bicycle and the rider. Different tires have different patterns on their outer surface known as tread. This bicycle has smooth tread tires for road racing. An off-road bicycle will have chunkier tread to provide better grip.

Gear cable

Rear derailleur ❯ The derailleur gear moves the chain to different gear cogs.

Spokes ❯ Thin and strong, spokes connect the wheel's rim to its center, or hub. They allow wheels to be built that are strong but light in weight, and they let air through when the wheel faces the wind.

Chainwheel

Bottom bracket

Chain

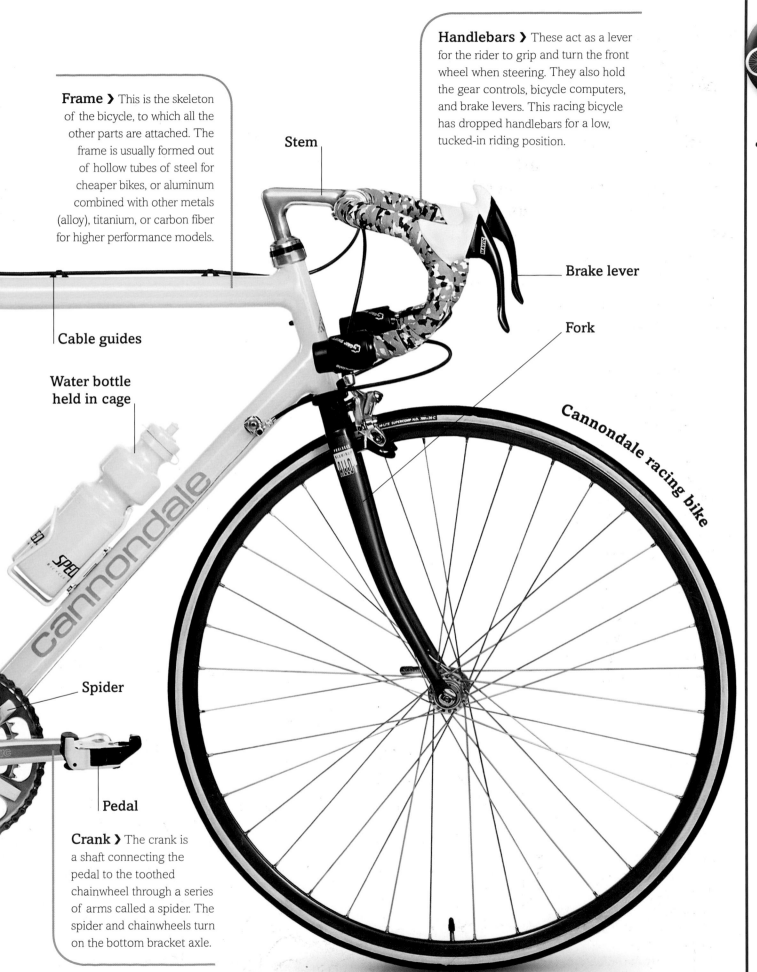

Frame > This is the skeleton of the bicycle, to which all the other parts are attached. The frame is usually formed out of hollow tubes of steel for cheaper bikes, or aluminum combined with other metals (alloy), titanium, or carbon fiber for higher performance models.

Handlebars > These act as a lever for the rider to grip and turn the front wheel when steering. They also hold the gear controls, bicycle computers, and brake levers. This racing bicycle has dropped handlebars for a low, tucked-in riding position.

Stem

Brake lever

Fork

Cannondale racing bike

Cable guides

Water bottle held in cage

Spider

Pedal

Crank > The crank is a shaft connecting the pedal to the toothed chainwheel through a series of arms called a spider. The spider and chainwheels turn on the bottom bracket axle.

Pedal power

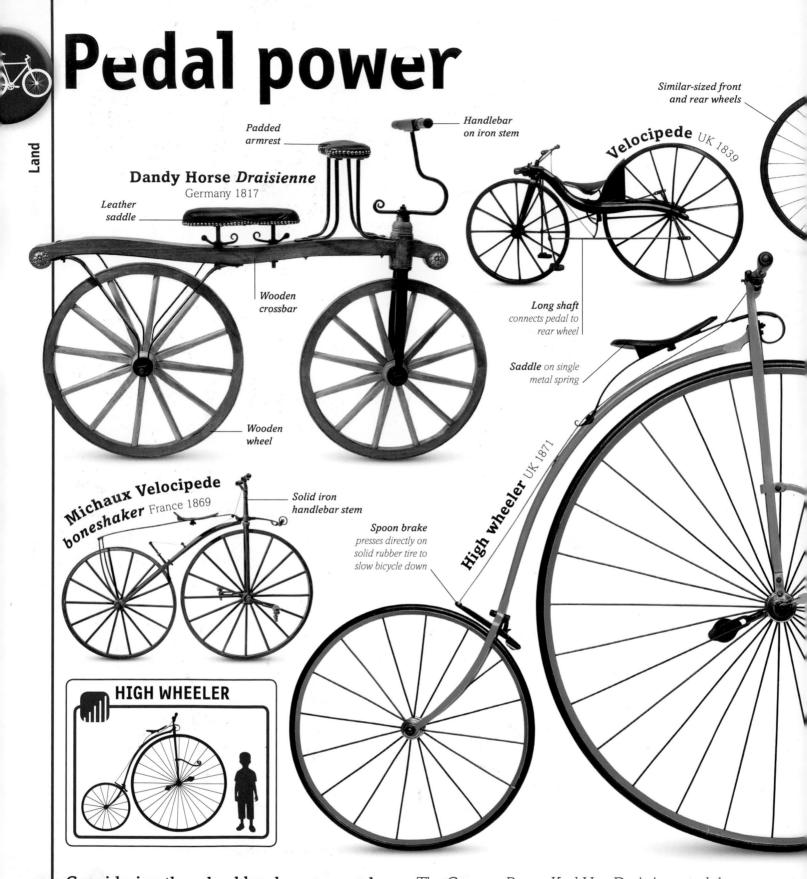

Dandy Horse *Draisienne*
Germany 1817

Padded armrest

Handlebar on iron stem

Leather saddle

Wooden crossbar

Wooden wheel

Similar-sized front and rear wheels

Velocipede UK 1839

Long shaft connects pedal to rear wheel

Saddle on single metal spring

Michaux Velocipede *boneshaker* France 1869

Solid iron handlebar stem

High wheeler UK 1871

Spoon brake presses directly on solid rubber tire to slow bicycle down

HIGH WHEELER

Considering the wheel has been around for more than 5,000 years, it is amazing to think that it was only 200 years ago people finally got the idea to place two wheels on a frame and create pedal-powered personal transportation.

The German Baron Karl Von Drais invented the **Dandy Horse** in 1817, which had a saddle and handlebars but was powered by a rider paddling his feet along the ground. It led to other human-powered machines, including the **Michaux Velocipede**, which had pedals fitted directly

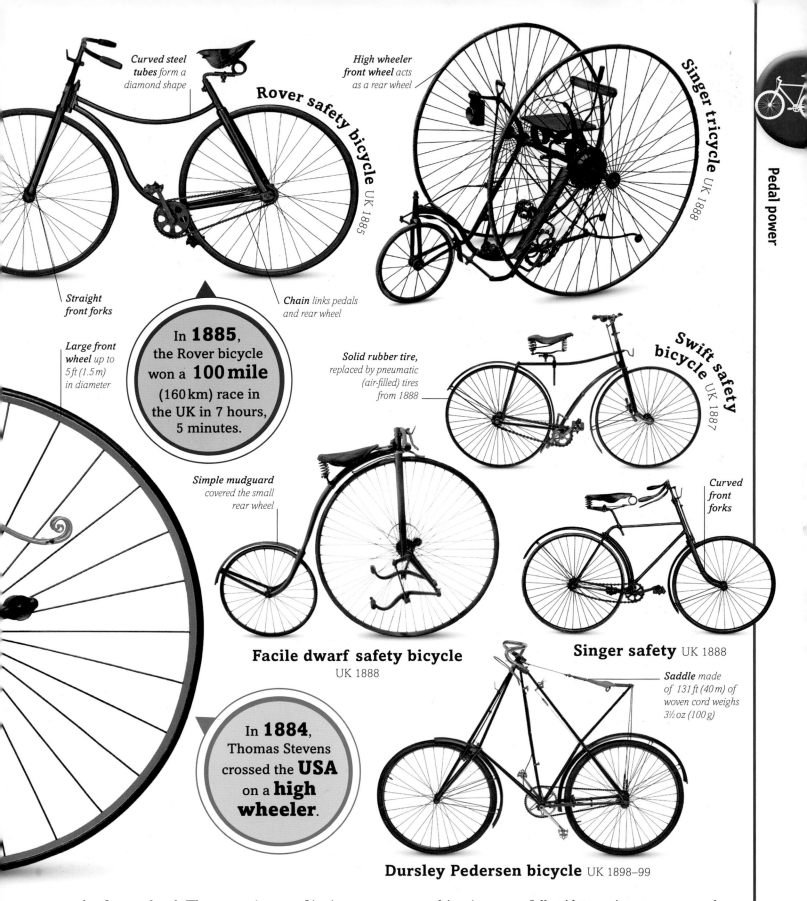

Curved steel tubes form a diamond shape

Rover safety bicycle UK 1885

High wheeler front wheel acts as a rear wheel

Singer tricycle UK 1888

Straight front forks

Chain links pedals and rear wheel

Large front wheel up to 5 ft (1.5 m) in diameter

In **1885**, the Rover bicycle won a **100 mile** (160 km) race in the UK in 7 hours, 5 minutes.

Solid rubber tire, replaced by pneumatic (air-filled) tires from 1888

Swift safety bicycle UK 1887

Simple mudguard covered the small rear wheel

Curved front forks

Facile dwarf safety bicycle UK 1888

Singer safety UK 1888

In **1884**, Thomas Stevens crossed the **USA** on a **high wheeler**.

Saddle made of 131 ft (40 m) of woven cord weighs 3½ oz (100 g)

Dursley Pedersen bicycle UK 1898–99

to the front wheel. The experience of its iron "tires" on cobbled streets earned it the nickname *boneshaker*. **High wheelers**, or Penny Farthings, in the UK, France, and the USA had no chains or gears, but had bigger front wheels to boost speed. It perched the rider high above the ground, resulting in many falls. Alternatives were sought, including pairing two high wheeler front wheels to form the rear wheels of the **Singer tricycle**, and using a chain-driven rear wheel, as in the **Rover safety bicycle**. This design ushered in the modern bicycle with wheels of similar size.

Speed wheels

Isaac Force Germany 2005

Seat post

Dedacciai Strada Assoluto Italy 2011

Rear wheel with spokes and carbon fiber rim

Dropped handlebars

Tires inflated with helium gas to save ⅜–⁹⁄₁₆oz (10–15 g) per tire

Molded carbon fiber frame

This revolutionary track bicycle weighed just **20 lb (9 kg)**.

Women's bicycles often have narrower handlebars

Single, fixed gear

Marin Ravenna A6WFG USA 2012

If you have a need for speed, then a racing bicycle is for you. Designed for fast riding on smooth surfaces, racing bicycles are light in weight with a high seat and low, dropped handlebars.

Not all racing bicycles are used for racing. Many are used by cyclists to commute rapidly to work or for a workout. Frames are designed for both men and women; the **Ravenna A6WFG** is a women's racing bicycle designed for endurance riding. Competition racing bikes are designed with super-

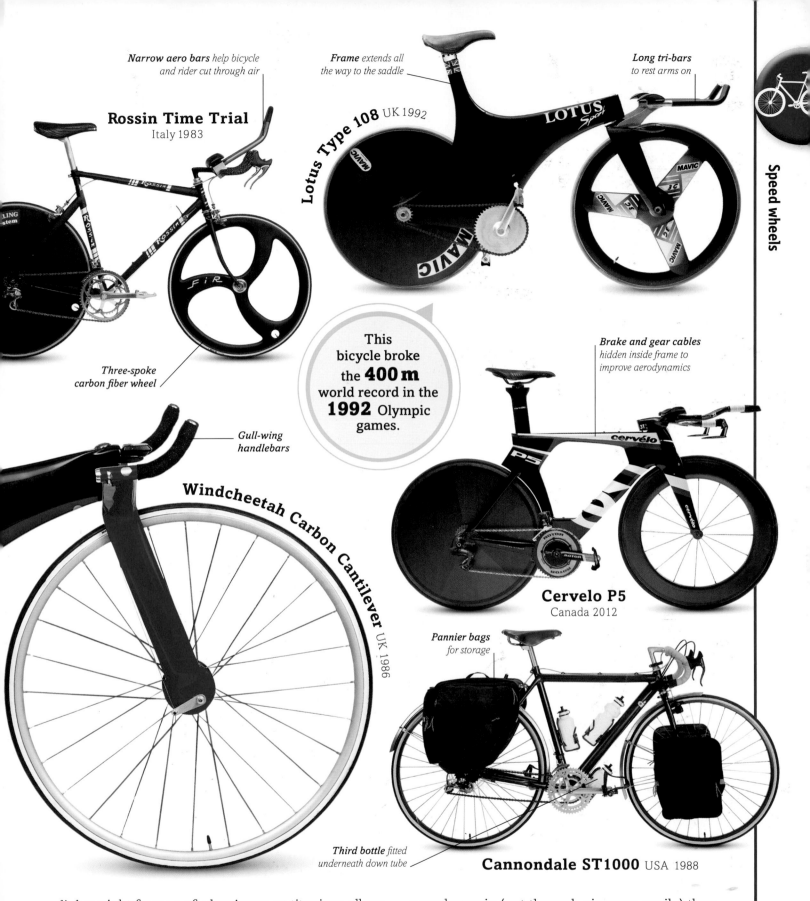

Narrow aero bars help bicycle and rider cut through air

Frame extends all the way to the saddle

Long tri-bars to rest arms on

Rossin Time Trial
Italy 1983

Lotus Type 108 UK 1992

Three-spoke carbon fiber wheel

This bicycle broke the **400 m** world record in the **1992** Olympic games.

Brake and gear cables *hidden inside frame to improve aerodynamics*

Gull-wing handlebars

Windcheetah Carbon Cantilever UK 1986

Cervelo P5
Canada 2012

Pannier bags *for storage*

Third bottle *fitted underneath down tube*

Cannondale ST1000 USA 1988

lightweight frames of aluminum or titanium alloys, or carbon fiber. The **Assoluto's** carbon fiber frame weighs just 2 lb 6 oz (1.1 kg), a little more than a baseball bat. Solid disk rear wheels are used on track racers, in time trials, and on triathlete's bikes such as the **Cervelo P5**, because they are more aerodynamic (cut through air more easily) than wheels with spokes. Solid-bodied track racers, such as the **Windcheetah Carbon Cantilever**, appeared in the 1980s with a solid carbon fiber body. They were tested in wind tunnels to ensure they were as aerodynamic as possible.

SPRINT FINISH
You can feel the pain just watching these sprinters pump the pedals at the end of another grueling stage of the world's most famous bike race, the Tour de France. This stage—the tenth of the 2011 Tour—started 98 miles (158 km) back. In a photo finish, André Greipel of Germany (right) crossed the line a fraction ahead of Mark Cavendish of the UK (left). Both are given the time of 3 hours, 31 minutes, and 21 seconds.

The Tour de France takes place over three weeks every summer. It covers more than 2,175 miles (3,500 km), broken up into 21 stages. Each year, the route across France changes, sometimes entering other European countries, but it always challenges riders over all sorts of terrain, with stages on the flat, in the hills, and in the mountains. Around 20 teams take part, each with nine riders. The cyclists' times for each day are added together and the rider with the overall lowest time gets to wear the prized *maillot jaune* (yellow jersey). But there are also prizes for the fastest sprinter (green jersey), the fastest climber (red polka dot jersey), the fastest rider under 25 (white jersey), and for the fastest team.

Bike business

Wicker basket holds up to 55 lb (25 kg) of goods

Pashley Delibike UK 1948

Pannier bag contains emergency medical equipment

Response bicycle UK 2000

Butterfly screw can be loosened to fold frame in half

Folding stand supports the bicycle when parked

Flashing side lights on rack bag

BSA Airborne UK 1943

Tool bag hung from top tube of frame

Police mountain bicycle
Germany 2000s

Folded-up bicycle is less than 23 in (57 cm) in height and 22 in (55 cm) in length

There are more than **1,200 parts** in a Brompton Folding Bicycle.

Brompton Folding Bicycle UK 1981–83

Cycling may be lots of fun, but many people ride their bicycles to and from work, or use them in order to do their jobs. Bicycles offer a cheap, quick, and convenient way to get around, and to transport people and deliver goods.

In both crowded towns and cities, and isolated countryside areas, **police mountain bicycles** allow officers to get to a crime scene quickly. **Response bicycles**, with their pannier bags filled with lifesaving medical equipment, can get through traffic or crowds to reach a patient where

Container for letters and small packages

Hooded canopy provides shade

DHL Parcycle Netherlands 2014

Penang Trishaw Malaysia 1980s

Seat for up to two passengers

Canopy keeps ice cream shaded from Sun

Cart handle acts as bicycle's handlebars

Tricycle ice cream cart India 1980s

Height and angle of the saddle can be adjusted for maximum comfort

Brake and gear cabling hang loose, so the bike can be folded

Luggage rack can hold large bag

Small wire basket to carry shopping

Public bicycle China 2000s

Small, 16-in (40.6-cm) wheel

larger vehicles cannot go. The **BSA Airborne** was used by British troops during World War II—its frame folded in half when two butterfly screws were loosened. Folding bicycles, such as the **Brompton Folding Bicycle**, continue to be used by thousands of commuters. Delivery bicycles are equipped with baskets or carriers to carry cargo. The **DHL Parcycle** fits a giant container onto a bike to carry packages. Bicycles can also be modified, and their frames attached to carts or carriages, such as the **ice cream cart** and the pedal-powered **Penang Trishaw** taxi.

31

Fun on wheels

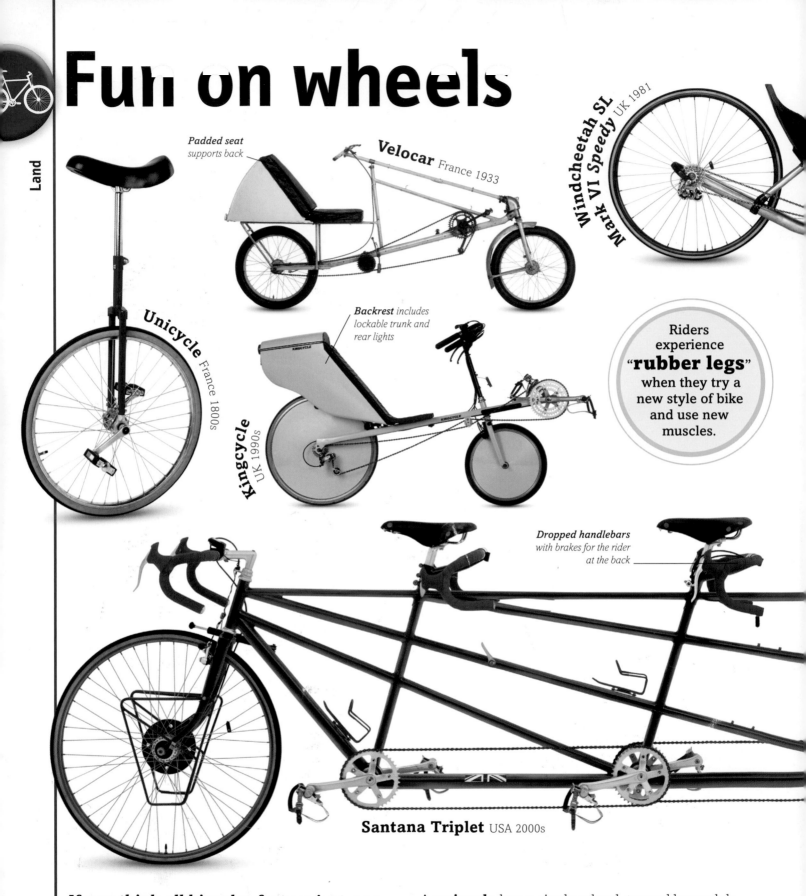

Padded seat supports back

Velocar France 1933

Windcheetah SL Mark VI Speedy UK 1981

Unicycle France 1800s

Backrest includes lockable trunk and rear lights

Kingcycle UK 1990s

Riders experience **"rubber legs"** when they try a new style of bike and use new muscles.

Dropped handlebars with brakes for the rider at the back

Santana Triplet USA 2000s

If you think all bicycles feature just one rider sitting upright, supported by two wheels, think again! Many variations on the bicycle's basic design have been attempted for greater speed, more comfort, or just for fun.

A **unicycle** has a single wheel, turned by pedals, and demands great balance from the rider to stay on. Three-wheelers are easier to ride, and some, such as the **Pashley Tri.1**, even offer a platform to carry large loads. Tandem bicycles, such as the **Dawes Galaxy Twin**, have two riders pedaling,

Joystick

Brakes on front wheel

Kingcycle Bean UK 1984

Body shell and bicycle weigh 82 lb (37.2 kg)

This slick bicycle has **joysticks** instead of **handlebars** for steering.

Hinged windshield acts as a door

Twike Switzerland 1995

Electric motor, plus pedal power, gives top speed of 15 mph (24 km/h)

Handlebars gripped under rider's knees

Twin seats

Sinclair C5 UK 1985

Platform to carry loads

Pashley Tri.1 UK 2013

Luggage rack

Hinged frame folds up for storage

Dawes Galaxy Twin UK 2008

Timing chain links two sets of pedals and chainwheels

but only the front rider steers. The **Santana Triplet** has seats for three riders, with a long chain linking each rider's chainwheel to ensure smooth pedaling. In recumbent bicycles, riders sit or lie down with their legs out in front; the bicycle is low and can slip through air at high speed.

The **Windcheetah** *Speedy* was cycled the length of the UK in just 41 hours, 4 minutes, 22 seconds. Some recumbents fit a body shell around the rider to let air flow past more smoothly. In 1990, the **Kingcycle Bean** set a world speed record of 47 mph (76 km/h) over one hour.

33

Extreme cycling

Trek 8900 Pro USA 1990

Suspension allows front forks to telescope down into lower tubes when hitting bumps

Frame made of carbon fiber tubes fitted to aluminum joints

Specialized Stumpjumper USA 1981

Gear changer on the handlebar helps select between the bicycle's 15 gears

Single gear cog on rear wheel

Raleigh Kool Max UK 2000s

2ft-6in- (6.4-cm-) wide tire for great grip in sand, dirt, and mud

Some mountain bicycles have up to **30 gears** to speed over different conditions.

Fat Chance Yo-Eddy USA 1991

Trek 6000 USA 1991

Toe straps secure rider's feet on pedals

Shock absorber cushions bumps

Hydraulic (fluid-operated) disk brakes

Stumpjumper FSR Pro USA 2004

While ordinary bicycles can be ridden off-road, their smooth tires and slender frames are not suitable for rough stuff. When bikers in the USA began redesigning bicycles for better off-road performances in the 1970s, mountain biking was born!

The first mountain bicycle made on a large scale was the **Specialized Stumpjumper**. Only 500 were initially produced, but they started a revolution. Soon, many manufacturers came up with their own designs. The **Trek 6000** had a lightweight, all-aluminum frame, while the **Trek**

Rubber grips on handlebar

Derailleur gear system has 20 different gears for rider to select from

Front forks have suspension that can slide as much as 3.8 in (99 mm) to cushion bumps

Cushioned saddle with plastic covering

Large frame

RALEIGH

KOOL max

Rigid forks

Chain guard stops clothing from snagging on chain

Marin Nail Trail
USA 2014

Reflector fitted to wheel spokes

Foot peg for stepping on when performing tricks

INSTINCT

MBM Instinct BMX stunt bicycle Italy 2000s

Saddle set low so that rider's weight is over rear wheel

Haro Freestyler BMX racing bike USA 2012

8900 Pro's frame was made of carbon fiber to keep its weight down. Many mountain bikes are fitted with suspension systems. Hardtail bicycles (with rigid frames), such as the **Marin Nail Trail**, have front forks that lessen the impact of bumps and landings. In contrast, full-suspension bicycles, such as the **Stumpjumper FSR Pro**, have shock absorbers for both wheels. BMX bikes are strong, small-wheeled bicycles, some of which are raced over dirt tracks. Freestyle (stunt riding) BMX bikes such as the **MBM Instinct**, are built for doing tricks and out-of-the-saddle moves.

MOUNTAIN BIKE MADNESS
MTB freerider Louis Reboul launches his mountain bike off a giant 52-ft- (16-m-) high ramp during the Red Bull Rampage 2014. He twists the bike and his riding position in midair to pull off a perfectly judged landing. One mistake and the result could be disastrous, with a huge drop onto the hard, unforgiving sandstone below.

Mountain bike (MTB) freeriding involves riders pulling moves and tricks as they take on a challenging run, full of dramatic natural features and, sometimes, man-made obstacles such as large ramps. Competitors ride bikes with full suspension on both wheels to allow for heavy impacts on landing, and their runs are judged for speed, control, and the execution and complexity of their tricks. These can involve full 360° spins, backflips, and no-hands riding. Held on the edge of Zion National Park in Utah, the Red Bull Rampage is an annual invite-only tournament for some of the hottest freeriders in the world. Each gets to pick their own route along the almost-vertical drops of ridges and cliffs.

Motorcycle

Bikes were first fitted with engines in the 19th century and have never looked back! Today, millions enjoy the fast, convenient travel and the freedom of the open road or trail that motorcycles provide. This **Yamaha XJR 1300** is called a "naked" bike, because its engine is not hidden behind body panels. With a top speed of 130 mph (210 km/h), it is faster than many cars.

Chassis ❯ The frame to which other parts of the motorcycle are attached, the chassis helps keep the wheels in line for good handling. It is usually made of steel or a combination of metals (alloy).

Rear seat ❯ Big motorcycles have a seat long enough for a passenger, who can grip the handle behind the seat.

Yamaha XJR 1300

Indicator light

Shock absorber ❯ A coil-spring and oil-filled cylinder cushion the bike and rider over bumps in the road.

Rear wheel ❯ This is driven by power from the engine through a shaft or belt, or on this motorcycle, a metal chain similar to a bicycle chain.

Exhaust pipe ❯ The exhaust pipe channels waste gases from the engine out behind the bike.

Side mirrors ❯ Mounted on the handlebars, these allow the rider to see what's going on behind the bike.

Throttle ❯ Controlled by twisting the right handlebar, the throttle controls the flow of gas and air mixture into the cylinders in the engine. More air means more power and a higher speed.

Windshield

Fuel tank ❯ The tank holds the gas and pumps it to the engine.

Headlight ❯ Powered by the motorcycle's alternator, this lights up the road ahead.

Front wheel ❯ Fitted with an air-filled tire, this wheel is steered by the handlebars.

Front forks

Brake disk

Engine ❯ Fueled by gasoline, the engine generates power, which is transmitted to the rear wheel. This engine generates around 107 horsepower, as much as a hatchback car.

Revving up

Michaux-Perreaux velocipede France 1867–71

Handlebars for steering

Saddle caught fire on its first journey because it was directly above the hot ignition tube

Metal-rimmed wooden wheel

This steam-powered motorcycle weighing 195 lb (88 kg) had **no brakes!**

Daimler Reitwagen Germany 1885

Hildebrand & Wolfmüller Motorrad Germany 1894

Mudguard was also the motorcycle's water tank

Cyklon Germany 1901

The first powered motorcycles used a small steam engine to drive the rear wheel, but motorcycles made a great leap forward once internal combustion engines were built small enough to attach to a bicycle-styled frame.

With its 0.5 horsepower engine, the **Daimler Reitwagen** is considered to be the first "real" motorcycle, even though it was crafted out of wood. It proved to be an uncomfortable ride due to its wooden wheels and lack of suspension. The faster **Motorrad** and the first widely made

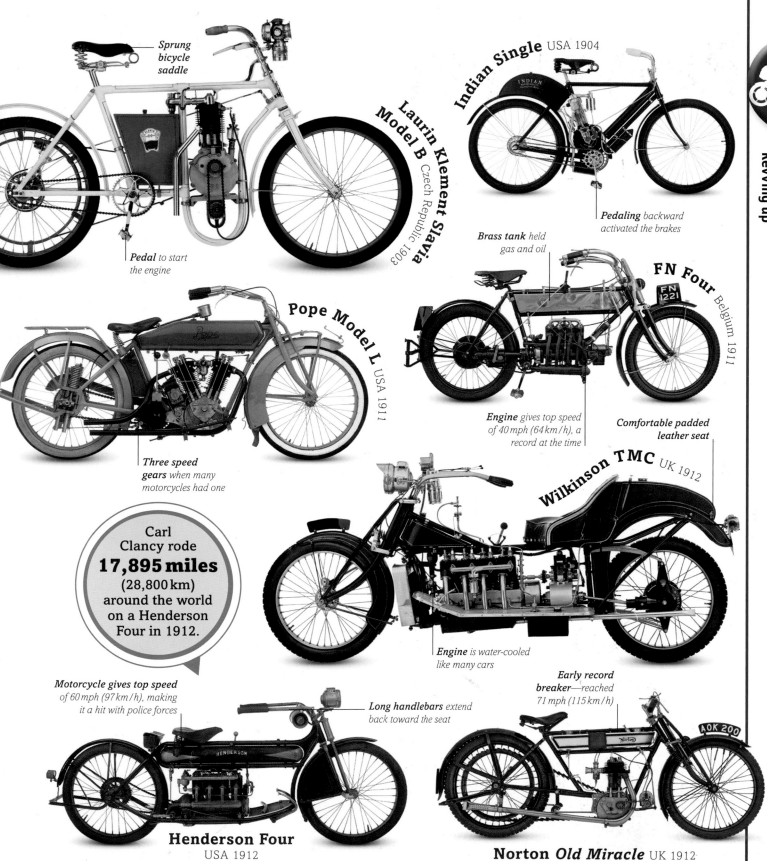

Sprung bicycle saddle

Laurin Klement Model B Czech Republic 1903

Indian Single USA 1904

Pedaling backward activated the brakes

Pedal to start the engine

Pope Model L USA 1911

Brass tank held gas and oil

FN Four Belgium 1911

Engine gives top speed of 40 mph (64 km/h), a record at the time

Comfortable padded leather seat

Three speed gears when many motorcycles had one

Wilkinson TMC UK 1912

Carl Clancy rode **17,895 miles** (28,800 km) around the world on a Henderson Four in 1912.

Engine is water-cooled like many cars

Early record breaker—reached 71 mph (115 km/h)

Motorcycle gives top speed of 60 mph (97 km/h), making it a hit with police forces

Long handlebars extend back toward the seat

Henderson Four USA 1912

Norton Old Miracle UK 1912

motorcycle, with around 2,000 built. Some early motorcycles had their engines mounted in strange places. The **Cyklon's** engine sat in front of the rider; it drove the front wheel around. The **Indian Single's** engine was so low, riding over a bump could knock it. Over time, engines were built with more than one cylinder. The **Pope Model L** had two cylinders and cost as much as a Ford Model T car. The **FN Four** was one of the first motorcycles with four cylinders. The four-cylinder **Wilkinson TMC** was designed for long-distance touring with a padded leather seat, but it had no front brake.

Bikes in battle

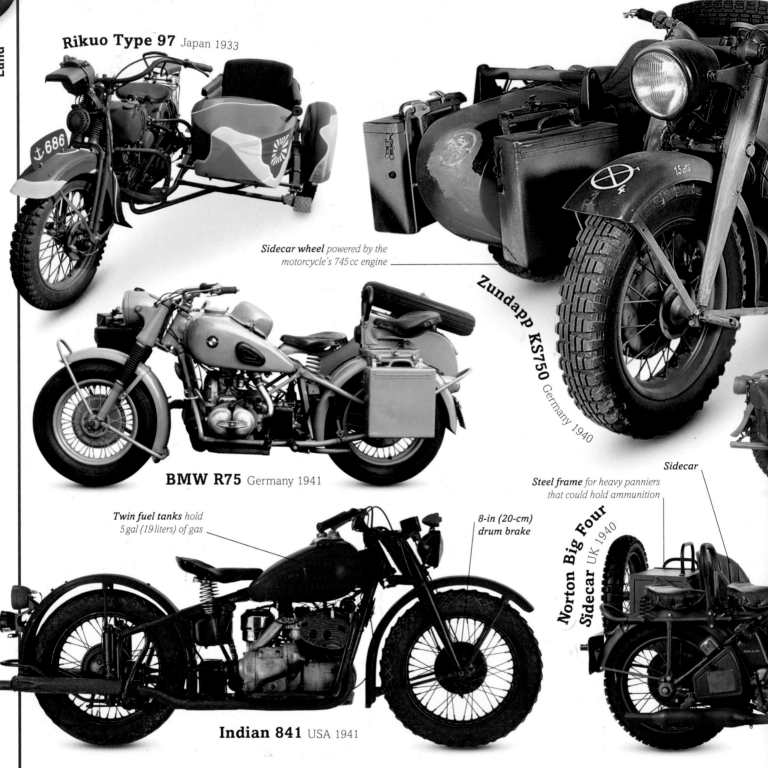

Rikuo Type 97 Japan 1933

Sidecar wheel *powered by the motorcycle's 745 cc engine*

Zundapp KS750 *Germany 1940*

BMW R75 Germany 1941

Steel frame *for heavy panniers that could hold ammunition*

Sidecar

Twin fuel tanks *hold 5 gal (19 liters) of gas*

8-in (20-cm) drum brake

Norton Big Four Sidecar *UK 1940*

Indian 841 USA 1941

As motorcycles became faster, sturdier, and more reliable, they were adopted by armed forces in their thousands. World War II saw heavy motorcycle use, as scouts, in convoys, and as couriers, transporting messages and people.

Many World War II motorcycles were adapted civilian models. More than 70,000 **Harley-Davidson WLAs** were made for the American forces, while 126,000 **BSA M20s** were built by the UK and its allies—making it the most produced motorcycle of the war. A prewar Harley-Davidson

Motorcycle could carry three soldiers and their weapons at speeds up to 59 mph (95 km/h)

Cannister, with the bike fitted inside, is just 13 in (33 cm) in diameter

Parachute

Welbike UK 1942

BSA M20 UK 1942

A **Welbike** could be put together in just **11 seconds**.

Rear-wheel canvas panniers

Holster to hold rifle or machine gun

Harley-Davidson WLA USA 1942

U.S. ARMY

Norton 16H Desert Duty UK 1942

Metal sheet "bash plate" to protect engine

The just 130-lb (60-kg) motorcycle could be dropped by parachute or carried by a glider

Small engine used 0.26 gal (1 liter) of gas per 33 miles (53 km)

Royal Enfield WD/RE125 *Flying Flea* UK 1948

built in Japan, the **Rikuo Type 97** served Japanese forces during wartime. Its sidecar was engine-powered, improving travel over rough ground, a feature also found in the sidecar of the **Norton Big Four**, used as a scout by British soldiers. The 930-lb (420-kg) **Zundapp KS750** was one of the biggest World War II sidecars. In contrast, the 71-lb (32-kg) **Welbike** could be folded inside a cannister, dropped from a plane, and parachuted to the ground. Another lightweight, the ***Flying Flea*** was used to carry messages when radio contact was impossible.

Scooting around

Steering column *folds down when not in use*

Autoped USA 1915

155 cc engine *directly over the front wheel*

Enclosed 202 cc engine *mounted under the seat*

Cushman Auto-glide
USA 1938

Lockable glove box

Large windshield

Rear wheel *is 10 in (25 cm) in diameter*

Exhaust pipe

Lambretta LD150 Italy 1957

M·TP 325

Padded bench saddle *seats two*

Vespa Rally 250
Italy 1976

Saddle *that can seat two people*

More than **60 million** Super Cubs have been built—the most produced motor vehicle ever.

Air vents *help cool engine, which can propel scooter to speeds up to 70 mph (113 km/h)*

Honda Super Cub C100
Japan 1958

Scooters are small motorcycles with a step-through design and the driver's seat above an enclosed engine. The term *mopeds* once meant motorized bikes that had to be pedaled to start, but now it applies to small scooters with 50 cc or lesser power engines.

The **Autoped** was one of the first scooters; its engine drove the front wheel using gears. The **VéloSoleX 45**, an early moped, had an engine that powered a ceramic roller that gripped the top of the front wheel to turn it. Lightweight and fuel-efficient, scooters and mopeds such as the

Safety cell *crumples in crash to protect rider*

BMW C1 200 Germany 2001

This scooter can go from **0–60mph** (100km/h) in under **7 seconds**.

Hooded instrument panel

Honda PCX 125 Japan 2010

Front wheel *fitted with hydraulic brake*

BMW C Evolution Germany 2014

Large lithium-ion battery *powers electric motors and can be recharged in 4 hours*

Scooter travels 60 miles *(100 km) on a single charge*

Small fuel tank *holds 1.3 gal (5 liters) of gas*

Carrier with storage box

Steel luggage rack

VéloSoleX 45 France 1949

Motobécane Mobylette France 1986

Hinged seat *with compartment underneath*

Yamaha Jog RR Japan 2011

Headlight *fitted into the plastic fairing*

PGO PMX Naked Taiwan 2011

Honda Super Cub proved to be a cheap form of transportation in the postwar years. A craze for stylishly designed Italian scooters in the 1950s and 1960s led to the popular **Lambretta LD150** with its large windshield, passenger seat, and top speed of 50mph (80km/h). Scooters and mopeds are still in demand. The **Yamaha Jog** and the **PGO PMX**, powered by small 50cc engines, are aimed at young riders. Future scooters may be enclosed with a roof, such as the **BMW C1 200** concept, or be powered by electric motors, like the **BMW C Evolution**.

Three-wheelers

Ariel Tricycle UK 1898

Fuel tank

Single-cylinder engine propelled bike to 24 mph (39 km/h)

Top box holds tools and spare clothing

Passenger seat in front of the driver

Raleigh Raleighette Tandem Tricar UK 1904

Steering wheel instead of handlebars

Coiled radiator tubes filled with water to cool engine

Rexette 5HP UK 1905

Rear light

Front fender

Harley-Davidson Servi-Car GE USA 1969

Police siren

Chopper-styled wide, padded seat

Honda Stream Japan 1982

Not all motorcycles have two wheels. Ever since bikes were first developed, engineers have experimented with three-wheeled machines, which are easier to learn to ride, have more space for engines or loads, and come with an extra tire for better grip.

Early three-wheelers were pedal-powered tricycles fitted with an engine. The **Ariel Tricycle** used the space between the rear wheels for the engine. Some manufacturers preferred to power a single rear wheel, so they placed a pair of wheels in the front. Both the **Rexette 5HP** and **Raleighette**

Honda Goldwing EML Trike
Japan/Netherlands 1994

Vandenbrink Carver One Netherlands 2007

Short, plastic **windshield** *deflects air up and over rider's head*

Three-wheeled car-like body *tilts up to 45 degrees, with wheels staying on the road*

Each Can-Am front wheel has its own **suspension** to ride out **bumps**.

Weighs 335 lb (152 kg), a quarter of the Carver One

Can-Am Spyder Trike
Canada 2011

Yamaha Tricity
Japan 2014

Twin six-spoked wheels
with 13.8 in (35 cm) diameter

Tricar had rear-wheel drive and used the space above the front wheels to fit a passenger chair. The **Harley-Davidson Servi-Car GE** served police forces and breakdown mechanics from the 1930s to the 1970s. In contrast, the **Can-Am Spyder** is built for fun and has as much power as a small hatchback car. Advances in technology have brought in new three-wheelers that can tilt their bodies as they turn. The **Vandenbrink** is like a three-wheeled car, with a fully enclosed cockpit and twin rear wheels, while the **Yamaha Tricity** resembles a motorcycle with twin wheels in front.

47

Road burners

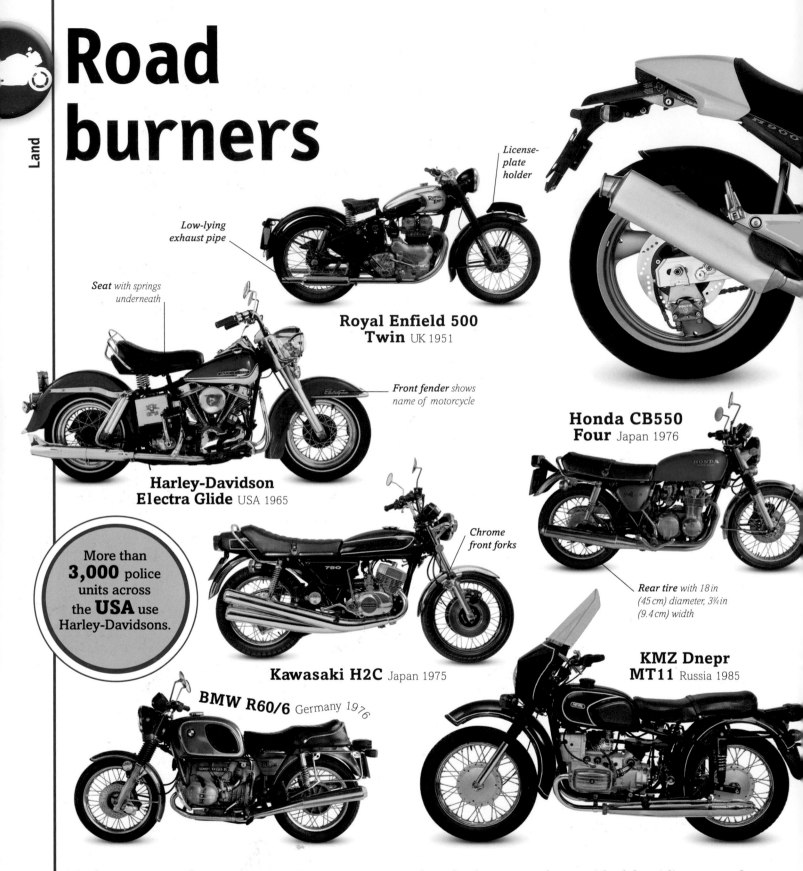

License-plate holder

Low-lying exhaust pipe

Royal Enfield 500 Twin UK 1951

Seat with springs underneath

Front fender shows name of motorcycle

Harley-Davidson Electra Glide USA 1965

Honda CB550 Four Japan 1976

More than **3,000** police units across the **USA** use Harley-Davidsons.

Chrome front forks

Rear tire with 18 in (45 cm) diameter, 3¾ in (9.4 cm) width

Kawasaki H2C Japan 1975

KMZ Dnepr MT11 Russia 1985

BMW R60/6 Germany 1976

Various types of motorcycles have been designed for road use, from standards to cruisers. Most standards offer a relatively upright riding style and have smooth tires. Cruisers are bigger, with a reclining back and relaxed riding position for long rides.

Standard motorcycles are ideal for riding around town and for short journeys. Popular midsize engine bikes in the 1970s included the **BMW R60/6** and the **Honda CB550**, with a top speed of 102 mph (164 km/h) from its 500 cc engine. For long-distance riding, cruisers are more

Powerful headlight

Ducati M900 Monster Italy 1994

Harley-Davidson FLSTF Fat Boy USA 1999

A **Fat Boy** starred in the **Terminator 2** movie.

Long exhaust pipe from engine cylinder

Large twin 12-ft-6-in- (32-cm-) diameter brake disks for high braking power

5.5 gal (21 liter) fuel tank

Yamaha FZS1000 Fazer Japan 2002

BMW R1200 RT Germany 2005

Engine gives top speed of 135 mph (217 km/h)

Instrument panel on top of fuel tank

Long bench seat is 29 in (74 cm) above ground

Triumph Bonneville UK 2011

Triumph Thunderbird UK 2010

popular. The **Electra Glide** was the first big Harley-Davidson motorcycle to have an electric engine starter. The **Thunderbird**, manufactured in UK, was Triumph's first belt-driven motorcycle since the 1920s. Muscle bikes have powerful engines and are shaped to look as modern as possible. The **Ducati M900** stands out with its large, sculpted fuel tank and unusual triangular frame. Other road motorcycles have picked up design elements from classic machines, such as the **Harley-Davidson Fat Boy** and the **Triumph Bonneville**.

Burning rubber

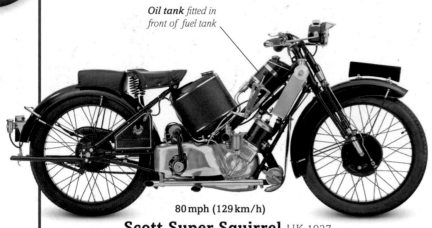

Oil tank fitted in front of fuel tank

80 mph (129 km/h)
Scott Super Squirrel UK 1927

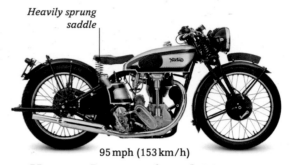

Heavily sprung saddle

95 mph (153 km/h)
Norton International 30 UK 1936

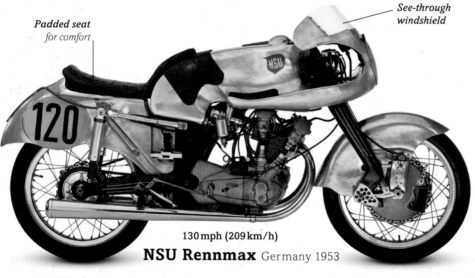

Padded seat for comfort

See-through windshield

130 mph (209 km/h)
NSU Rennmax Germany 1953

The RC166's engine could turn at **20,000 rpm**, which is 333 turns every second!

Rider has to lean over large aluminum fuel tank

Three of the motorcycle's six exhaust pipes

178 mph (286 km/h)
Moto Guzzi V8 Italy 1957

Windshield

Honda RC166 Japan 1966

150 mph (241 km/h)

Racing motorcycles are built and tuned for ultimate performance, and maximum speed, acceleration, and braking power on the track. Sports bikes also boast high performance, but are used on roads. Some mimic the style and features of racers.

Early racing motorcycles, like the **Scott Super Squirrel** and the **Norton International 30**, competed in different kinds of races, from track races to time trials. In 1934, the Nortons finished first, second, third, and fourth in the famous Isle of Man TT (time trial). Track racers compete

Kawasaki Dragster UK/Japan 1977

Low fairing with built-in windshield

283

GOODYEAR

DOHC

Two Kawasaki 850 cc motorcycle engines work together

220 mph (354 km/h)

Sculpted seat for low riding position

Suzuki RG500 Japan 1986

SUZUKI

147 mph (237 km/h)

Bimota Mantra Italy 1996

125 mph (201 km/h)

The Dragster could reach **149 mph** (240 km/h) in just **7.7 seconds**.

Castrol

Wide, slick, treadless tire for racing on smooth tracks

DUNLOP

200 mph (320 km/h)

Honda CBR1000RR Fireblade Japan 2009

Yamaha YZF R1 Japan 1998

YAMAHA

DELTABOX

EXUP

YAMAHA

171 mph (275 km/h)

Aprilia RSV4 Italy 2011

aprilia

Single racing exhaust made of titanium metal

180 mph (290 km/h)

according to their type and engine size. The **Honda RC166** weighed 247 lb (112 kg) and had a 250 cc engine, yet it could race at speeds up to 150 mph (241 km/h). Modern racers, such as the **Aprilia RSV4**, are packed with electronic wizardry. An RSV4 rider can adjust the motorcycle's suspension, gearbox, and engine performance while riding. Manufacturers can produce street versions of their more successful racers. The **Suzuki RG500** was based on the racing RG500s, which had won four 500 cc Grand Prix World Championships in seven years.

JUMPS AND FLICKS
Woooah! Pedro Moreno pulls a spectacular midair move during the 2013 freestyle competition in Zurich, Switzerland—the largest freesport event in Europe. Moreno is a professional freestyle motocross (FMX) rider. This is a sport in which motocross riders perform routines, throwing stunning shapes and pulling wicked tricks in the air as their bikes leap off giant ramps.

Freestylers use modified motocross racing motorcycles with a number of adjustments. These include shaving the foam saddle down to narrow it, replacing components with lighter variations, and rerouting cables to keep from getting boots tangled up in them as they perform their tricks and moves. These can be spectacular, such as full backflips by both bike and rider; "the cliffhanger," where the rider hooks his or her toes under the handlebars; and "the tsunami," where the rider performs a handstand over the handlebars while keeping the bike horizontal! Riders can also twist in the air, grab the saddle, and even let go of the bike completely, but they must nail a safe landing to get great scores from the judges.

Off-roaders

Harley-Davidson Hillclimber USA 1930

Raised mudguard to keep mud and water from flinging up

BSA Gold Star Scrambler UK 1959

Metal chains wrapped around rear tire to grip loose ground

Hollow aluminum **wheels** meant this motorcycle could **float** in water!

Rokon Trail-breaker USA 1963

Large, steel cargo rack

Husqvarna Enduro Sweden 1973

Chain driving front wheel

Road-legal bike weighs 240.3 lb (109 kg)

2.8 gal (10.6 liters) plastic fuel tank

Knobbly, deep-tread tire for gripping soft ground

Race number

CZ 250 Motocross Czech Republic 1974

Suzuki Enduro PE250X Japan 1981

Off-road motorcycles let you get away from the traffic, unless you are competing in a motocross race with 30 or 40 riders over a bumpy dirt course. Off-roaders are tough and strong, and equipped with plenty of suspension to soak up impacts.

The **Rokon Trail-breaker** is the only widely produced motorcycle to offer an all-wheel drive. Other off-roaders rely on rear-wheel drive and chunky tires with deep tread to grip sand or mud. The **KTM 65SX** is ideal for 8 to 13 year olds, but young riders may progress to a top motocross bike

Speedway bikes take under **3 seconds** to accelerate from **0–60 mph** (100 km/h).

Small tank holds enough methanol fuel for four laps of racing

Forks steeply angled to give more response when steering

Weslake Speedway UK 1981

Honda Africa Twin Japan 1990

Twin headlights

Motorcycle can travel 373 miles (600 km) on one tank of gas

Yamaha XT Tenere Japan 2010

KTM 65SX Austria 2011

Long-travel front forks

Aluminum exhaust silencer tucked up under seat rear

Motorcycle gives top speed of 50 mph (80 km/h)

KTM 350 SX-F Austria 2012

such as the **KTM 350 SX-F**. KTMs won the Motocross MX2 World Championships from 2008 to 2014. Enduro bikes, such as the lightweight **Suzuki Enduro PE250X**, race off-road but are usually used for competing over longer courses than motocross. Adventure motorcycles are big off-roaders with large fuel tanks, such as the **Yamaha XT Tenere**, which is based on the bike that won the Dakar Rally seven times. Speedway bikes, such as the **Weslake Speedway**, have no brakes and just one gear. They are raced in laps on a tight, oval dirt track in competitions.

Fastest on two wheels

A 1929 SS100 once sold for a record **£315,100** (about $460,000) at auction in the UK.

Engine's two cylinders form a V-shape

Excelsior 20R USA 1920

100 mph (160 km/h)

Pannier bags for storage

102 mph (164 km/h)

Brough Superior SS100
UK 1927

Vincent Black Shadow UK 1949

Wheelie bar stops front of bike flipping up as it accelerates

Vincent Mighty Mouse UK 1966

Single exhaust from V-twin engine

160 mph (257 km/h)

122 mph (196 km/h)

Body shell, made of carbon fiber, is 21-ft (6.4-m) long

Two Suzuki Hayabusa engines power the bike

367 mph (591 km/h)

Ever since motorcycles were built, they have been raced or tested to see just how fast they would go. Designers, engineers, and riders would push everything to the limit to squeeze every drop of speed from their magnificent machines.

The **Excelsior 20R** was one of the first motorcycles to reach 100 mph (160 km/h). It was overtaken by the **Brough Superior SS100** and later the **Vincent Mighty Mouse**, which became the fastest single-cylinder motorcycle when it raced along drag strips in the 1960s. Most modern

BMW R90S
Germany 1975

Winner of the first AMA Superbike Championship in 1976

125 mph (200 km/h)

Ducati 916 Italy 1995

160 mph (257 km/h)

Streamlined fairing channels air past bike

Hinged fuel tank lifts up for access to parts inside

186 mph (299 km/h)

Suzuki GSX 1300R Hayabusa
Japan 1999

Powerful disk brakes

Giant exhaust for jet engine gases

250 mph (402 km/h)

MTT Turbine Superbike
USA 2001

Top 1 Ack Attack USA 2004

WWW.TOP1OIL.COM

376 mph (606 km/h)

BUB Seven Streamliner USA 2006

Giant 1,441 cc engine has power of two cars

187 mph (301 km/h)

Kawasaki ZZR1400 Japan 2011

SPEED Top three record breakers

Top 1 Ack Attack

376 mph (606 km/h)

BUB Seven Streamliner

367 mph (591 km/h)

MTT Turbine Superbike

250 mph (402 km/h)

motorcycles have engines with multiple cylinders. The **Ducati 916** won four World Superbike Championships with its twin-cylinder engine, while the four-cylinder **Suzuki GSX 1300R Hayabusa** was the fastest production motorcycle of last century, and the **Kawasaki ZZR1400** is the fastest so far. Even faster are modern streamliners, motorcycles with low-slung aerodynamic bodies inside which riders lie flat. The **BUB Seven Streamliner** was the first to break 350 mph (563 km/h) in 2006, while the **Top 1 Ack Attack** is currently the world's fastest motorcycle.

Easy riders

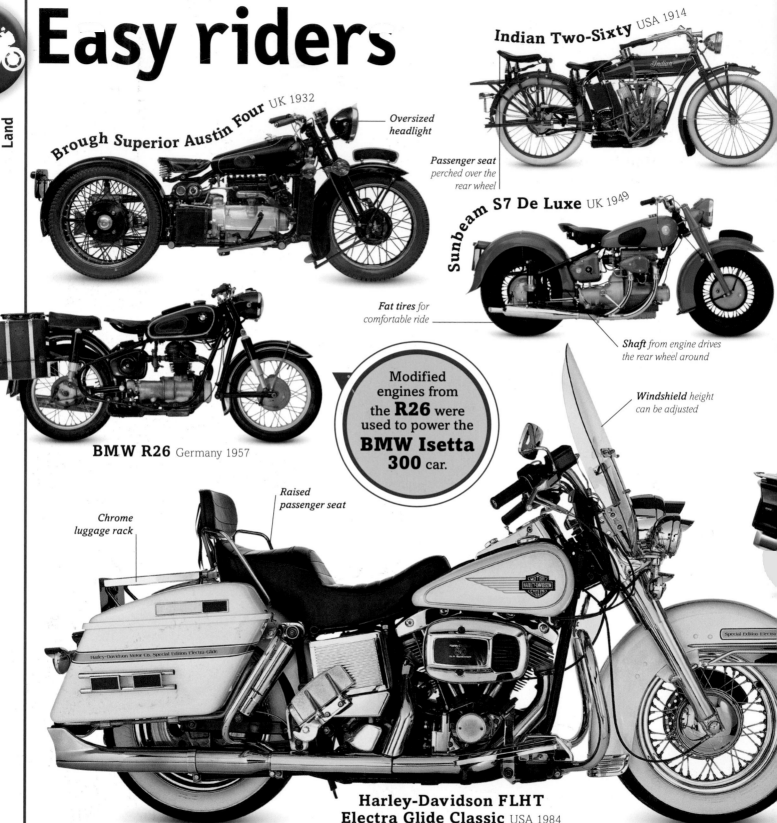

Indian Two-Sixty USA 1914

Brough Superior Austin Four UK 1932

Oversized headlight

Passenger seat perched over the rear wheel

Sunbeam S7 De Luxe UK 1949

Fat tires for comfortable ride

Shaft from engine drives the rear wheel around

Windshield height can be adjusted

BMW R26 Germany 1957

Modified engines from the **R26** were used to power the **BMW Isetta 300** car.

Chrome luggage rack

Raised passenger seat

Harley-Davidson FLHT Electra Glide Classic USA 1984

Large, heavy, and powerful, touring and sports-touring motorcycles are designed for comfortable long-distance riding. Some of these big beasts are the last word in luxury, with high-quality audio systems and comforts not found on other bikes.

Early big motorcycles often copied features usually found in cars. The **Indian Two-Sixty** was the first bike to come with electric lighting as a standard feature. The **Brough Superior Austin Four** used an engine and a gearbox from a car to drive two closely set rear wheels for a smoother

Cruise control *allows motorcycle to travel at set speed*

Honda Goldwing GL1500 Japan 1999

Suzuki M1800R Intruder Japan 2007

Harley-Davidson CVO Softail Convertible USA 2010

Carbon fiber body panels

1,078 cc engine *gives top speed of 196 mph (315 km/h)*

MV Agusta F4CC Italy 2008

Cast aluminum front wheel

Adaptive headlight *changes brightness according to conditions*

Twin disk brakes, *normally found on racing motorcycles*

With a cost of **$300,000**, this motorcycle comes with a **$20,000** watch.

BMW K1600GT Germany 2011

Frame *made of light but strong titanium metal*

Air bag *inflates in 0.1 seconds during crash*

Ecosse Titanium USA 2011

Honda Goldwing GL1800 Japan 2014

ride. In the 1970s and 1980s, big motorcycles got even larger and heavier. The **Electra Glide Classic** weighed more than 738 lb (335 kg) empty. Modern luxury motorcycles continue to offer innovative features. The **Honda Goldwing GL1500** comes with foot heaters and some feature a built-in jukebox. The **BMW K1600GT** has heated seats and handlebar grips for cold weather, and an onboard computer with a color touch screen. The **Honda Goldwing GL1800** has an electric reverse gear and an air bag for the rider.

Car

The car revolutionized transportation in the 20th century, and more than half a billion cars are found on the world's roads today. While some are powered fully or partly by electric motors, most cars use an internal combustion engine in which gas and air are mixed and burned to produce power to drive the wheels. The **Toyota Yaris** (or the *Vitz*) is a popular, small family car, with more than 200,000 manufactured every year.

Engine ❯ Under the hood sits an internal combustion engine that generates around 90 horsepower to give a top speed of 109 mph (175 km/h).

Headlight ❯ Protected by transparent plastic cover, headlights light up the path ahead.

Turn indicator

Side mirror

Steering wheel

Rearview mirror

Disk brakes ❯ Brakes apply pads onto discs, which are attached to the wheels. The friction between the pad and disc slows the wheel down.

Interior › Inside the car, the driver and passengers are protected by a number of air bags, which inflate when there is a severe impact, to cushion the occupants. The Yaris has front and side air bags.

Hatchback › A full-height rear lifting trunk door gives this car 71.8 gal (272 liters) of storage space. Cars with a rear door like this are known as hatchbacks.

Radio antenna

Rear indicator and brake light

Toyota Yaris / Vitz

Passenger door › These are fashioned out of steel panels, aluminum, or carbon fiber. This car is fitted with remote central locking. The driver presses a button on the key to open or close the locks on all four doors.

Pioneering cars

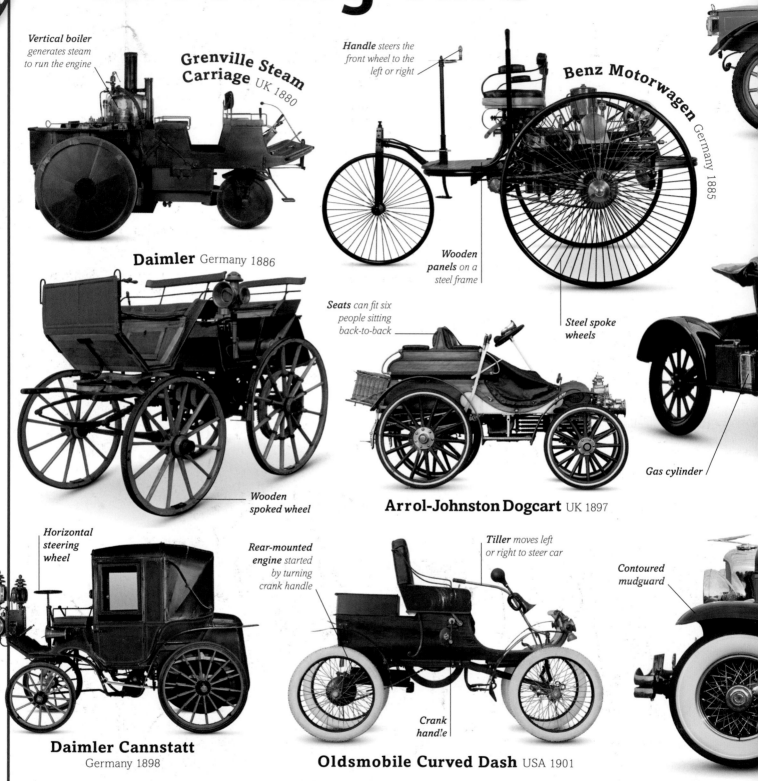

Vertical boiler generates steam to run the engine

Grenville Steam Carriage UK 1880

Handle steers the front wheel to the left or right

Benz Motorwagen Germany 1885

Daimler Germany 1886

Wooden panels on a steel frame

Seats can fit six people sitting back-to-back

Steel spoke wheels

Gas cylinder

Wooden spoked wheel

Arrol-Johnston Dogcart UK 1897

Horizontal steering wheel

Rear-mounted engine started by turning crank handle

Tiller moves left or right to steer car

Contoured mudguard

Crank handle

Daimler Cannstatt
Germany 1898

Oldsmobile Curved Dash USA 1901

Early attempts to take to the road were in steam-powered vehicles, such as the Grenville Steam Carriage. It took the development of reliable internal combustion engines fueled by gasoline, to produce the first popular cars.

Karl Benz's three-wheeled **Benz Motorwagen** was the first car with a working internal combustion engine. A year later, the **Daimler**, a motorized horse carriage became the first gas-driven four-wheeler. While Daimler continued to develop motorized horse carriages, more car

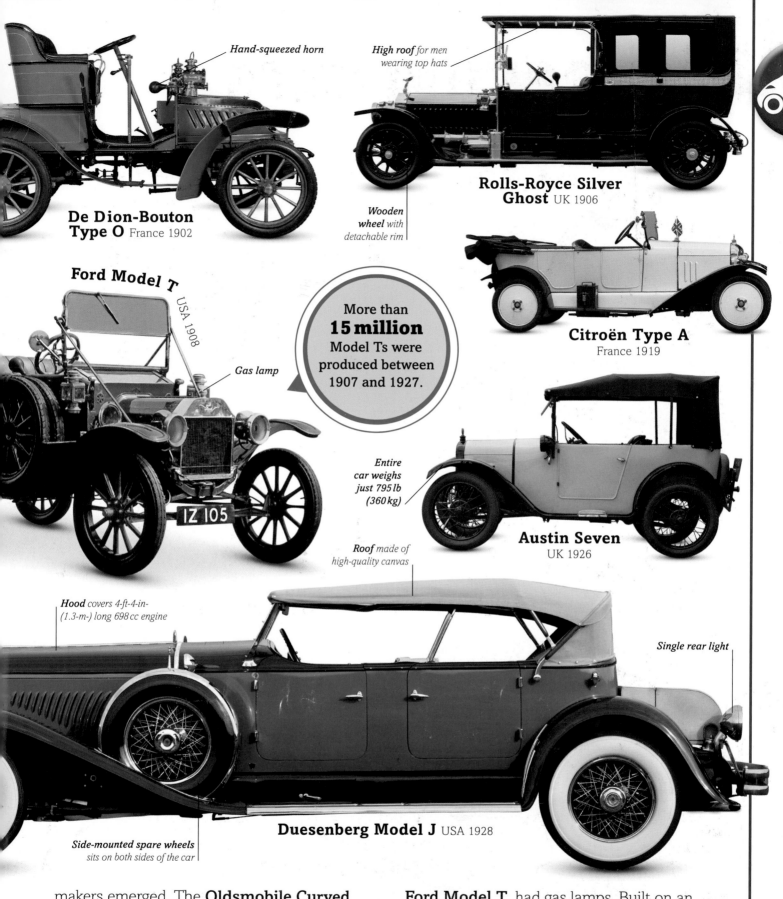

De Dion-Bouton Type O France 1902

Hand-squeezed horn

Rolls-Royce Silver Ghost UK 1906

High roof for men wearing top hats

Wooden wheel with detachable rim

Ford Model T USA 1908

Gas lamp

More than **15 million** Model Ts were produced between 1907 and 1927.

Citroën Type A France 1919

Entire car weighs just 795 lb (360 kg)

Austin Seven UK 1926

Roof made of high-quality canvas

Hood covers 4-ft-4-in- (1.3-m-) long 698 cc engine

IZ 105

Single rear light

Duesenberg Model J USA 1928

Side-mounted spare wheels sits on both sides of the car

makers emerged. The **Oldsmobile Curved Dash** was the world's first mass-produced car, with more than 19,000 sold. Some early cars had somewhat primitive features. The engine of the **Arrol-Johnston Dogcart** was started by pulling on a rope, and many cars, including the **Ford Model T**, had gas lamps. Built on an assembly line, the Model T made motoring affordable for the masses. The 1920s saw an explosion in car design, from the **Duesenberg Model J**, driven by American gangsters and movie stars, to the compact **Austin Seven**.

THRILLS AND SPILLS
At first, this dramatic tangle of men and machines looks like a horrible accident. In fact, it's all fun and games. A clue is the ball on the ground on the right of the picture—and, if you look closely, you can see that the two passengers in the cars are wielding mallets. Welcome to the sport of "auto polo," and a crunch moment during a game in Florida, in 1928.

Polo is usually played by riders on horseback. In the USA in the early 1900s, the sport was spiced up a little when the horses were replaced with cars. It is said that the inventor was a Ford automobile dealer who came up with the idea as a publicity stunt, and it caught on. The game was played by two teams, each made up of two cars and four players, and their steeds were stripped-down Ford Model Ts. The driver was held in place with a seat belt, while his malletman leaned out and tried to hit a basketball into a goal. The cars tore around the field at furious speeds up to 40 mph (64 km/h), while the referee chased the action on foot. By the end of the game, most of the cars were destroyed.

Early race cars

Some early race cars had a **mechanic** onboard to make repairs.

Small, round windshield known as a monocle

Cylindrical fuel tank

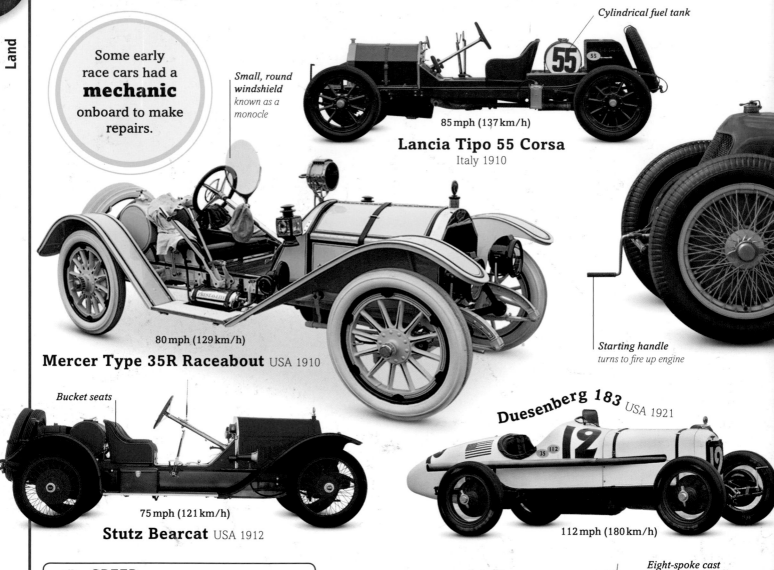

85 mph (137 km/h)

Lancia Tipo 55 Corsa
Italy 1910

80 mph (129 km/h)

Mercer Type 35R Raceabout USA 1910

Starting handle turns to fire up engine

Bucket seats

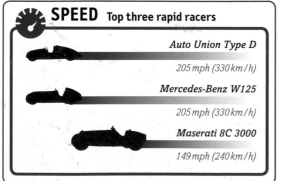

75 mph (121 km/h)

Stutz Bearcat USA 1912

Duesenberg 183 USA 1921

112 mph (180 km/h)

Bugatti Type 35B France 1927

Eight-spoke cast aluminum wheels

127 mph (204 km/h)

SPEED Top three rapid racers

Auto Union Type D
205 mph (330 km/h)

Mercedes-Benz W125
205 mph (330 km/h)

Maserati 8C 3000
149 mph (240 km/h)

As soon as cars were mass produced, people became eager to race them. Early racing tested speed as well as reliability, since early cars broke down a lot. But advances in technology quickly saw race cars develop into speed demons.

Some early race car drivers turned into car builders. Italy's Vincenzo Lancia, who won the 1904 Coppa Florio race, manufactured the **Lancia Tipo 55 Corsa**. Across the Atlantic, the **Stutz Bearcat** won 25 of the 30 races it entered, while the **Mercer Type 35R Raceabout** won

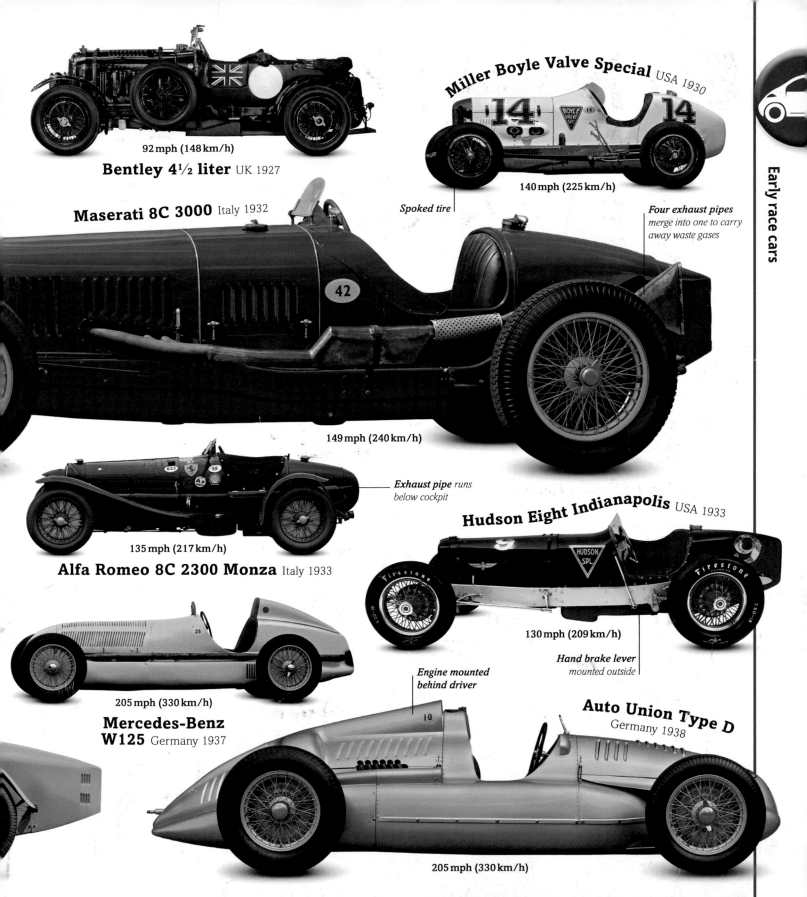

Bentley 4½ liter UK 1927
92 mph (148 km/h)

Miller Boyle Valve Special USA 1930
140 mph (225 km/h)

Spoked tire

Four exhaust pipes merge into one to carry away waste gases

Maserati 8C 3000 Italy 1932
149 mph (240 km/h)

Exhaust pipe runs below cockpit

Alfa Romeo 8C 2300 Monza Italy 1933
135 mph (217 km/h)

Hudson Eight Indianapolis USA 1933
130 mph (209 km/h)

Hand brake lever mounted outside

Mercedes-Benz W125 Germany 1937
205 mph (330 km/h)

Engine mounted behind driver

Auto Union Type D Germany 1938
205 mph (330 km/h)

five of its first six races in 1911. Race cars remained box-shaped until after World War I, when sleeker, more rounded shapes started to emerge. In 1921, the **Duesenberg 183** became the first all-American car to win a Grand Prix race in Europe. Stunning speedsters, such as the

Alfa Romeo 8C 2300 Monza and the **Bugatti Type 35B**, were produced throughout the 1920s and 1930s. Type 35 cars won more than 1,000 races and battled it out with German cars such as the **Mercedes-Benz W125**, which dominated at the 1937 European Grand Prix Championship.

67

Machines with style

Mercedes-Benz 500K Special Roadster Germany 1934

Electric, hard-metal, foldable roof

Peugeot 401 Eclipse
France 1934

Vents in the hood cool the engine

Bugatti Type 57SC Atalante France 1935

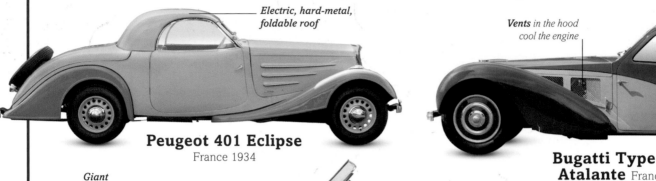

Giant wheel fenders or "wings"

Auburn Speedster USA 1935

Metal plate prevents damage from gravel

Spare tire fits in trunk to keep car streamlined

MG TA Midget UK 1936

Spare wheel

Gas tank can hold 18 gal (68 liters)

Low-cut sloping door hinged at the back

Lincoln-Zephyr USA 1936

Fashionable, full whitewall tire

BMW 328 Germany 1936

In the 1930s, some cars got slick and sleek as research revealed the importance of airflow around a car, especially at higher speeds. Streamlining vehicles to improve performance resulted in some stylish and eye-catching designs.

The **Lincoln-Zephyr** created a sensation at the 1936 New York Auto Show with its teardrop shape. On the road, the **Auburn Speedster** roared with a 148 horsepower engine that generated a top speed of around 100 mph (160 km/h). While some European sports cars

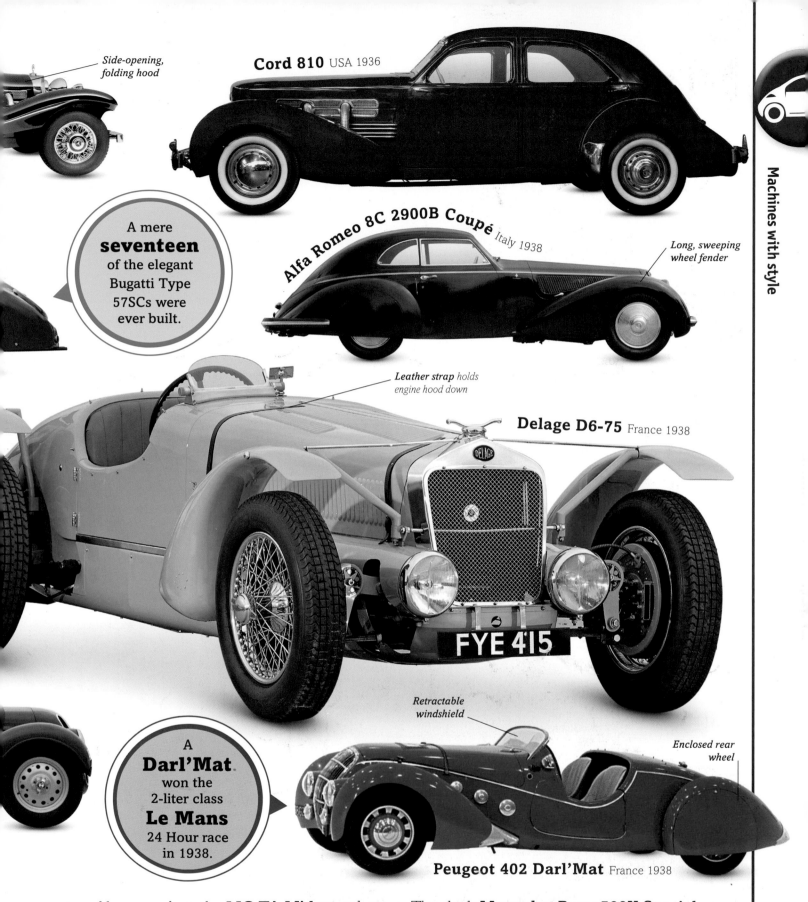

Side-opening, folding hood

Cord 810 USA 1936

A mere **seventeen** of the elegant Bugatti Type 57SCs were ever built.

Alfa Romeo 8C 2900B Coupé Italy 1938

Long, sweeping wheel fender

Leather strap *holds engine hood down*

Delage D6-75 France 1938

FYE 415

Retractable windshield

Enclosed rear wheel

A **Darl'Mat** won the 2-liter class **Le Mans** 24 Hour race in 1938.

Peugeot 402 Darl'Mat France 1938

stayed boxy, such as the **MG TA Midget**, others like the **Alfa Romeo 8C 2900B Coupé** were designed with sweeping, rounded body shapes. The exotic **Peugeot 402 Darl'Mat** showcased extreme streamlining with a lightweight aluminum body and an advanced gearbox.

The sleek **Mercedes-Benz 500K Special Roadster** was packed with advanced features for its time, including electric door locks, turn indicators, hydraulic brakes, and separate suspension systems for each wheel for a comfortable ride.

Fins and finery

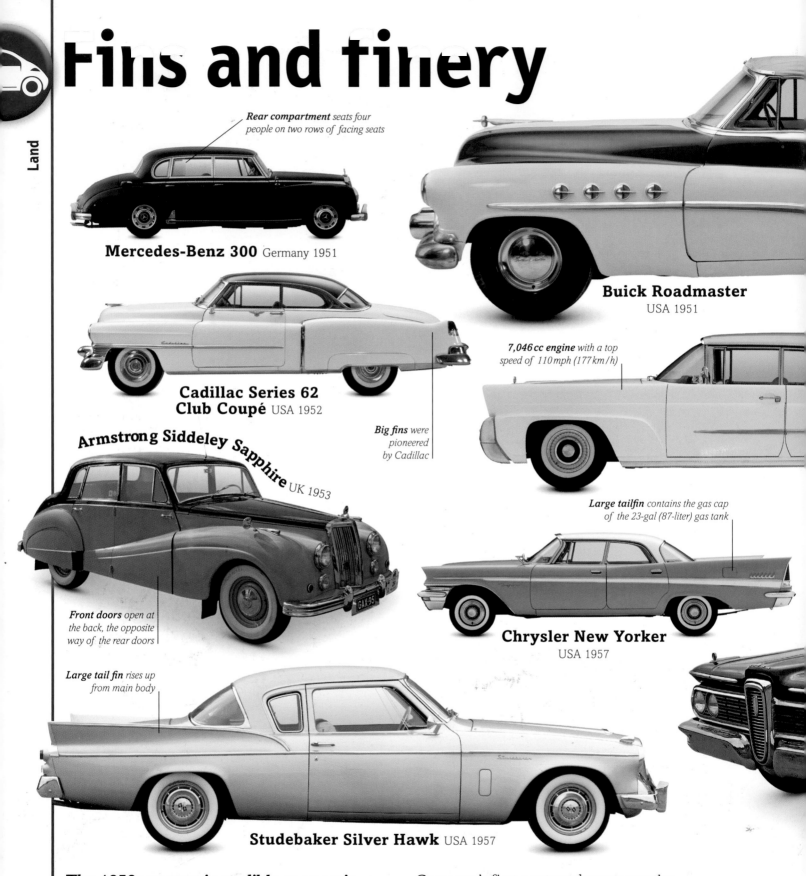

Rear compartment seats four people on two rows of facing seats

Mercedes-Benz 300 Germany 1951

Buick Roadmaster
USA 1951

**Cadillac Series 62
Club Coupé** USA 1952

7,046 cc engine with a top speed of 110 mph (177 km/h)

Big fins were pioneered by Cadillac

Armstrong Siddeley Sapphire UK 1953

Large tailfin contains the gas cap of the 23-gal (87-liter) gas tank

Front doors open at the back, the opposite way of the rear doors

Chrysler New Yorker
USA 1957

Large tail fin rises up from main body

Studebaker Silver Hawk USA 1957

The 1950s saw an incredible economic boom in the USA; 30 million more cars had taken to its roads by the end of the decade. Cars went from everyday transportation to chrome-covered status symbols, packed with innovative new features.

Germany's first postwar luxury car, the **Mercedes-Benz 300**, seated six people and was called the **Adenauer** after the West German chancellor who installed a writing desk inside one of his 300s. In contrast, the American **Buick Roadmaster** was a riot of two-tone color and

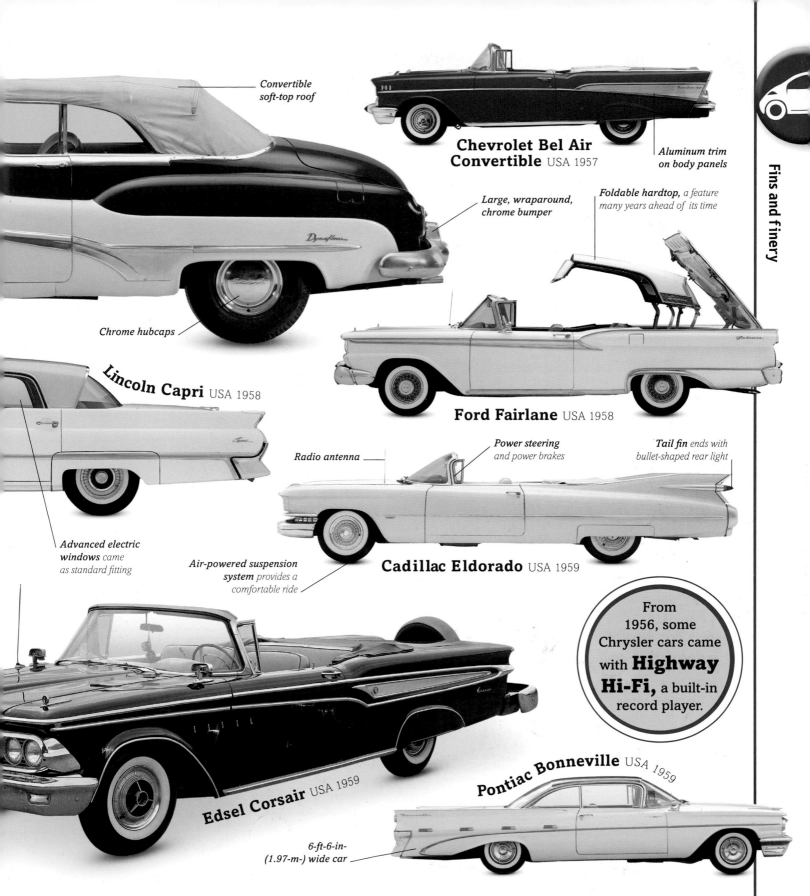

*Convertible
soft-top roof*

**Chevrolet Bel Air
Convertible** USA 1957

*Aluminum trim
on body panels*

*Large, wraparound,
chrome bumper*

*Foldable hardtop, a feature
many years ahead of its time*

Chrome hubcaps

Lincoln Capri USA 1958

Ford Fairlane USA 1958

*Power steering
and power brakes*

*Tail fin ends with
bullet-shaped rear light*

Radio antenna

*Advanced electric
windows came
as standard fitting*

*Air-powered suspension
system provides a
comfortable ride*

Cadillac Eldorado USA 1959

From
1956, some
Chrysler cars came
with **Highway
Hi-Fi,** a built-in
record player.

Edsel Corsair USA 1959

Pontiac Bonneville USA 1959

*6-ft-6-in-
(1.97-m-) wide car*

chrome, including chrome engine vents. The USA had entered the jet-aircraft age and this was reflected in the design of many cars—such as the **Pontiac Bonneville,** with its futuristic styling and large tail fins. Some cars also grew in length. The **Chrysler New Yorker** was more than 18 ft

(5.5 m) long, while the **Lincoln Capri** was even longer at over 20 ft (5.8 m). Automatic transmission was popular in big cars such as the **Chevrolet Bel Air Convertible,** which also had fuel injection and luxurious styling. It remains one of the most collectable cars from the fifties.

Faster and faster

Single, two-eared wheel nut for quick replacement

Mercedes-Benz W196 Germany 1954

Removable steering wheel

196

10

Large 53-gal (200-liter) gas tank carries 50 percent methanol

Maserati 250F Italy 1954

63

Large stabilizing fin

Jaguar D-type UK 1956

83

This Formula 1 racer won **8 Grand Prix** between 1954 and 1960.

Driver's headrest

Aston Martin DBR1 UK 1956

101

5

Roll bar to protect driver if car turns over

Huffaker-Offenhauser Special USA 1964

Jack Morrison owner
Kjell Quale owner
Walt Hansgen driver
Joe Huffaker crew

MG **LIQUID SUSPENSION** *Special*

STP

76

Race car design developed greatly from the 1950s onward. Engineers and designers were constantly looking for improvements to increase speed, enhance handling, and boost performance in order to be the first to cross the finish line.

Track racing began in the 1950s with mostly front-engined race cars, such as the **Maserati 250F** and the **Mercedes-Benz W196**, which won the Formula 1 (F1) Championships in 1954 and 1955. By the end of the 1950s, rear-mounted engines became all the rage in

Ford GT40 MKII USA 1966

Lotus 49 UK 1967

Lola-Cosworth T500 UK 1978

Nose fitted with low front wing

FIRST NATIONAL CITY TRAVELERS CHECKS

Benetton-Ford B193 UK 1993

Carbon fiber body

UNITED COLORS OF BENETTON.

Adjustable rear spoiler

Castrol

Holden VR Commodore SS Australia 1993

Williams-Renault FW18 UK 1996

Williams-Renault FW18 won **12** of the **16 F1 races** in 1996.

Windshield clipped in for easy removal

Large, aerodynamic wing keeps the car stable at high speed

Goodwrench Service

Chevrolet Monte Carlo USA 2000

3,000 cc engine gives top speed of 220 mph (354 km/h)

Front wing ensures car grips the track

F1 and Indy Cars. Sports car racing also saw change. Open cockpit cars such as the **Jaguar D-Type**, which won the Le Mans 24-hour endurance race in 1955, 1956, and 1957, were replaced by cars with a roof. The sleek **Ford GT40 MkII** finished first, second, and third at Le Mans in 1966. In some parts of the world, track racing featuring modified sedan cars gained popularity. A **Holden VR Commodore SS** won the 1995 Australian Touring Car Championships, while the **Chevrolet Monte Carlo** was driven by many NASCAR racers.

Fast and furious

Bentley Speed 8 UK 2001

Le Mans 205 mph (330 km/h)

Rear wing deflects air to keep car stable

Aston Martin DBR9 UK 2005

Le Mans 186 mph (299 km/h)

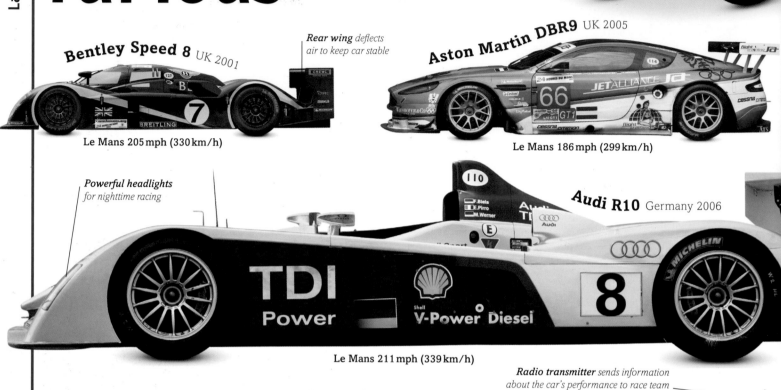

Powerful headlights for nighttime racing

Audi R10 Germany 2006

Le Mans 211 mph (339 km/h)

Radio transmitter sends information about the car's performance to race team

Roll cage frame protects driver if car rolls over

BMW M3 GT2 Germany 2008

Le Mans 180 mph (290 km/h)

Ferrari F2008 Italy 2008

Powerful disk brakes can stop a car at 125 mph (200 km/h) in three seconds

Modern high-speed racers packed with electronics are designed and modeled on computers, and tested in wind tunnels to ensure their design offers maximum performance. No expense is spared on these sleek speed machines.

All successful race cars must be fast, but different forms of racing place different demands on the vehicle. A power-packed rally car must be rugged and able to handle roads, tracks, and rough ground. The World Championship winning **Volkswagen WRC Polo R** can accelerate from

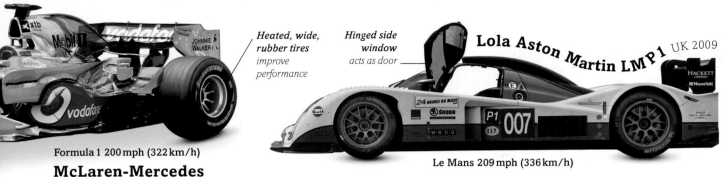

Heated, wide, rubber tires *improve performance*

Hinged side window *acts as door*

Lola Aston Martin LMP1 UK 2009

Le Mans 209 mph (336 km/h)

Formula 1 200 mph (322 km/h)

McLaren-Mercedes MP4/23 UK 2008

Chevrolet SS USA/Australia 2013

Large roof flaps lift up to ground car during crash

NASCAR 196 mph (316 km/h)

F1 drivers **shift gears** more than **3,600** times in a Grand Prix race.

Indycar Series 230 mph (370 km/h)

Team Penske Dallara/Chevrolet USA 2014

Volkswagen WRC Polo R Germany 2014

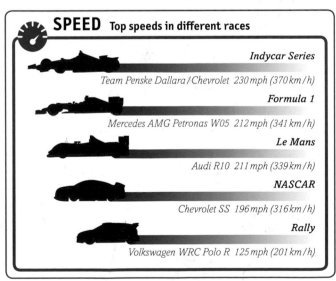

Rally 125 mph (201 km/h)

Formula 1 200 mph (322 km/h)

Mercedes AMG Petronas W05 Germany 2014

Formula 1 212 mph (341 km/h)

SPEED Top speeds in different races

Indycar Series
Team Penske Dallara/Chevrolet 230 mph (370 km/h)

Formula 1
Mercedes AMG Petronas W05 212 mph (341 km/h)

Le Mans
Audi R10 211 mph (339 km/h)

NASCAR
Chevrolet SS 196 mph (316 km/h)

Rally
Volkswagen WRC Polo R 125 mph (201 km/h)

0–60 mph (0–100 km/h) in 3.9 seconds. Cars built for endurance racing must be very reliable. In 2009, the **Lola Aston Martin LMP1** raced 3,159 miles (5,084 km) in 24 hours at Le Mans. Its driver, Tom Kristensen, also won the race a record nine times in the **Bentley Speed 8** and the **Audi**

R10. Danica Patrick, in a **Chevrolet SS**, became the first woman to win pole position for NASCAR's Daytona 500. Lewis Hamilton won the World Championship with the **McLaren-Mercedes MP4/23** in 2008, and again in 2014, with the **Mercedes AMG Petronas W05**.

THE ULTIMATE TEST

Powering through giant sand dunes, some more than 66 ft (20 m) high, is just one of the many challenges facing this Monster Energy X-Raid Mini in the 2013 Dakar Rally. Considered the toughest test of car and driver on the planet, competitors race across more than 5,280 miles (8,500 km) of the toughest terrain imaginable, from rocky pavements to giant deserts and forest trails.

The Dakar was first held in 1979 across the unforgiving Sahara in Africa, but since 2009 it has run through South America. More than 400 cars, motorcycles, quad bikes, and trucks take part in each race, but fewer than 60 percent of these reach the finish line. This Mini is built tough and equipped with four-wheel drive, a powerful engine giving it a 111 mph (178 km/h) top speed, and tanks able to hold up to 106 gallons (400 liters) of gas. Driver Stéphane Peterhansel is a Dakar legend. He won the motorcycle class of the rally six times before switching to cars. Over two solid weeks of phenomenal off-road racing in his Mini, Peterhansel won the 2013 Dakar—his fifth victory in the car class.

Fun in cars

Willys MB *Jeep*
USA 1941

Fold-down windshield
with hand-operated
wipers in early models

Chunky-tread tire
provides grip over
rough ground

S 20103442

Mini Moke
UK 1964

Rear spoiler

MICHEL

Leyland Mini Moke Australia 1968

Dune Buggy USA 1960s

*Small
9¾in- (25 cm-)
diameter wheel*

Steel side box holds car battery

Between
1960 and 1980,
every **second
car** on Magnetic
Island, Australia
was a Mini
Moke.

Suzuki Jimny LJ10 Japan 1970

Spare wheel
in place of
a fourth seat

*Bucket seats with
harness* to keep driver
and passenger secure

*Fold-down
windshield*

Volkswagen Beetle Baja Bug Germany 1970s

Grille lets air into
engine compartment

Ford Escort RS1800 UK 1973

Toughened body
for rallying

DUCKHAMS **ROTHMANS** ROTH

PIRELLI 26th ACROPOLIS RALLY

BILSTEIN

8

Strong towing bar
to pull car out if
stuck in sand or mud

Driving can be enjoyable, but some cars are more fun than others! A number of cars have been modified or designed from scratch to offer a fun drive on open roads, across stretches of sand, or along trails and rally courses.

The **Willys MB *Jeep*** could be driven just about anywhere, with more than 600,000 produced during World War II. Civilian Jeeps followed until 1986 when they were replaced by the **Jeep Wrangler**, which allowed drivers to switch between two- or four-wheel drive. Several fun

Peugeot 205 T16 Evo 2 France 1985

Gas cap of 76.6-gal (290-liter) gas tank

V12 engine from a Lamborghini Countach supercar

Lamborghini LM002 Italy 1986

Steel half-door

Spare wheel

Rear door for passengers to enter

Jeep Wrangler USA 1987

Heavy-duty suspension to withstand bumps

MCC Smart Crossblade France 2002

Cut-out sides offer open-air driving

Doors are optional on this two-seater

Secma F16 Sport France 2008

The Crossblade has **no doors**, **no windshield**, and **no roof**.

cars started life as military prototypes, such as the **Lamborghini LM002**, an off-roader with four-wheel drive, air conditioning, and a roof-mounted stereo. The **Leyland Mini Moke**, on the other hand, was a bare-bones vehicle with no frame around the driver. **Dune Buggies** were tailor-made for beaches, while some modified cars, such as the **Baja Bug**, had raised bodies and strong suspensions to overcome the most difficult terrains. Buggy-styled cars are still made today, such as the **Secma F16 Sport**, which has plastic body panels and a convertible roof for rainy days.

Crazy cars

Lightweight plywood body

Leyat Hélica France 1919

34-ft- (10.4-m-) long wings

Aerocar USA 1954

Brooke Swan UK 1910

Whitewash came out of the back to simulate bird droppings

Aluminum disc wheel

BMW Isetta 600 The Detonator Germany 1958

Colorful, hot-rod paint scheme

This **James Bond** car can race in reverse gear at speeds above 112 mph (180 km/h).

Gull-wing doors

Body made of brushed stainless-steel

DeLorean DMC-12 UK 1981

Aston Martin Vanquish UK 2002

Machine guns

KE02 EWW

Rockets fire from radiator grille

Wienermobile USA 2004

Oscar Mayer

Think all cars are simple, straightforward boxes-on-wheels? Think again! Over the years, designers and engineers have let their imaginations run wild, and some outrageous and surprising designs have left the drawing board and turned into reality.

Some of these wacky machines, such as the **Brooke Swan**, which hissed hot water and steam out of its beak, were special one-of-a-kind models built for eccentrics, or for movies such as the **Batmobile** *Tumbler*. The **Flatmobile**, however, was made to break records. At just 19 in (48.2 cm)

Batmobile *Tumbler* USA 2005

Four rear tires

LOWEST STREET CAR

19 in (48.2 cm) tall

Homemade jet engine from a Volvo F10 truck turbocharger

Flatmobile UK 2007

Terrafugia Transition USA 2009

Electromagnets lock wings into place

Cockpit has an aircraft control stick and a car steering wheel

The Transition can **convert** from a car to a plane in less than **60 seconds**.

Giant Buick-Rover V8 engine fitted to the rear

Toyota FV2 Japan 2013

Controlled by driver's body movements

Cab shaped like a hot dog

Onda Solare Emilia 3 Italy 2013

Small cockpit pod

Solar panels produce more than 1,200 watts of electricity to drive motors

tall, it is the lowest street-legal car in the world. Flying cars are among the craziest of all, but the **Aerocar** and **Terrafugia Transition** did work, using folding wings and a pusher-propeller at the rear to thrust the car forward. The **Leyat Hélica** couldn't fly but was pushed into action by an aircraft propeller and could reach speeds of up to 106 mph (170 km/h). Some strange-looking cars are experiments to test out new ideas, such as the solar-powered **Onda Solare Emilia 3**, or the **Toyota FV2**, whose body can change color to reflect the driver's mood!

A SPIN ACROSS THE WAVES

Is it a car? Is it a boat?
The answer is it's both!

The WaterCar Panther is an American amphibious vehicle equally at home on water as it is on land.
When on a lake, river, or bay, its engine powers jet thrusters that suck in water and then push it out
behind the craft, propelling it forward at speeds up to 43 mph (70 km/h).

On the road, the car's 1-gal (3.7-liter) Honda Acura engine powers the Panther's rear wheels, giving it a top speed of around 80 mph (128 km/h). The 15-ft- (4.6-m-) long waterproof, Jeep-shaped body can carry four people and is sculpted out of fiberglass fitted to a steel frame. Parts of its body are filled with incredibly lightweight Styrofoam to help it float. When reaching the water, the driver only has to pull a knob to engage the jet thrusters, and press a button. The Panther does the rest, using its hydraulic suspension system to retract its wheels up into its body. This all takes under 15 seconds! Once on the water, the Panther can glide with ease and can even tow a water-skier or wakeboarder.

Family cars

Radio antenna

Engine at the rear of car

Hillman Imp UK 1963

Volkswagen Kombi Germany 1950

The Cortina was the **UK's bestselling** car from 1972 to 1981.

Ford Cortina MK I GT UK 1963

Chrome hubcaps

18 ft (5.5 m) long

Oldsmobile Starfire USA 1964

Fake air vents, only for show

Austin Maxi 1750 UK 1969

Rear seats fold flat to form cargo area

Morris Marina UK 1971

Gas tank can hold 13.7 gal (52 liters)

A family car needs to be economical and have space for four to five people, as well as for plenty of storage. Many manufacturers work hard to build affordable cars that have the perfect balance of space, performance, and price.

Family cars in the 1960s, such as the **Oldsmobile Starfire**, were often based on a three-box design, with an engine compartment, passenger cabin, and large trunk. The **Hillman Imp** changed things by putting the engine in the rear, while early hatchbacks, such as the **Austin Maxi 1750**,

Volkswagen Golf GTI Germany 1975

Front wheels drive
110-horsepower engine

*Top speed of just
58 mph (93 km/h)*

Fiat Strada/Ritmo Italy 1978

*Front-wheel
drive*

Trabant East Germany 1989

Peugeot 406 France 1995

*Engine gives top speed
of 60 mph (100 km/h)*

OF·921 A

*Body panels made
of recycled materials*

Volvo V70 T5 Sweden 1997

Mercedes-Benz A-Class MKII Germany 2004

*Top speed of
135 mph (218 km/h)*

came with a sloping rear door to offer more versatile storage space. The affordable **Morris Marina** was built to compete with the highly popular **Ford Cortina**, which was bought by more than two million customers, mostly in the UK. Sleeker family cars appeared from 1970s, with more hatchbacks such as the **Fiat Strada/ Ritmo**—and the **Volkswagen Golf GTI**, which launched a new class of cars, the "hot hatch." These offered a hatchback design with a faster, sportier output than most family cars. More than 29 million Golfs have been built to date.

Outdoor warriors

Spyker 60HP
Netherlands 1903

Wheels powered by 8-liter engine

Jeep Wagoneer USA 1972

Low height to enable easy loading of cargo

Rear seats fold down to create large cargo space

Subaru Leone Estate Japan 1972

Car switches between four- and two-wheel drive

Audi Sport Quattro Germany 1983

Top speed of 154 mph (248 km/h)

Low rear spoiler

Small 7 ft 2 in (2.2 m) wheelbase

Daihatsu Sportrak Japan 1987

STEEP CLIMB

Most 4x4s can climb at angles up to 45°

Turbocharger boosts engine power to 185 horsepower

Lancia Delta Integrale
Italy 1987

Most cars transmit power from their engine to either the front or rear wheels, but not four-wheel drives. Known as "4x4s," these cars direct power to all four wheels, offering better grip on slippery roads and tricky off-road conditions.

In 1903, the **Spyker 60HP** used the first four-wheel drive on a gasoline-fueled car. However, only military and special purpose off-road 4x4s, such as Land Rovers, were built in large numbers until the 1960s and 1970s. The **Subaru Leone Estate** was one of the first everyday 4x4s. It was

Land Rover Discovery series II UK 1998

Rubber impact bumper

Top speed of 98 mph (158 km/h)

Volvo XC90 Sweden 2002

Electronic suspension allows car to have better grip for twisting roads

Range Rover Sport UK 2005

Open cargo area

Lincoln MK LT USA 2005

Fold-down tailgate

Hummer H3 USA 2005

Mounted rear tire takes length to 15 ft 8 in (4.8 m)

Saturn Outlook USA 2006

Three rows of seats accommodate up to eight people

The H3 was the **smallest** among the Hummer models, and the **only** one to be built by **GM**.

designed mainly for driving on roads in all conditions, with some light, off-road action. In the 1980s, rallies became dominated by fast, rugged 4x4s, such as the **Lancia Delta Integrale** and the **Audi Sport Quattro**, which won many World Rally Championship titles between them. By then, the first sports utility vehicles (SUVs) had emerged. These rugged cars, like the **Daihatsu Sportrack** and **Volvo XC90**, had high-set bodies for better ground clearance over bumpy roads. The **Hummer H3** can travel through 24 in (60 cm) of deep water and drive up 60-degree slopes.

Convertibles and sports cars

Soft-top roof had to be folded by hand

MGB Convertible UK 1962

Austin-Healey 3000 MKIII UK 1963

Wire-spoked wheels

Porsche 911 Germany 1965

Ford Mustang Fastback USA 1965

Small, narrow trunk wide enough to hold spare tire

Rear-mounted engine

Ferrari Dino 246GT Italy 1969

Headlight with transparent plastic cover

559 VF

Fast to accelerate and quick to brake, sports cars are built to thrill. Mostly two-seaters, they offer higher performance and sharper handling than everyday cars. Convertibles have a folding roof for open-top driving on sunny days.

There's no mistaking the love for sports cars—old and new! The first generation of **Chevrolet Corvettes** were built in 1953 and the seventh generation came out in 2014. More than 820,000 high-performance **Porsche 911s** have been built, while **Ford Mustang Fastbacks** were

Datsun 260Z Japan 1973

Pontiac Trans Am
USA 1975

Large V8 engine
under steel hood

Turning indicator lights

The 260Z series was one of the world's **best-selling** sports car in the 1970s.

Chevrolet Corvette USA 1980

Long, sloping hood

Mazda MX-5 (MkI) Japan 1989

Alloy wheel fitted with disc brake

Fiberglass body on top of aluminum frame

More than **940,000 MX-5s** were sold by 2015.

Lotus Elise UK 1996

Morgan Aero 8 UK 2001

Audi TT Roadster
Germany 1999

Louvers channel air over front brakes to keep them cool

among the two million Mustangs sold in the first two years of production. Many Mustangs in the late 1960s and 1970s were fitted with large V8 engines to offer the brute force provided by fellow muscle cars such as the **Pontiac Trans Am**. Sports cars fitted with smaller engines, even

if not as powerful and fast, also proved fun to drive due to their light weight. The **Mazda MX-5** weighed 1,962 lb (890 kg), while the **Lotus Elise** tipped the scales at just 1,598 lb (725 kg). The popular British soft-top **MGB Convertible** sold half a million models in the UK alone.

Mini motors

Volkswagen Beetle Germany 1945

Rear engine air-cooled via vents

1

13 ft 6in (4.1 m) long

BMW Isetta 300 Germany 1955

2

Front of car opens out as a single door

7 ft 6in (2.3 m) long

Messerschmitt KR200 Germany 1956

3

9 ft 4in (2.8 m) long

Shallow doors open out at the front

Frisky Family Three UK 1958

4

10 ft 2in (3.1 m) long

The Subaru 360 took **37 seconds** to do 0–60mph (0–100km/h).

Subaru 360 Japan 1958

5

Austin Mini Seven UK 1959

6

Space for four seats

9 ft 8in (2.9 m) long

Peel P 50 UK 1963

7

Car has a handle at the back for driver to pull it into parking spaces

4 ft 4in (1.3 m) long

Small is beautiful when you need a car to dodge and weave through narrow city streets, and to squeeze into the smallest parking spaces. Light in weight and easy on the pocket, their small engines make these mini motors cheap to run.

Partly inspired by the success of the **Volkswagen Beetle**, a wave of tiny cars hit the roads in the 1950s and 1960s. The compact **Messerschmitt KR200** could accommodate only a driver and one passenger, while the egg-shaped **BMW Isetta 300** had two front wheels placed close

⑧ **Reliant Robin** UK 1973

10 ft 10 in (3.3 m) long

Single front wheel

SIZE Smallest to biggest

7 2 12 9 3 5 6
4 11 8 10 1

⑩ **Fiat 500** Italy 2007

Small trunk area above engine

11 ft 6 in (3.5 m) long

⑨ **Smart City-Coupé** Germany/France 1998

8 ft 3 in (2.5 m) long

Fiberglass roof

Gas cap underneath hood

⑪ **Tata Nano** India 2009

nano twist

10 ft 3 in (3.1 m) long

⑫ **Renault Twizy ZE** France 2012

XPX 193F

9 ft 8 in (2.9 m) long

Storage space under hood as engine in the back

Small 1-ft-1-in- (32.5-cm-) long wheels

Scissor doors open upward

7 ft 6 in (2.3 m) long

together, no hood, and a motorcycle engine tucked behind the seat. Many three-wheeled cars, such as the **Reliant Robin** and the **Frisky Family Three**, could be driven on a motorcycle license. While the Frisky sold only in hundreds, the sales of the hugely popular **Austin Mini Seven** reached more than four million by 1976. Today, mini cars such as the **Smart City-Coupé** and the **Tata Nano** are popular in crowded cities. However, all of them still dwarf the **Peel P50**, the world's smallest car, which weighs a mere 130 lb (59 kg).

THE MOPETTA MICROCAR
In 1958, the passionate German car designer Egon Brütsch decided he was going to build the world's smallest car for the International Bicycle and Motorcycle Exhibition in Frankfurt that year. His idea was to use a new material called fiberglass to make two shell-like panels, which would fit together to form an egg-shaped microcar.

Brütsch built the prototype of the Mopetta overnight, but he did not have time to sort out the mechanics before the exhibition, so the microcar was displayed up high, away from prying eyes. Success at the show meant Brütsch then had to make his design work. The result was a single-seat three-wheeler that was 5 ft 7 in (1.75 m) long, 3 ft (0.9 m) wide, and had a 50 cc engine that took it to a top speed of 22mph (35 km/h). With its fiberglass body, Brütsch thought the car would also work as a boat. Although publicity photographs showed the Mopetta crossing a shallow stream, it could never be made fully watertight. Sadly, the Mopetta never became popular and only 14 were ever made.

Supercars

Lamborghini Countach, LP 400 Italy 1974

170mph (274km/h)

Engine mounted sideways just behind driver's seat

Lamborghini Miura
Italy 1966

177 mph (285 km/h)

Marcello Gandini designed the Miura before he turned **28**.

Rear wing keeps wheels on the ground at high speeds

Lamborghini Diablo Italy 1990

202 mph (325 km/h)

Driver sits in the center and slightly in front of two passenger seats

McLaren F1 LM UK 1995

230 mph (370 km/h)

Five-spoke magnesium wheels fitted with tires specially made for the car

0–62 MPH (0–100 KM/H)

Caparo T1

2.5 seconds

Porsche 918 RSR Spyder

3.0 seconds

Koenigsegg CCX-R

3.1 seconds

Pagani Zonda Italy 1999

Body panels made of light but strong carbon fiber

220 mph (354 km/h)

Some cars are just too hot to handle. These high-performance sports cars, known as supercars, are phenomenally fast and often very expensive. Hand-crafted in small numbers, they offer the last word in speed and handling.

The first supercar emerged in the 1960s. High-performance cars such as the **Lamborghini Miura** had sleek lines, powerful engines, and were built low to the ground. Miura's successor, the **Countach, LP 400**, was just 3 ft 7 in (1.1 m) tall. Some supercars were made of high-tech

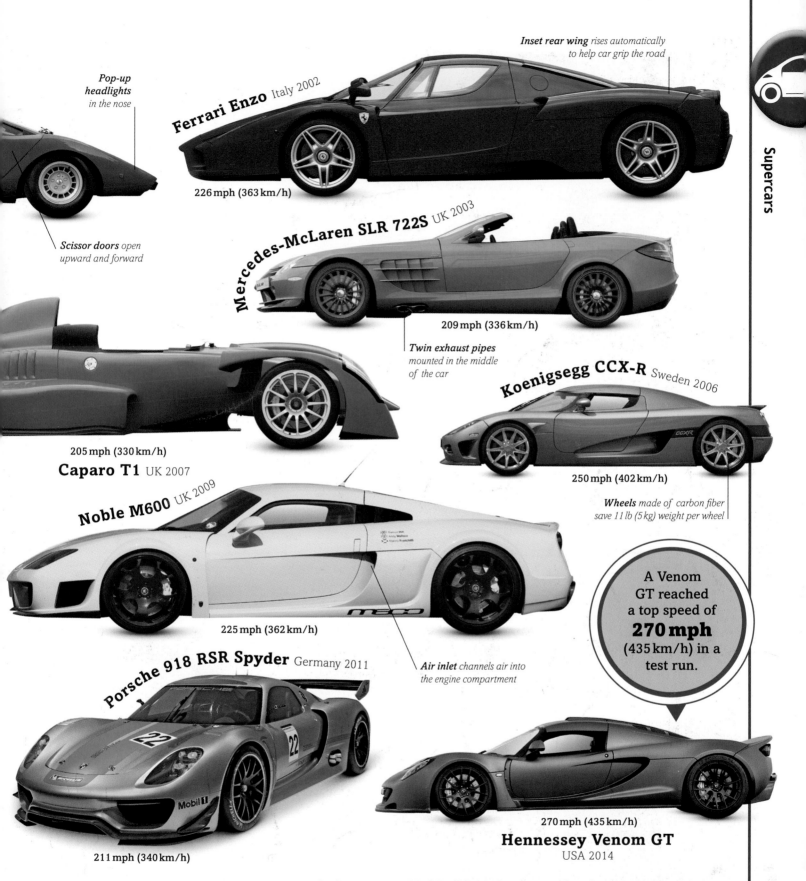

Pop-up headlights in the nose

Scissor doors open upward and forward

Inset rear wing rises automatically to help car grip the road

Ferrari Enzo Italy 2002

226 mph (363 km/h)

Mercedes-McLaren SLR 722S UK 2003

209 mph (336 km/h)

Twin exhaust pipes mounted in the middle of the car

205 mph (330 km/h)

Caparo T1 UK 2007

Koenigsegg CCX-R Sweden 2006

250 mph (402 km/h)

Wheels made of carbon fiber save 11 lb (5 kg) weight per wheel

Noble M600 UK 2009

225 mph (362 km/h)

Air inlet channels air into the engine compartment

Porsche 918 RSR Spyder Germany 2011

A Venom GT reached a top speed of **270 mph** (435 km/h) in a test run.

270 mph (435 km/h)

Hennessey Venom GT
USA 2014

211 mph (340 km/h)

material to keep their weight down, with the 1,036 lb (470 kg) **Caparo T1** being the lightest. The heavier supercars compensate with incredibly powerful engines. The **Hennessey Venom GT** can deliver up to 1,244 horsepower, which is 10 times the power of a hatchback. The **Noble M600's** twin turbochargers give it a top speed of 225 mph (362 km/h), while the **McLaren F1 LM** can hit 230 mph (370 km/h). Some supercars feature the latest in race car technology, like the **Mercedes-McLaren SLR 722S**, which has fly-by-wire (electronic) brakes.

Luxury rides

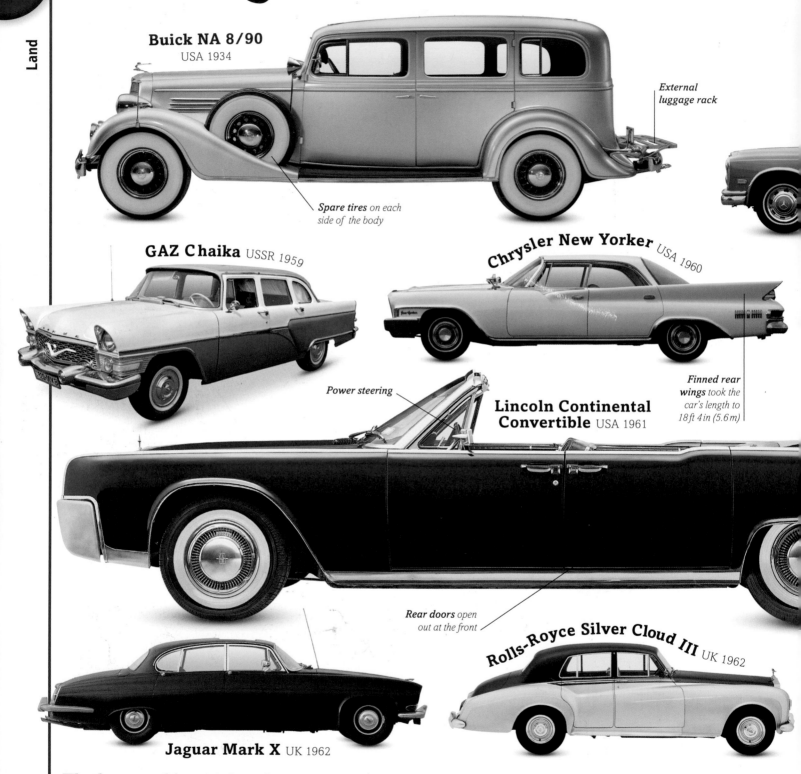

Buick NA 8/90
USA 1934

External luggage rack

Spare tires on each side of the body

GAZ Chaika USSR 1959

Chrysler New Yorker USA 1960

Finned rear wings took the car's length to 18 ft 4 in (5.6 m)

Power steering

Lincoln Continental Convertible USA 1961

Rear doors open out at the front

Rolls-Royce Silver Cloud III UK 1962

Jaguar Mark X UK 1962

The last word in comfort, luxury cars are often packed with the most advanced driving and passenger features. These grand, superexpensive cars offer a quiet, cushioned ride for the rich, the powerful, and the famous.

Celebrities and dignitaries did not have to shut the doors of the **Mercedes-Benz 600**. This 2.9-ton car did it for them! Owners ranged from the Pope and presidents of many countries to the rock 'n' roll legend Elvis Presley. In the Soviet Union, the 18 ft-4 in- (5.6 m-) long, seven-seater

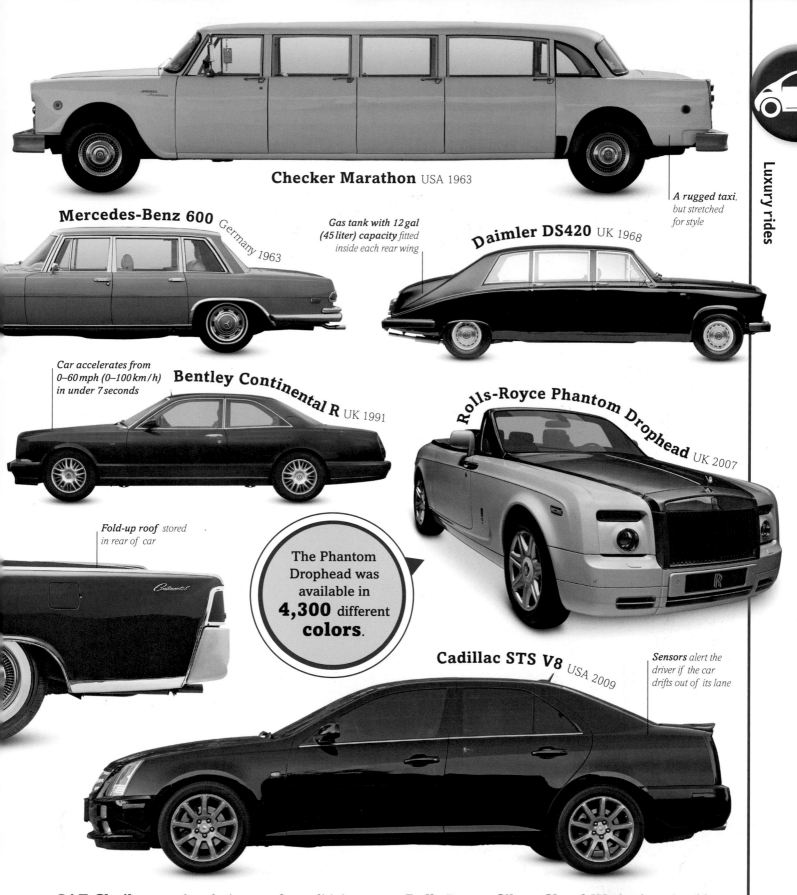

Checker Marathon USA 1963

A rugged taxi, but stretched for style

Mercedes-Benz 600 Germany 1963

Gas tank with 12 gal (45 liter) capacity fitted inside each rear wing

Daimler DS420 UK 1968

Car accelerates from 0–60 mph (0–100 km/h) in under 7 seconds

Bentley Continental R UK 1991

Rolls-Royce Phantom Drophead UK 2007

Fold-up roof stored in rear of car

The Phantom Drophead was available in **4,300** different **colors**.

Cadillac STS V8 USA 2009

Sensors alert the driver if the car drifts out of its lane

GAZ Chaika was the choice car for politicians, while the stately **Daimler DS420** was used by the British, Swedish, and Danish royal families. The car was based on the **Jaguar Mark X**, which came with a wood-paneled interior, plenty of legroom, and fold-down picnic tables. Some

Rolls Royce Silver Cloud IIIs had cocktail bars and televisions, while the **Lincoln Continental Convertible** turned heads with its convertible, four-door design. The statue on the hood of the **Rolls-Royce Phantom Drophead** sinks into the hood when the car is locked up.

Record breakers

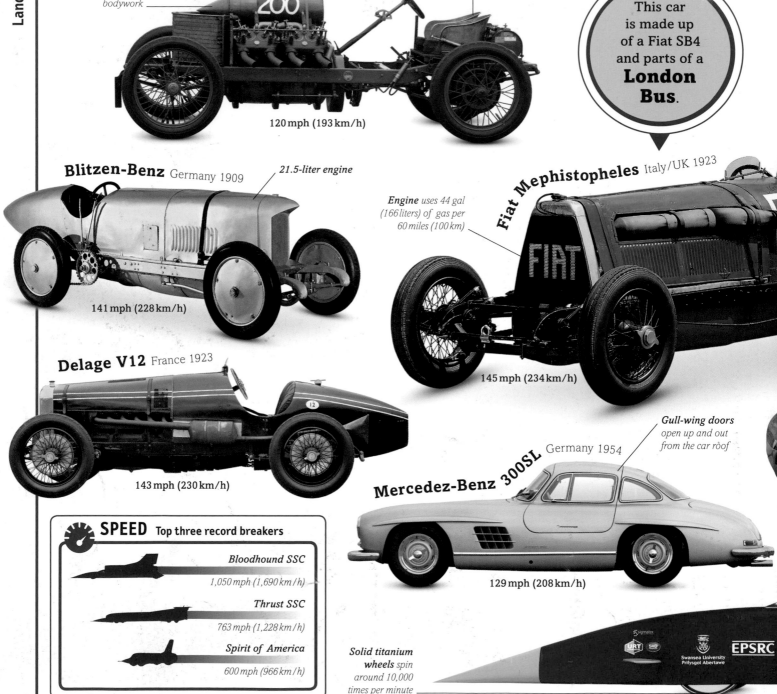

Exposed engine without any bodywork

Darracq 200HP France 1905

Basket seat

120 mph (193 km/h)

This car is made up of a Fiat SB4 and parts of a **London Bus**.

Blitzen-Benz Germany 1909

21.5-liter engine

141 mph (228 km/h)

Engine uses 44 gal (166 liters) of gas per 60 miles (100 km)

Fiat Mephistopheles Italy/UK 1923

145 mph (234 km/h)

Delage V12 France 1923

143 mph (230 km/h)

Gull-wing doors open up and out from the car roof

Mercedez-Benz 300SL Germany 1954

129 mph (208 km/h)

SPEED Top three record breakers

Bloodhound SSC
1,050 mph (1,690 km/h)

Thrust SSC
763 mph (1,228 km/h)

Spirit of America
600 mph (966 km/h)

Solid titanium wheels spin around 10,000 times per minute

Cars have always been valued for their speed. Some people have built one-of-a-kind fast cars in an attempt to break land-speed records, while car manufacturers have competed to produce the fastest production cars.

The **Blitzen-Benz** was the first car with an internal combustion engine to break the 125 mph (200 km/h) barrier. In 1924, the **Delage V12** held the land-speed record for six days before it was broken by the **Fiat Mephistopheles** with a bomber aircraft engine. The **Bluebird CN7**, also

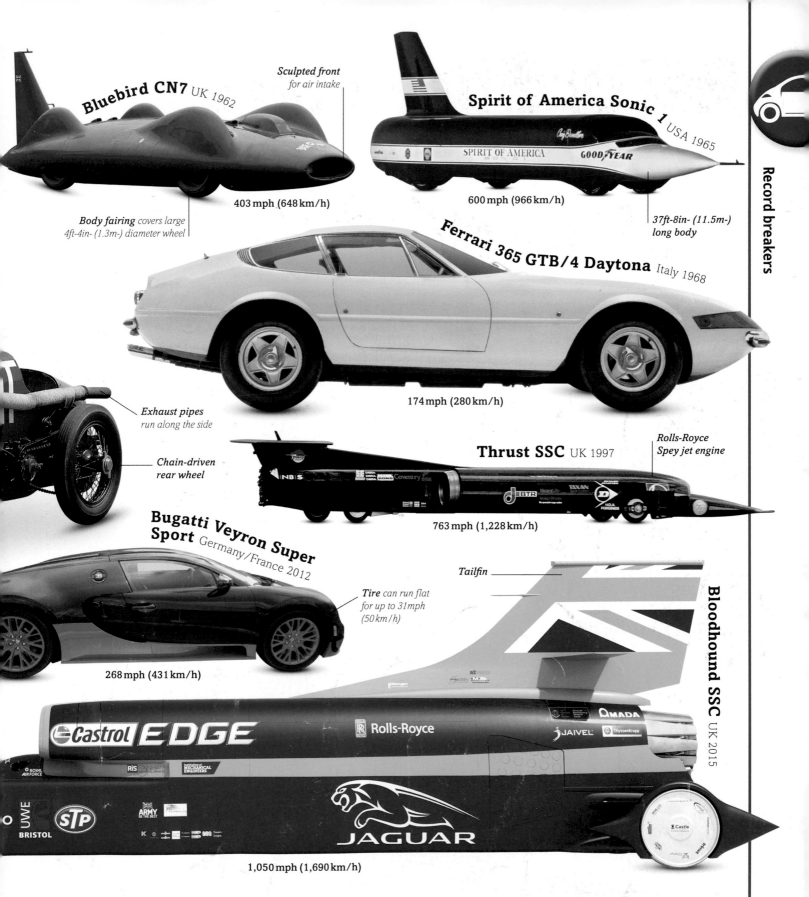

Bluebird CN7 UK 1962

Sculpted front for air intake

403 mph (648 km/h)

Body fairing covers large 4ft-4in- (1.3m-) diameter wheel

Spirit of America Sonic 1 USA 1965

SPIRIT OF AMERICA GOOD✦YEAR

600 mph (966 km/h)

37ft-8in- (11.5m-) long body

Ferrari 365 GTB/4 Daytona Italy 1968

174 mph (280 km/h)

Exhaust pipes run along the side

Chain-driven rear wheel

Thrust SSC UK 1997

Rolls-Royce Spey jet engine

763 mph (1,228 km/h)

Bugatti Veyron Super Sport Germany/France 2012

Tire can run flat for up to 31mph (50 km/h)

268 mph (431 km/h)

Tailfin

Bloodhound SSC UK 2015

Castrol **EDGE**   Rolls-Royce   JAIVEL   AMADA ThyssenKrupp

ROYAL AIR FORCE   STP   ARMY BE THE BEST   JAGUAR   UWE BRISTOL

1,050 mph (1,690 km/h)

with an aircraft engine, was the last record-breaking car with wheels driven directly by the engine. Record breakers since then, such as the current holder **Thrust SSC**, are propelled by jet engines. The **Bloodhound SSC** team is hoping that their machine, using a Jaguar car engine, a jet engine, and a rocket engine, will set a new record at supersonic speeds. The **Mercedes-Benz 300SL** set a record for fastest production car in 1955, which was broken by the **Ferrari 365 GTB/4**. The **Bugatti Veyron Super Sport** is the current fastest production car.

DRAGSTER BURNOUT

Vrrrm, Vrrrm! Dave Gibbons revs up his Rough Diamond T dragster at the UK's Santa Pod Raceway in 2014. These mean machines race along straight pieces of tarmac track, known as drag strips, in high-speed races that last as little as five or six seconds. Blink and you'll miss the contests between these epic racers—the fastest-accelerating cars in the world.

Dragsters feature ridiculously powerful engines that burn an explosive fuel mixture. The most powerful, found in a class of dragster called Top Fuel, can generate a staggering 8,000 horsepower. That's more than the power created by all of the first 10 NASCARs or Formula One cars on a starting grid put together. This phenomenal force carries dragsters from 0–100 mph (0–160 km/h) in less than 0.8 seconds. After two or three seconds, they're rocketing along at more than 250 mph (400 km/h) while the fastest can cross the line at 310 mph (500 km/h). Dragsters need plenty of braking assistance, usually provided by large parachutes that open out behind the car to generate drag and slow it down.

Truck

Trucks come in many shapes and sizes. Articulated trucks come in two parts. At the front is a tractor, containing the engine and driver's cab. It is connected to the cargo-trailer by a pivoting joint, which allows the truck to go around tight corners. The **Kenworth C540** is a powerful long-distance truck that can haul a fully loaded trailer over long distances.

Sleeper cab ❯ This cab contains a bed, storage space, and, often, cooking facilities for long-distance truckers.

Kenworth C540

WALKER BROS.

ABCODE HOLLAND

Trailer side curtain

Semitrailer ❯ This is called a semitrailer, because it does not have a front set of wheels. It is designed to hook up to the tractor. This model is a curtain-sider, with fabric side panels that can be pulled aside for loading or unloading.

Wheels ❯ Two sets of tractor rear wheels support the weight of the trailer.

Gas tank

Side lights

Cab light

Exhaust stack ›
Vertical exhaust pipes
release waste gases
from the engine.

Windshield

Rearview
mirror

Radiator grille ›
The grille lets in air
to cool the large
diesel engine that
powers the truck.

NILRAH EQUIPMEN
407-855-870
ORLANDO, F

BE·16·88

MARLINS

Steps to
driver's cab

Fender

Bumper

Tons of trucks

Stack from steam engine

Wallis & Steevens Wagon 7279 UK 1912

Flatbed to carry sacks, boxes, or other loads

Thornycroft Type J UK 1917

THE SOUTHERN COUNTIES AGRICULTURAL TRADING SOCIETY LTD.
CORN & SEED MERCHANTS
WINCHESTER.
TELEGRAMS, FARMERS. TELEPHONE, 382

UW 450

Solid-rubber tires

During World War I, some Type Js were fitted with **guns** to shoot at enemy aircraft.

Two-doored cab seats only one

Piaggio Ape Model D Italy 1967

Frame for protective cover

Subaru Sambar Kei truck Japan 1969

Tree logs carried in trailer from forest to lumber mill

Chevrolet C10 USA 1960s

Driver's cab contains sleeping bunk in roof

Renault TR 280 France 1971

There are almost as many types of trucks as there are jobs they perform—from whisking packages around town to hauling farm animals, cars, or goods on trailers. The first motorized trucks ran on steam power, but today most have diesel engines.

In Japan, tiny Kei trucks, such as the **Subaru Sambar,** carry small cargos around cities, while in Italy, the even smaller **Piaggio Ape Model D** runs on three wheels, with a motorcycle engine powering its rear wheels. Pickup trucks, such as the **Chevrolet C10,**

MCD DAF 85 Netherlands 1992

Mercedes-Benz 1838 tanker truck Germany 1996

DAF XF105 Netherlands 2008

Racing
DAF 85 trucks reach speeds of up to **100 mph** (160 km/h) on race tracks.

Rear supported by three sets of wheels

Vertical exhaust

Large 793-cu in (13-liter) engine situated below driver's cab

Volvo Bobtail semi-truck Sweden 2011

Living quarters contain bed for driver

Radiator grille

Scania P400 Sweden 2009

are often just a little larger than a sedan, and have an open cargo bed behind the driver's cab. Many large trucks, such as the **Volvo Bobtail** and **Scania P400**, are designed to haul a range of trailers carrying very different loads. These trucks have a tractor unit with a driver's cab and

an engine, and are articulated, which allows the truck to turn around tight corners. Trailers can be box-shaped, open, or specialized, such as the ramped car transporter hauled by the **MCD DAF 85**, or a tanker containing liquid pulled by the **Mercedes-Benz 1838**.

Special task trucks

Alvis Stalwart UK 1966

Three-seater cab can be entered from the roof

Douglas P3 UK 1970

Aircraft Engineering

Underside of vehicle is waterproof to travel through water

Walter Snowfighter USA 1972

56

WALTER SNOWFIGHTER

FD 22B

Water-and-foam cannon can fire hundreds of liters of liquid per minute

Gloster Saro Javelin UK 1987

4

B·A·A
Stansted
Airport Fire Service

JAVELIN

E188 KDF

Large blades push snow to the sides

Telescopic ladder can extend upward to reach into multistory buildings

59

Large hopper to collect garbage

MIAMI-DADE

American La France Metrostik 75 USA 2000

Six-wheel drive with engine powering all wheels

Extended cab carries firefighters and equipment

Clean TRUCK
0 – 00
I'm a fuel efficient hybrid
automated garbage truck
Miami-Dade green

Outrigger provides stable base when ladder is extended

M·A HAZ MAT TEAM

MIAMI INTERNATIONAL AIRPORT

MIAMI-DADE
FIRE RESCUE

While some trucks are designed to be versatile and carry a wide range of loads, others are designed and specially built to do one job and do it extremely well. Meet some of the more extraordinary special task trucks.

Every airport has tugs, such as the **Douglas P3**, which can pull a giant aircraft into position, and crash tenders such as the **Gloster Saro Javelin**. These high-speed firefighting vehicles often have four-, six-, or eight-wheel drive and can rush to a stricken aircraft to cover it in water and foam.

Powerful crane can lift smaller tow trucks

Kenworth W900 tow truck
Australia 2007

Flashing warning lights

Mercedes-Benz Citaro ambulance Germany 2009

Driver's cab windows are protected from branches and debris by metal mesh

John Deere 843K USA 2010

KEEP BACK 300 FT / 90 M

Citaro is the **largest** civilian ambulance, with space for **20 patients**.

Holder C270 Germany 2010

Giant tires support weight of the 27,990-lb (12,696-kg) vehicle and its load

Vertical exhaust pipe

Autocar E3 refuse truck USA 2011

MIAMI-DADE COUNTY 061022
55176
061022

Rapidly spinning brushes remove dirt

Hyundai 700S-7E South Korea 2012

Special purpose trucks are also found every day on city streets. Street sweepers, such as the small **Holder C270**, can turn their cabs to sweep around tight corners, while garbage trucks, such as the **Autocar E3**, collect and compact garbage in their rear hoppers before taking it to dumps or recycling centers. The **Walter Snowfighter** can clear roads of snow, and the **Kenworth W900** lifts and recovers broken-down vehicles. Out in the countryside, tree fellers such as the **John Deere 843K** use powerful saws and grippers to fell and remove trees.

SHUTTLE CRAWLER
Meet the ultimate heavy hauler—NASA's gigantic Crawler Transporter. This picture shows it inching the Space Shuttle Discovery from the Vehicle Assembly Building to Launchpad 39B at the Kennedy Space Center in Florida in 2005. Fully loaded, the Shuttle spacecraft weighs more than 2,500 tons (2 million kg), so it takes a serious machine to carry such an extreme load.

NASA's two Crawler Transporters, nicknamed Hans and Franz, were built in the 1960s to carry Saturn V launch vehicles. The loading platform is 295 sq ft (27.4 sq m)—about the same size as a baseball diamond. Each Crawler Transporter is 131 ft (40 m) long, 115 ft (35 m) wide, and weighs 3,000 tons (2,721,000 kg). When loaded with a space vehicle, the crawlers move along a special, heavy-duty road, known as a crawlerway, at a top speed of 1 mph (1.6 km/h). The vehicle is powered by 16 electric engines, and the electricity is supplied by an onboard generator run by two diesel engines. Burning fuel at 126 gal per mile (297 liters per km), the Crawler Transporter is a real gas-guzzler.

Bus stop

Bollée L'Obeissante
France 1873

Steam stack

Open cab for driver

Engine radiator

LCOG B-type
UK 1911

27 ft 6 in (8.4 m) long

AEC Regent III RT UK 1938

Open platform to enter and exit

Foremost Terra bus
Canada 1986

Be Trendy... Hire a Bendy!

Door powered by compressed air

Volvo B10MA *Bendy Bus* Sweden 1996

The first motorized buses were steam-powered and carried people for short distances in the 19th century. The arrival of the internal combustion engine led to bigger and more powerful buses for commuters, tourists, and school runs.

Driven by twin steam engines, one for each rear wheel, the **Bollée L'Obeissante** could carry 12 passengers at speeds up to 25 mph (40 km/h). Gradually, gasoline-engine buses took over the first mass-produced bus, the **LCOG B-type**, had seats for 16 passengers inside and 18 on the

Volvo B12M Sweden 2001

Underfloor-mounted engine

Joint covered by flexible rubber seals

The bendy, 92-ft- (28-m-) long B12M can seat up to **270 passengers**.

R.L. HANSON
STOP

School bus USA 2002

High-mounted driver's cab

Rails for a flexible roof

ROMA CRISTIANA
Hop on Hop off

Roma Cristiana open bus Italy 2003

Fold-down steps

49 ft 2 in (15 m) long

Wi-fi onboard for using gadgets

luxury travel day and night
megabusGold.com
luxury travel day and night

Van Hool sleeper bus Belgium 2009

xury Seats

top deck. Double-decker buses proved popular, with room for many more people. The **AEC Regent III RT** used to carry up to 64 passengers around London, UK, while today's open-topped buses, such as the **Roma Cristiana**, give tourists spectacular city views. The rugged, single-decker **Foremost Terra Bus** transports tourists and workers around ice-bound regions in Canada and Antarctica. The **Volvo B10MA** can bend in the middle to travel around corners, while the **Van Hool sleeper bus's** seats convert into 42 beds for long, overnight journeys.

Tractor

Tractors are a farm's workhorses, used to pull plows and other tools in fields, or to carry and lift a range of loads. These machines vary in size, from tiny tractors used in gardens and parks to giant beasts with massive pulling power. The **Massey Ferguson 7618** is a versatile, large tractor that can perform lots of different jobs in the field.

Engine ❯ A large engine burns diesel fuel. This tractor has a top speed of around 31 mph (50 km/h) on the road and 17 mph (28 km/h) on the field.

Engine hood

Vertical exhaust

Massey Ferguson 7618

MASSEY FERGUSON 7618

Radiator grille

Mudguard

Weight frame ❯ Weights can be added to the front of the tractor to balance out the weight of the tools or loads it carries behind it.

Fuel tank

Tire tread ❯ Deep tread on the rubber tire helps the tractor grip the soft ground and move forward or backward.

Driver's cab

Warning light

Cab light ❯ Equipped on all the four corners of the cab, these light up the area around the tractor.

Rear wheel ❯ Huge rear wheels equipped with giant tires, 5 ft 1 in (1.8 m) in diameter and 22¾ in (58 cm) wide, support the tractor's weight.

Steps to the cab

Total tractor

Stack funnel

Clayton & Shuttleworth Dorothy UK 1914

Steering chains turn front wheels

Canopy covered driver and engine

Twin City 40-65
UK 1916

Waterloo Boy
USA 1917

Steel wheels equipped with blades dig into the ground to provide more grip

Caterpillar Sixty
USA 1931

Driver's cab sits high above ground

Big Bud 16V 747 USA 1978

Each tire measures 7 ft 10 in (2.4 m) in diameter

Ferguson TE-20 UK 1946

Rubber tires with heavy tread for better grip

Powered by steam, the first farm tractors were often heavy and slow, but they could pull objects with great force. Over time, diesel and gas engines replaced steam, while solid steel wheels made way for tracks and wide rubber tires.

The **Clayton & Shuttleworth Dorothy** steam-powered tractor weighed 22,046 lb (10,000 kg) and had a top speed of 5 mph (8 km/h). In contrast, the 15,212-lb (6,900-kg) **JCB Fastrac 185-65** can reach 50 mph (80 km/h). The **Ferguson TE-20** became so

Hydraulic arms raise and lower farm tools

Storage area

JCB Fastrac 185-65 UK 1994

Bar protects the driver if the tractor rolls over

Wheel turned by steam engine

A Fastrac **push-started** the world's fastest diesel car on its record run.

Massey Ferguson 1540
USA 2005

Weights balance heavy tools or loads pulled by the tractor

Renault Ares 710 RZ France 2009

Challenger MTF 7650 USA 2012

Rear linkage hook to pull plows or other farm tools

Steps to driver's cab

Xenon lights illuminate field around tractor

John Deere 6150 RH USA 2013

Kingpin around which both halves of the body can turn

New Holland T9.505 USA 2013

popular that over half a million were built. Some tractors run on a continuous belt called a track, which spreads weight evenly over the ground, giving good stability and grip. The **Caterpillar Sixty** had steel tracks, while the modern **Challenger MTF 7650** has rubber tracks.

Tractors today range greatly in size. The small **Massey Ferguson 1540** is used in parks and gardening, while the **New Holland T9.505** is so long that its body is hinged in the middle. At 27 ft (8.23 m) long, the **Big Bud 16V 747** was used on large American cotton farms.

On the farm

This harvester can pick and wash as many as **one million** pumpkins in a week!

Pumpkin Harvester UK 2006

Massey Ferguson 9240 UK 1995

Sharp metal discs of the harrow break up soil

Tank provides water to wash pumpkins

Large, chunky tire provides grip over rough and muddy ground

Folding crop-spray boom can stretch out to a width of almost 60 ft (18 m)

John Deere 5430i USA 2008

Steps to driver's cab

Forks can lift up to 7,716 lb (3,500 kg)

Catterpillar TH406 USA 2010

Reel gathers in stalks of cereal crops toward cutting bar

Cutting head cuts grass and stalked crops

John Deere W260 USA 2013

Cutting bar slices the stalks off the plant

John Deere S690 USA 2013

Farming involves a vast amount of hard work but, fortunately, machines have come to the rescue. Farm machines automate and speed up many tasks, which previously had to be done by hand or by using animals.

Some farm tools like plows and disk harrows can be pulled or operated by multipurpose tractors such as the **Massey Ferguson 9240**. Growing crops are protected by crop-dusting machines, such as the **John Deere 5430i**, whose giant booms spray large areas of fields

Hydraulic-powered grippers can hold and lift hay bales

New Holland 740TL USA 2013

Unloading pipe discharges 35.7 gal (135 liters) of grain per minute

New Holland T6.140
USA 2013

Grain tank can hold up to 3,725 gal (14,100 liters) of grain

Driver's cab

New Holland Braud 960L USA 2013

Cutter head removes flowers from top of corn plant

Narrow wheels fit into gaps between rows of corn crops

Hagie 204SP Detassler USA 2013

with pest-removing chemicals. Come harvest time, different machines speed up the collection of crops, such as the **New Holland Braud 960L**, which travels above rows of vines, harvesting grapes, or the **Pumpkin Harvester**, which picks, washes, and packs pumpkins. Large combine harvesters, such as the **John Deere S690**, cut the stalks of cereal crops, separate the grain, and shoot the remaining straw out the back. This straw is packed into hay bales that can be lifted by forklifts, such as the **Caterpillar TH406**, or held by grippers, as on the **New Holland 740TL**.

MONSTER LEAP
At the Monster Mania festival in the UK, Ian Batey flies high in his *Lil' Devil* monster truck over a row of old cars. Fueled by high octane racing methanol in its hefty V8 engine, this powerful vehicle boasts ten times as much power as a regular family car. It weighs more than 8,800 lb (4,000 kg)—guaranteeing a crushing ending for any of the wrecked cars should it land on them.

Ever since Bob Chandler built the original Bigfoot monster truck in 1979 in the USA, these mean machines have been entertaining crowds all over the world with their antics. Events include races over dirt courses in arenas as well as stunts, jumps off ramps, and plenty of car crushing. Many monster trucks begin life as a humble pickup, a Chevrolet Silverado in the case of *Lil' Devil*. Only the body is kept, as the vehicle is tricked out with a tubular steel frame chassis and mighty 5-ft-7-in- (1.7-m-) high "terra" tires. These ride on suspension systems capable of absorbing enormous impacts on landing while the driver, held firmly in his seat in a racing harness, focuses on pulling amazing monster truck moves.

Construction and mining

Front roller *can be moved left or right to turn the vehicle*

Arm *can move bucket to dig down to depths of more than 14 ft 10 in (4.5 m)*

The **hopper** can hold **90 tons** of rock—as heavy as **20** monster trucks.

Steel bucket

Hamm HW90/10 Germany 1987

Case Poclain 688B USA 1993

Vertical exhaust pipe

Steel loader *can lift more than 2,200 lb (1,000 kg) in a single scoop*

Hopper *can be tipped by hydraulic arms*

75570

Caterpillar 950G USA 1998

Tire *is 8 ft 11 in (2.7 m) tall and weighs more than 3,307 lb (1,500 kg)*

BELAZ-75570

31 ft 10 in (9.7 m) tall

Liebherr LTM1500 Germany 2000

Outriggers *stabilize the crane when it is raised*

AINSCOUGH HEAVY CRANE DIVISION

Construction sites and mines have a lot of digging, leveling, and heavy lifting going on, and big, rugged machines do most of the work. They have to be strong to withstand the stresses of the tasks, and reliable to work all day long.

Excavators are digging machines usually fitted with a steel bucket that cuts into the earth. Some, such as the **Case Poclain 688B**, run on wheels, while others, such as the **John Deere 160DL C**, run on continuous tracks, which are ideal for crossing muddy ground. Front loaders, such as

Drum *mixes concrete for building purposes*

Mercedes-Benz Germany 2007

John Deere 160DL C USA 2007

Diesel engine *turns the tracks to move digger*

BelAZ-75570 Belarus 2008

Excavator *can dig up to a depth of 21 ft 4 in (6.5 m)*

Backhoe bucket *to dig holes or trenches for pipelines*

Front loader *can carry and push large amounts of soil and other materials*

JCB 3CX UK 2009

The **Dancing Diggers** are a team of JCBs that perform routines to music.

Long blade *levels materials for a smooth surface*

Caterpillar 12M2 USA 2011

John Deere 650K XLT USA 2012

the **Caterpillar 950G**, feature a large front-scoop, and backhoe loaders, such as the **JCB 3CX**, have both a front-loader and a rear bucket-digger. The **John Deere 650K XLT** is a bulldozer equipped with a long, strong blade to push materials along the ground, while compactors, such as the **Hamm** HW90/10, use heavy rollers to press down and make a firm surface. Giant cranes lift materials when building tall structures and some, such as the **Liebherr LTM1500**, are mobile, with an arm that telescopes out and up to a distance of 276 ft (84 m)—longer than a Boeing 747 jumbo jet.

Tanks and tracks

Stabilizer prevents tank from tipping over backward

Renault FT-17 France 1917

Mark V UK 1918

Gun originally used in ships and coastal forts

Continuous metal tracks around side of body

M4A1 Sherman USA 1941

Turret hatch, below which tank commander sits

Panzerkampfwagen IV Germany 1936

Turret holds three of the five crew members

T-34/85 Soviet Union 1941

Large gun can fire shells more than 3 miles (5 km)

Tough armor made of ceramics and metals

CHURCHILL

CHALLENGER 1 MBT

9 ft 8 in (3 m) tall

Tanks are heavily armored vehicles that run on tracks so they can cross muddy ground and other difficult terrain. They are usually equipped with a powerful, shell-firing artillery gun. The first tanks saw service in World War I.

The **Mark V** had an eight-man crew and a top speed of 5 mph (8 km/h), the same as the two-man **Renault FT-17**—the first tank with a rotating gun turret. The **Panzerkampfwagen IV's** powerful gun could pierce the armor of other tanks. It had a top speed of 24 mph

M4 Sherman V *Crab* USA 1943

Heavy, spinning chains pound the ground to set off land mines

With a top speed of 57 mph (92 km/h), this was the **fastest tank** of World War II.

Amphibious landing craft

M-29C Weasel tank transported inside

Landing Vehicle Tracked Mk IV Buffalo USA 1943

M18 Hellcat USA 1944

16-ft- (4.9-m-) long aluminum body holds a crew of three

Alvis FV107 Scimitar UK 1971

Smoke-grenade launchers generate smokescreen for defense

Tracks can travel through 6-ft- (1.8-m-) deep water

Challenger 1 MBT UK 1983

FV104 Samaritan UK 1978

Leopard C2 Germany 2000

Armored skirt protects upper tracks

(39 km/h) and a range of 125 miles (200 km). The **T-34/85**, one of its opponents, could travel twice as far. Other military vehicles are also armored and tracked but perform different tasks. The **FV104 Samaritan** is a battlefield ambulance, carrying up to six patients on stretchers, while the

Sherman *Crab* has flailing chains to clear paths through minefields. Main battle tanks, such as the 68-ton **Challenger 1 MBT**, are large and equipped with powerful weapons. In contrast, the **Alvis FV107 Scimitar** weighs less than 9 tons and can travel at 50 mph (80 km/h).

Steam train

Steam trains have engines that burn fuel in their firebox. The heat boils water to produce steam, which is fed into cylinders where it expands to drive the pistons. The movement of the pistons turns the wheels with the help of a rod and a crank, moving the train. This American locomotive from 1863, *Thatcher Perkins*, weighs 45 tons and could haul several wagons or carriages at 50 mph (80 km/h).

B&O Class B No. 147
Thatcher Perkins

Steam-powered whistle

Cab

Tender ❯ On many trains, this stored both water and fuel, often in the form of coal or, on this train, wood, to power the engine.

Wheel brakes ❯ To slow down the train, the driver pulls a lever, which presses brake shoes directly onto the driving wheels.

Driving wheel

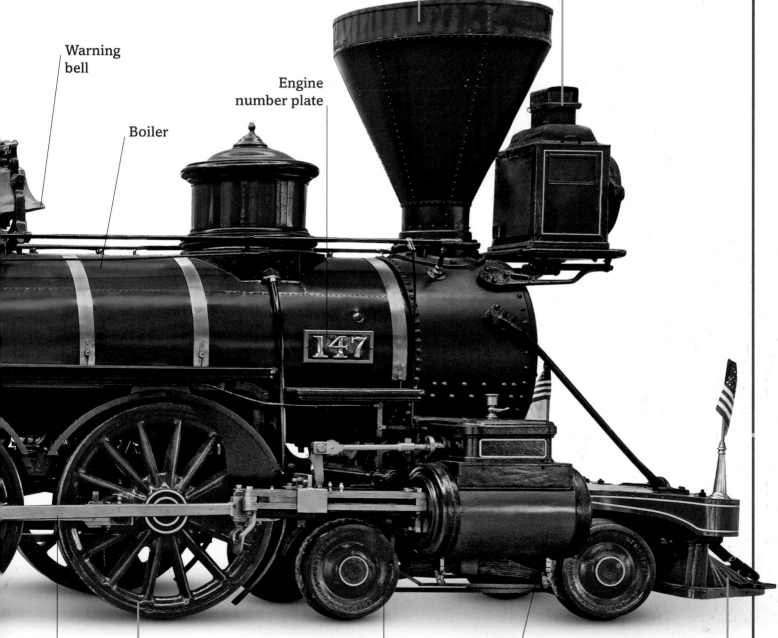

Stack › The smoke from the burning fuel in the firebox is channeled up and out through the stack. This one is fitted with layers of mesh to stop any dangerous sparks from escaping.

Headlamp › A large lamp burned oil to light up the tracks ahead.

Warning bell

Boiler

Engine number plate

147

Coupling rod

Wheel arrangement › Steam engines are defined by the number of wheels they have. This one has four leading wheels and six driving wheels.

Leading wheel

Engine cylinder

Pilot › Also known as the cowcatcher, this brushes aside obstacles, such as tree branches, from the train's path.

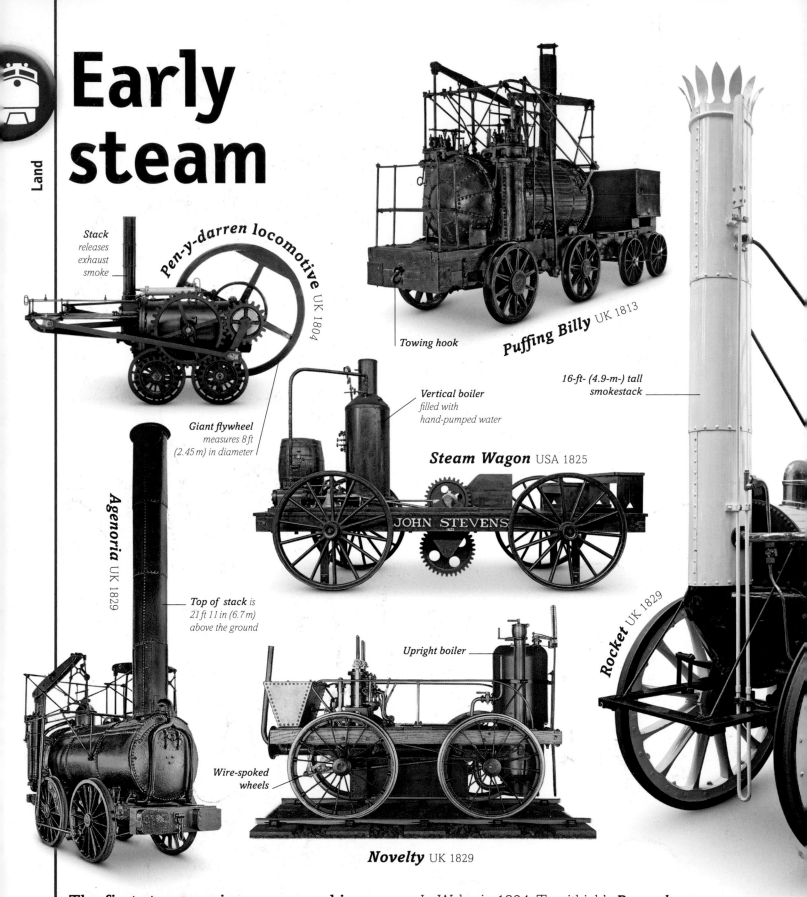

Early steam

Pen-y-darren locomotive UK 1804

Stack *releases exhaust smoke*

Puffing Billy UK 1813

Towing hook

Giant flywheel *measures 8 ft (2.45 m) in diameter*

Vertical boiler *filled with hand-pumped water*

Steam Wagon USA 1825

JOHN STEVENS

16-ft- (4.9-m-) tall *smokestack*

Agenoria UK 1829

Top of stack *is 21 ft 11 in (6.7 m) above the ground*

Upright boiler

Rocket UK 1829

Wire-spoked *wheels*

Novelty UK 1829

The first steam engines were used in factories to run machines, or in mines to pump out water. Richard Trevithick, a mining engineer, was one of the first to use steam to power a moving locomotive, sparking a transportation revolution.

In Wales in 1804, Trevithick's **Pen-y-darren** made the first railroad journey at less than 2 mph (4 km/h), hauling 12 tons of cargo and 70 people over 8.9 miles (14.4 km). Other steam engines, such as the **Puffing Billy** and **Agenoria**, quickly followed, ferrying coal or goods from factories.

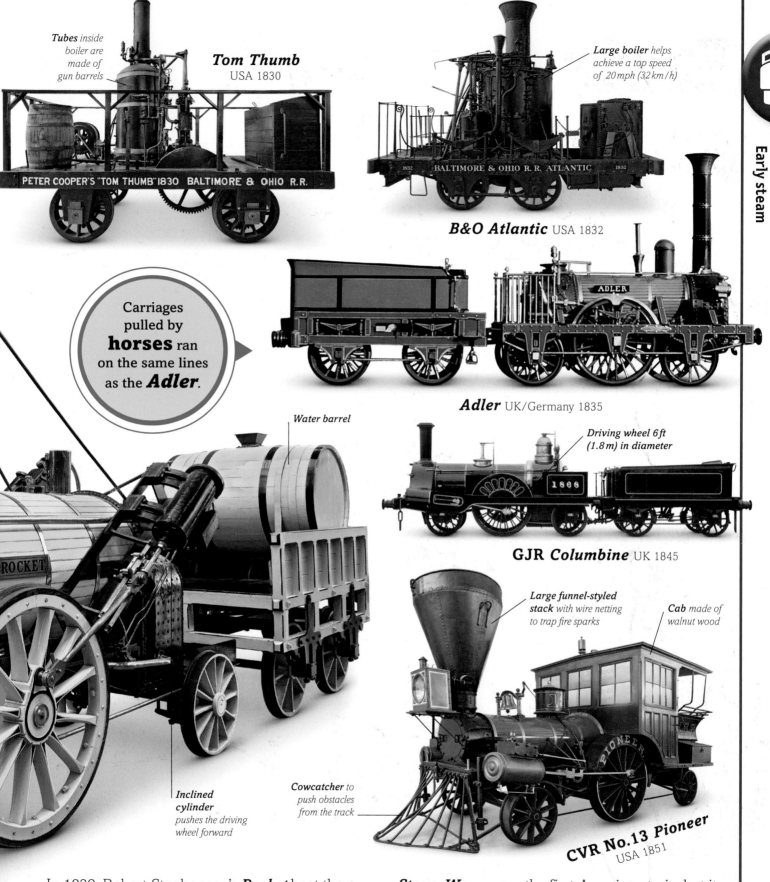

Tom Thumb USA 1830

Tubes inside boiler are made of gun barrels

PETER COOPER'S "TOM THUMB" 1830 BALTIMORE & OHIO R.R.

B&O Atlantic USA 1832

Large boiler helps achieve a top speed of 20 mph (32 km/h)

BALTIMORE & OHIO R.R. ATLANTIC

Carriages pulled by **horses** ran on the same lines as the *Adler*.

Adler UK/Germany 1835

ADLER

GJR Columbine UK 1845

Driving wheel 6 ft (1.8 m) in diameter

1868

Water barrel

ROCKET

Inclined cylinder pushes the driving wheel forward

Large funnel-styled stack with wire netting to trap fire sparks

Cab made of walnut wood

Cowcatcher to push obstacles from the track

PIONEER

CVR No.13 Pioneer USA 1851

In 1829, Robert Stephenson's **Rocket** beat the **Novelty** at the Rainhill Trials in the UK, where engines competed to run on the Liverpool and Manchester Railway—the world's first intercity line. Stephenson's company later built the **Adler**, the first German commercial train. John Steven's **Steam Wagon** was the first American train, but it ran on a small circular track. The first engine used on regular service in the USA was **Tom Thumb** on the Baltimore & Ohio Railroad (B&O). By 1840, the country had over 2,796 miles (4,500 km) of track, more than found in the whole of Europe.

Mainstream steam

SNB *Limmat*
Germany/Switzerland 1847

Wooden-clad cylinder

Engine named after the river it traveled alongside

Fairy Queen was given **national treasure** status by India in 1972.

Headlight

B&O L Class No. 57 Memnon USA 1848

Crown-shaped stack opening

Headlight

Hinged door to access smokebox

Driver's cab

EIR 22

FAIRY QUEEN

22 EIR

EIR No. 22 Fairy Queen UK/India 1855

Steam railroads boomed in the later half of the 19th century, opening up new territories and connecting towns and cities. Locomotives developed rapidly, to become faster, more reliable, and able to pull more cars or cargo wagons.

The **SNB *Limmat*** ran on the first railroad line in Switzerland, while the **EIR No. 22 *Fairy Queen*** operated in India for 54 years. The **DHR Class B**, also from India, had a short wheelbase, which helped it grip the track of the Darjeeling Mountain Railway that rose 6,500 ft (2,000 m) in

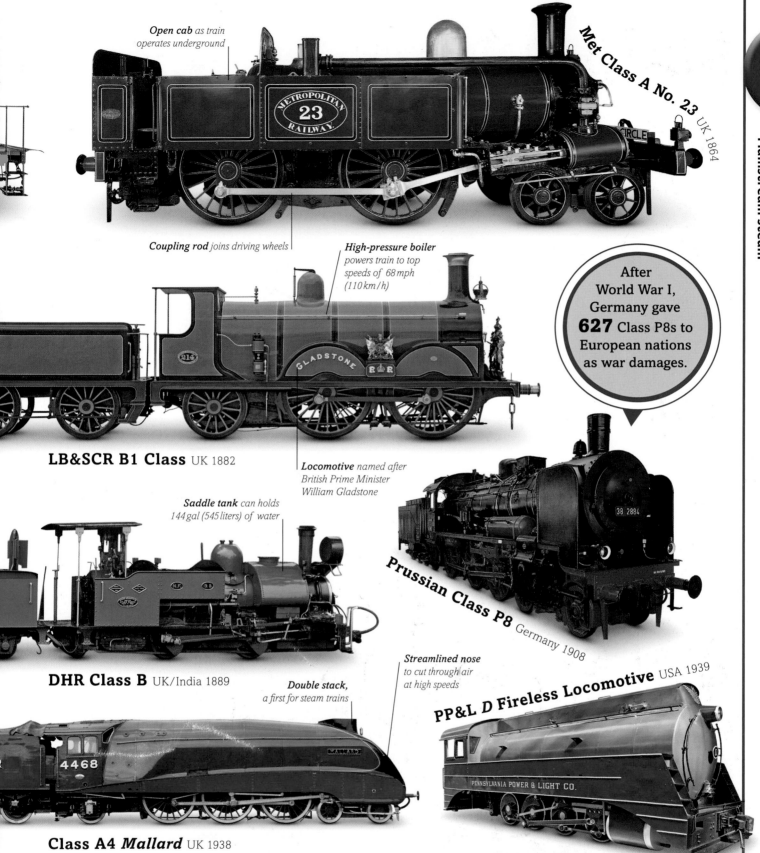

Open cab as train operates underground

Met Class A No. 23 UK 1864

Coupling rod joins driving wheels

High-pressure boiler powers train to top speeds of 68 mph (110 km/h)

After World War I, Germany gave **627** Class P8s to European nations as war damages.

LB&SCR B1 Class UK 1882

Locomotive named after British Prime Minister William Gladstone

Saddle tank can holds 144 gal (545 liters) of water

Prussian Class P8 Germany 1908

DHR Class B UK/India 1889

Double stack, a first for steam trains

Streamlined nose to cut through air at high speeds

PP&L D Fireless Locomotive USA 1939

Class A4 Mallard UK 1938

altitude. In contrast, the **Met Class A** ran on the world's first underground train line, the Metropolitan Railway in central London. Steam trains were built well into the 20th century. More than 3,700 **Prussian Class P8** engines were built and used in Romania, Poland, France, and elsewhere. Innovations included the **PP&L D Fireless**, which stored steam in its boiler so it could work in places where flammable fuel was a hazard. Steam engines were also streamlined for extra speed. The **Class A4 Mallard** was the fastest, with a top speed of 125 mph (202 km/h).

FLYING SCOTSMAN
The No. 4472 *Flying Scotsman* powers along the tracks of the Carlisle to Settle line in the north-west of England, a service known as the "Cumbrian Mountain Express." The 71-ft-2-in- (21.7-m-) long locomotive weighed more than 109 tons, but generated enormous pulling power. In 1934, it became the first steam locomotive officially recorded to exceed 100 mph (160 km/h).

The *Flying Scotsman* was designed by the British engineer Sir Nigel Gresley, who had joined the railroad as a 17-year-old apprentice. The locomotive was built in 1923, and soon after was painted its famous apple-green color. During World War II, however, it was painted black. After 40 years of faithful service, the *Flying Scotsman* was retired by British Rail in 1963, but the engine's travels weren't over. It was saved from being scrapped by enthusiast Alvin Pegler and, after restoration, underwent a five-year tour of the USA, before being taken to Australia, where she set a new world record for the longest nonstop locomotive run, traveling 422 miles (679 km) on the Alice Springs to Melbourne route.

Diesel train

Diesel trains contain one or more large internal combustion engines that generate hauling power. This power is transferred to the wheels by different transmission systems. Locomotives using the diesel-mechanical system, such as this **BR Class 05**, transfer the power directly to the wheels by means of shafts and cranks. In a diesel-electric system, the power is converted into electricity in a generator, which drives the motors that turn the locomotive's wheels.

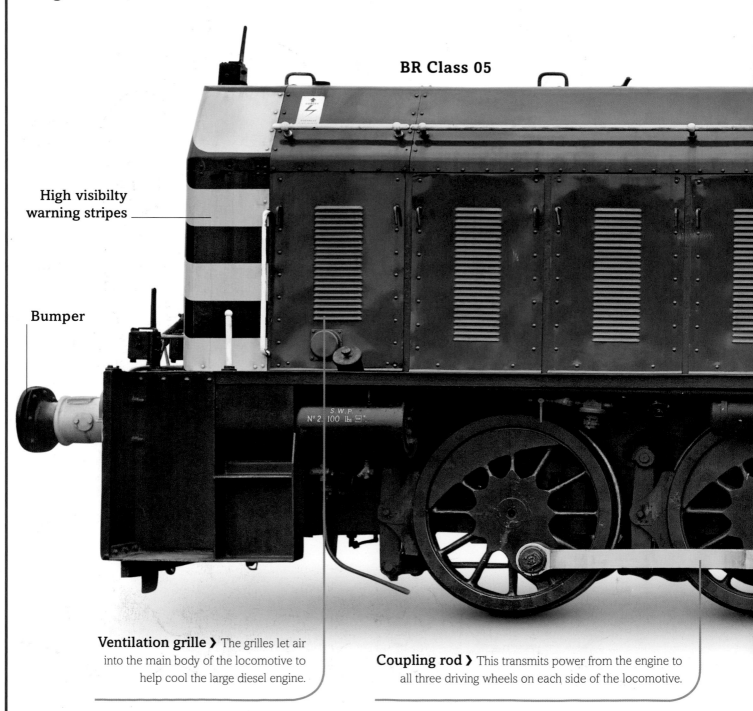

BR Class 05

High visibilty warning stripes

Bumper

Ventilation grille › The grilles let air into the main body of the locomotive to help cool the large diesel engine.

Coupling rod › This transmits power from the engine to all three driving wheels on each side of the locomotive.

Engine ❯ A large Gardiner eight-cylinder diesel engine gives this locomotive a lot of pulling power with the help of a four-speed gearbox. However, it has a low speed—18 mph (29 km/h).

Cab ❯ The 11-ft-6-in- (3.5-m-) high cab gives a good view down the long hood, while twin rear windows allow the driver to see what is going on behind. Inside, a series of dials gives the driver details of the engine's speed, temperature, and status.

Signaling horns

D 2595

Narrow cab door

Hand rail

Driving wheel is 3 ft 4 in (1.02 m) in diameter

Counterweight ❯ This helps to balance the force of the coupling rod.

Steps to driver's cab

Dawn of diesel

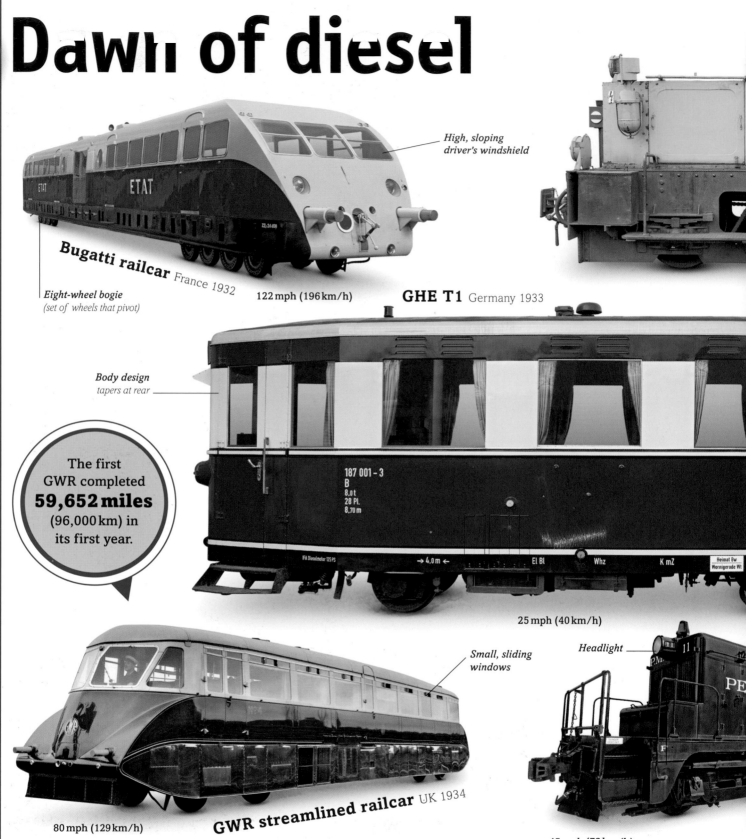

High, sloping driver's windshield

Bugatti railcar France 1932

122 mph (196 km/h)

Eight-wheel bogie
(set of wheels that pivot)

GHE T1 Germany 1933

Body design
tapers at rear

187 001-3
B
8,0 t
28 Pl.
8,70 m

IFA Dieselmotor 125 PS → 4,0 m ← El Bt Whz K mZ Heimat Bw Wernigerode Wt

The first GWR completed **59,652 miles** (96,000 km) in its first year.

25 mph (40 km/h)

Small, sliding windows

Headlight

GWR streamlined railcar UK 1934

80 mph (129 km/h)

45 mph (72 km/h)

As engine technology developed in the early 20th century, some engineers turned away from steam in favor of locomotives that ran on diesel fuel. Diesel-engined trains entered service in numbers from 1930s onward.

Diesel engines required less maintenance than steam locomotives and could be operated without extra crew to stoke the boiler. This made some, such as the **VC Porter No.3** and **DR Class Kö**, ideal as low-speed switchers. Many early diesel trains used their engines to drive the wheels

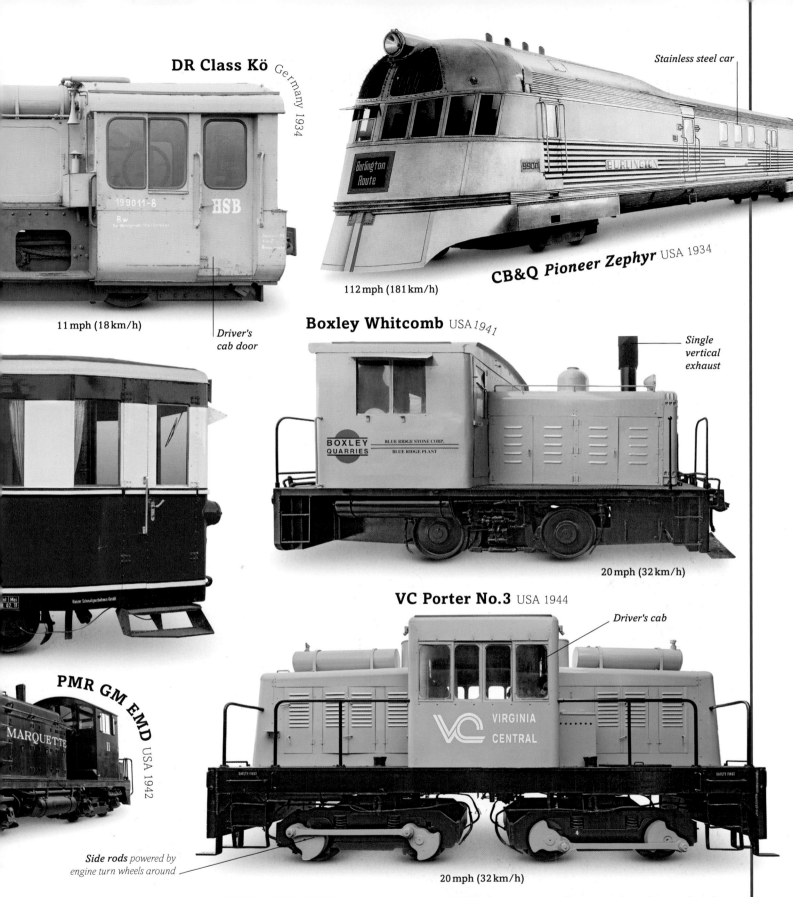

DR Class Kö *Germany 1934*

199011-8 Rw
HSB

11 mph (18 km/h)

Driver's cab door

CB&Q *Pioneer Zephyr* USA 1934

Burlington Route 9900 BURLINGTON

Stainless steel car

112 mph (181 km/h)

Boxley Whitcomb USA *1941*

BOXLEY QUARRIES BLUE RIDGE STONE CORP. BLUE RIDGE PLANT

Single vertical exhaust

20 mph (32 km/h)

VC Porter No.3 USA 1944

VC VIRGINIA CENTRAL SAFETY FIRST

Driver's cab

20 mph (32 km/h)

PMR GM EMD USA 1942

MARQUETTE

Side rods powered by engine turn wheels around

mechanically, but not the **PMR GM EMD**. A diesel-electric locomotive, its diesel engine powered a generator that supplied electricity to its four electric motors. Diesel engines were also used to power railcars—train passenger cars with motors fitted below. The **GHE T1** railcar could carry 34 passengers and ran on just four wheels. The **GWR streamlined railcar** had a top speed of 80mph (129km/h), while the **Bugatti railcar** was even faster. This sleek machine broke the record for high-speed trains in 1934 with a top speed of 122mph (196km/h).

Mainstream diesel

106 mph (171 km/h)

Powerful headlight to illuminate track ahead

Logo of the Norfolk and Western Railway

Baldwin Class DS-4-4-660 USA 1946

60 mph (96 km/h)

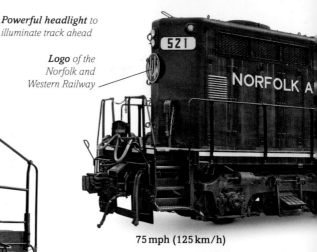

521

NORFOLK A

75 mph (125 km/h)

Stainless steel body is 85 ft (25.9 m) long

Budd RDC railcar USA 1949

85 mph (137 km/h)

2188

Two **jet aircraft** engines were fitted to the roof of a Budd to set a speed record in 1966.

B&O F7 Class USA 1949

MARC 7100

Ladder to driver's cab

50–120 mph (80–193 km/h)

Diesel locomotives became common after World War II. Although they were often more expensive to build, many were much cheaper and easier to operate than steam locomotives, and they spent less time in repair shops as well.

Baldwin Class DS-4-4-660 switchers were used to move cars and wagons in railroad yards. With their 660-horsepower diesel engines, some 139 were built. The rugged and reliable **N&W EMD GP9 Class** served all over the USA and Canada as a switcher, with more than

English Electric DP1 *Deltic* UK 1955

Spacious cab provided at either end of the locomotive

N&W EMD GP9 Class USA 1955

Driver's cab mounted on the roof

DB VT11.5 Germany 1957

100 mph (160 km/h)

UP GM EMD Class SD60 USA 1984

Radiator cooling fans

Rounded fuel tanks

65 mph (105 km/h)

Sliding double doors

Upper deck connected to lower by two spiral staircases

BR GM EMD Class 66 UK/USA 1998

60 mph (100 km/h)

DWA Class 670 railcar
Germany 1996

75 mph (121 km/h)

4,000 produced. The **DB VT11.5** hauled first-class passengers at speeds of up to 100 mph (160 km/h) on the famed Trans-Europ Express services, which linked 130 cities throughout Europe. Diesel-powered railcars, such as the **Budd RDC**, proved very versatile. On small lines, each railcar could operate by itself to carry a limited number of passengers, or they could be linked together for greater capacity. Another option was a double-decker, such as the **DWA Class 670 railcar**, which could hold up to 110 people on two decks.

Rail workhorses

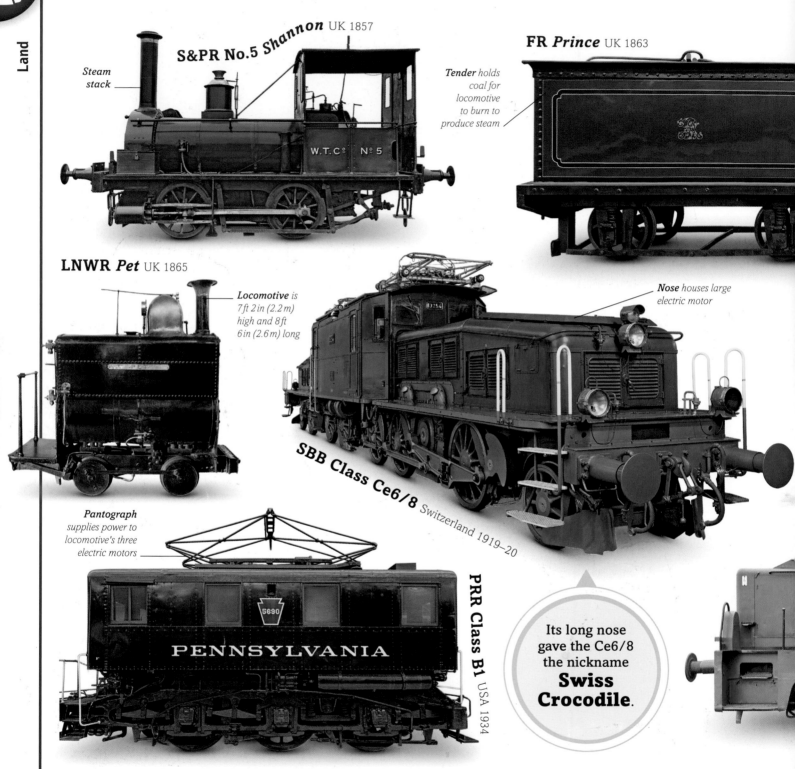

S&PR No.5 *Shannon* UK 1857

Steam stack

W.T.Cº Nº 5

FR *Prince* UK 1863

Tender holds coal for locomotive to burn to produce steam

LNWR *Pet* UK 1865

Locomotive is 7ft 2in (2.2m) high and 8ft 6in (2.6m) long

Nose houses large electric motor

SBB Class Ce6/8 Switzerland 1919–20

Pantograph supplies power to locomotive's three electric motors

PENNSYLVANIA

5690

PRR Class B1 USA 1934

Its long nose gave the Ce6/8 the nickname **Swiss Crocodile**.

While passenger trains grab all the attention, thousands of other trains are busy at work every day. These rail workhorses haul vast amounts of freight, and move other trains and cars around railroad yards.

Freight trains often use diesel engines, such as the **DR V100**, more than 1,100 of which have served across the world. The electric **SBB Class Ce6/8**, similar in design to the DR V100, has a central cab with a protruding nose at each end. The engine was hinged so that it could turn on

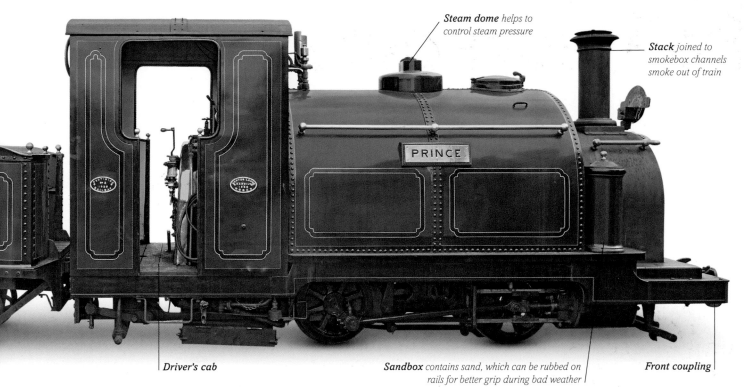

Steam dome helps to control steam pressure

Stack joined to smokebox channels smoke out of train

PRINCE

Driver's cab

Sandbox contains sand, which can be rubbed on rails for better grip during bad weather

Front coupling

50 BALTIMORE & ANNAPOLIS R.R.

B&A GE 70-ton switcher USA 1946

604 PHANTOM

BR Class 08 *Phantom* UK 1953

Central driver's cab gives excellent visibility in all directions

Driver's cab

DR V100 Germany 1966

112 331-4

Deutsche Reichsbahn

101 691-4

DR V15 Germany 1959

tight tracks in the Swiss mountains. Not all freight is carried cross-country. Many trains move goods and equipment on lines serving docks, mines, and factories, such as the **FR** *Prince*, which hauled slate from Welsh mines. Many small locomotives are also used to move around cars, wagons, and larger locomotives, to assemble and disassemble train services. These switchers, such as the **DR V15** and the **BR Class 08**, had to be robust and reliable. More than 100 Class 08s are still in service more than 50 years later.

Going electric

Trolley pole *transfers electricity from overhead cable to train's motor*

Door *to engineers's cab*

10 BALTIMORE AND OHIO

B&O Bo Switcher USA 1895

Pantograph *collects power from overhead cable*

GIPR Class WCP1 UK/India 1930

GIPR

NORTH EASTERN

NER Electric Locomotive UK 1905

Each half *of locomotive has two motors to drive the wheels*

Streamlined nose

4935

DRE04 Germany 1933

4935 PENNSYLVANIA

PRR Class GG1 USA 1934

A GG1 pulled the **funeral train** of President Franklin D. Roosevelt.

92042

The 1880s saw electric streetcars and trolleys rattling around cities, and it was not long before electric trains appeared. They offered advantages over smoke-belching steam trains, but they needed electrified railroad lines on which to run.

Experimental electric trains had been built since the 1830s, but the first main line electric service was in Baltimore in the 1890s. The **B&O Bo Switcher** operated in Baltimore's docklands at a top speed of 9 mph (16 km/h). Electric trains get their power supply either from overhead cables or

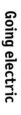

Cowcatcher pushes obstructions from the track

SNCF Class BB9000 France 1954

Single pantograph connects with overhead power lines of 11,000 volts

Penn Central/Budd Metroliner USA 1969

DR Class 243 Germany 1982

The BR Class 92 was built to run in the **Channel Tunnel** linking England and France.

Locomotive weighs 141 tons

BR Class 92 UK 1993

DB SCHENKER

via a third rail running along the track. The **NER** used both systems. After World War I, many countries began the electrification of their lines. The **GIPR Class WCP 1s** were the first electric engines to run in India. The 79-ft-3½-in- (24.2-m-) long **PRR Class GG1** was designed to travel around tight bends on American tracks. Electric railcars, such as the **Budd Metroliner**, also ran on American railroads. Electric trains proved to be reliable workhorses; more than 600 **DR Class 243s** were built for East German railroads to haul freight and passengers.

High-speed electric trains

Birmingham Airport Maglev UK 1984

26 mph (42 km/h)

Train is held ½ in (15 mm) above the track by magnets

VT Class *Pendolino* UK 2002

140 mph (225 km/h)

Cabin tilts up to 8 degrees when traveling on bends

DB ICE 3 Germany 2000

Engineer's cab separated from passenger seats by a glass panel

199 mph (320 km/h)

Shanghai Transrapid Maglev China 2004

249 mph (400 km/h)

Magnets raise the train around ⅜ in (10 mm) above the guideway

199 mph (320 km/h)

SNCF TGV POS France 2006

The need for speed has never been greater as high-speed trains take on aircraft and road traffic to get passengers from one point to another in the quickest possible time. Meet some of the most rapid railroad vehicles of all time.

The superfast **JRN700 Shinkansen** train can accelerate from 0 to 168 mph (270 km/h) in three minutes and can tilt slightly to keep its speed when moving around bends. While most high-speed electric trains, such as the **Hyundai Rotem KTX**, have powerful wheel-turning

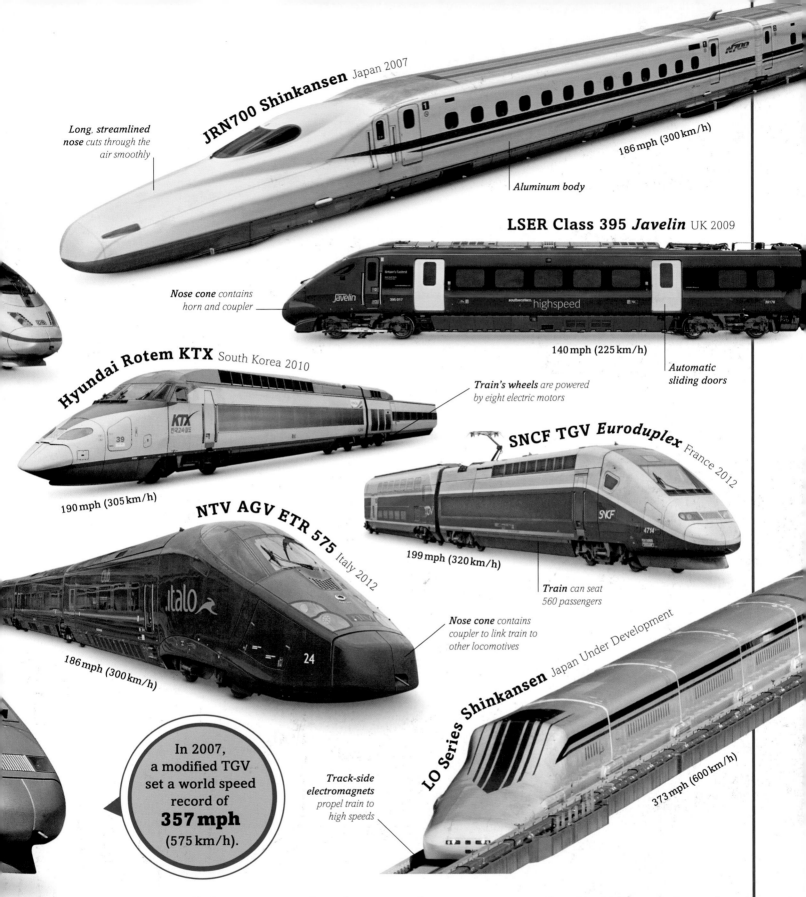

JRN700 Shinkansen Japan 2007

Long, streamlined **nose** cuts through the air smoothly

186 mph (300 km/h)

Aluminum body

LSER Class 395 *Javelin* UK 2009

Nose cone contains horn and coupler

140 mph (225 km/h)

Automatic sliding doors

Hyundai Rotem KTX South Korea 2010

Train's wheels are powered by eight electric motors

190 mph (305 km/h)

SNCF TGV *Euroduplex* France 2012

NTV AGV ETR 575 Italy 2012

199 mph (320 km/h)

Train can seat 560 passengers

186 mph (300 km/h)

Nose cone contains coupler to link train to other locomotives

LO Series Shinkansen Japan Under Development

In 2007, a modified TGV set a world speed record of **357 mph** (575 km/h).

Track-side electromagnets propel train to high speeds

373 mph (600 km/h)

electric motors housed in a power unit at the front of the train, the **DB ICE 3** has its motors spread out over the entire length of the train to distribute the weight. The **SNCF TGV *Euroduplex*** is a rare example of a high-speed double-decker train. Some trains use powerful electromagnets to raise them above their track and move them along. This is called magnetic levitation (maglev). The first public passenger maglev train was the **Birmingham Airport Maglev** in the UK, while the fastest is the **Shanghai Transrapid Maglev**, in China.

BULLET TRAIN
Sleek, streamlined, and super-fast, a Japanese Shinkansen high-speed "bullet train" speeds across Honshu Island past snow capped Mount Fuji. In 2014, Japan celebrated 50 years since Shinkansen trains ran for the very first time, just before the 1964 Tokyo Olympic Games. Today, Japan's high-speed rail network has carried more than 11 thousand million passengers.

The first Shinkansen trains ran at speeds of up to 130 mph (210 km/h). The latest classes of trains take their power from 25,000 volt overhead electricity lines and can reach a top speed of 200 mph (320 km/h). The trains run on their own lines, separate from slower rail traffic—a total of 1,483 miles (2,387 km) of high-speed track crosses Japan. As many as 13 bullet trains per hour fly between Japan's two biggest urban areas, Tokyo and Osaka, providing an unrivalled high-speed service. Before the bullet trains were introduced, journey time between the two cities was around 6 hours, 40 minutes. The fastest services today complete the route in just 2 hours, 35 minutes.

Urban railroads

Single, large wiper cleans entire windshield

Mud Island Monorail USA/Switzerland 1982

Mud Island River Park

Suspended car can hold up to 180 passengers

Gatwick Adtranz C-100 UK/Canada 1987

Gatwick

Gatwick

Train runs on wheels fitted with rubber tires

SMRT North-South Line C151 Singapore 1987

Train travels at speeds up to 50 mph (80 km/h)

U55 Hauptbahnhof

Berlin U-Bahn Germany 1992

Trains on the Berlin U-Bahn carry over **508 million** passengers every year.

Articulated joints between short cars

Rail services in towns and cities ferry millions of people every day. Some travel for work or for school, others for fun and leisure. There are urban railroads that link airports with towns, while others help reduce congestion on city roads.

Rapid transit systems, such as the **Matra Taipei Metro**, offer quick and reliable transportation between city stations separated by short distances. To avoid cluttering up the streets, many train lines run underground. The **Berlin U-Bahn** has 80 percent of its 90 miles

Siemens Avanto Germany 1995

Matra Taipei Metro Taiwan/France 1996

Rail supplies
750-volt electricity to
power train's motors

*Hollow box
girder contains
cable along which
train's wheels run*

Bombardier MOVIA Canada/Singapore 2000s

Düsseldorf H-Bahn Skytrain Germany 2002

Large windshield
on engineer's cab

Moscow Monorail Russia 2004

*Driverless train has a
maximum speed of
56 mph (90 km/h)*

*Automatic coupler,
to link with other trains*

Vossloh Wuppertal Schwebebahn
Germany 2015

(146 km) of lines running below the surface of the city. Monorails are trains that run on a single rail. Many, such as the **Moscow Monorail**, have their trains running on top of the rail, while some, such as the **Mud Island Monorail**, are suspended below the rails. While many urban trains are controlled by a human driver, some systems run automatically. The **Gatwick Adtranz**, the **Düsseldorf H-Bahn Skytrain**, and the popular **Bombardier MOVIA**, which runs in Singapore and China among other countries, are driverless vehicles.

Streetcars and trolleybuses

Great Orme Tramway UK 1902

5

Streetcar pulled uphill by cable moved by electric motors

Hand-operated double doors

JEN VELIMSKÁ ZRNITA JE TA PRAVÁ

22

352

ELEKTRICKÉ DRÁHY HLAVNÍHO MĚSTA PRAHY.

Electric tram Czech Republic 1907

Pantograph connects tram with overhead electricity supply

W2 Class Melbourne tram Australia 1927

This W2 Class has been converted into a restaurant on wheels

RESTAURANT

RESTAURANT

Wheels powered by four electric motors

STARR GATE BLACKPOOL BEACH

Several **Balloon** streetcars run in Blackpool, England, **80 years** after they were built.

English Electric Balloon
UK 1934

Hong Kong Tramways
China 1980s

Streetcars run on tracks, are powered by electricity supplied by overhead cables, and share space on streets with other vehicles. They are also known as trams. Trolleybuses are also electrically powered, but they run on tires instead of tracks.

Britain's first electric tramway was built in Blackpool in 1885. The double-decker **English Electric Balloon**, which could hold up to 94 passengers, ran along at speeds of up to 43 mph (70 km/h). The **Hong Kong Tramways** is an all-double-decker service—the only one in the

Flexity Swift M5000 Canada / Germany 2009

Bury

3002

Metrolink

3002B

Aluminum body panels

Some **CAF** trams run an average distance of **59,030 miles** (95,000 km) per year.

Five articulated segments allow tram to travel around bends

CAF Urbos 3 Spain 2009

Seats up to 66 passengers

Low floor sits 13¾in (35cm) above the track

Trolley pole channels electricity from overhead wire to trolleybus

Solaris Trollino 15 Poland 2001

LISTAS
Ferencas
(1811–1886)
Ferenz Liszt
VENGRIJOS SŪNUS. PIANISTAS VIRTUOZAS IR KOMPOZITORIUS ROMANTIKAS.

San Francisco Trolleybus USA 2003

31 BALBOA
Ferry Plaza

Belkommunmash 42003A Belarus 2007

world—and uses narrow trams, only 6 ft 5 in (1.98 m) wide. Modern streetcars such as the **Flexity Swift** are found in Manchester, Istanbul, and Cologne, while the **CAF Urbos 3** runs on tramways all over the world, from Australia and Brazil to Taiwan and Spain. Trolleybuses, such as the **San Francisco Trolleybus** and the **Solaris Trollino 15**, run on regular roads and need only a series of roadside poles from which their overhead power line is suspended. The Trollino is quieter and generates much less pollution than buses powered by gasoline or diesel engines.

HOLD ON TIGHT! Followers of the Hindu religion crowd a train on its way to the northern Indian town of Govardhan, to take part in the Guru Purnima festival. Indian locomotives and train cars are not normally as crowded as this, but the country does run one of the largest and busiest railroad systems in the world, with enough track—some 71,500 miles (115,000 km) in total—to circle the Earth almost three times.

This WDM-3A class locomotive is just one of 5,345 diesel engines that runs along the tracks of Indian Railways. The company also operates 4,568 electric locomotives and 43 steam engines. These haul more than 62,000 passenger cars and 239,000 freight wagons, stopping at more than 7,200 stations throughout India. Some services also travel over the border, into the neighboring countries of Pakistan, Nepal, and Bangladesh. In India the cost of train fares is low, and the number of car owners relatively small, so rail travel is incredibly popular. In 2014, more than 8.5 billion passengers took the train, giving Indian Railways' 1.3 million employees plenty of work to do.

WATER

Taking to the water

Water

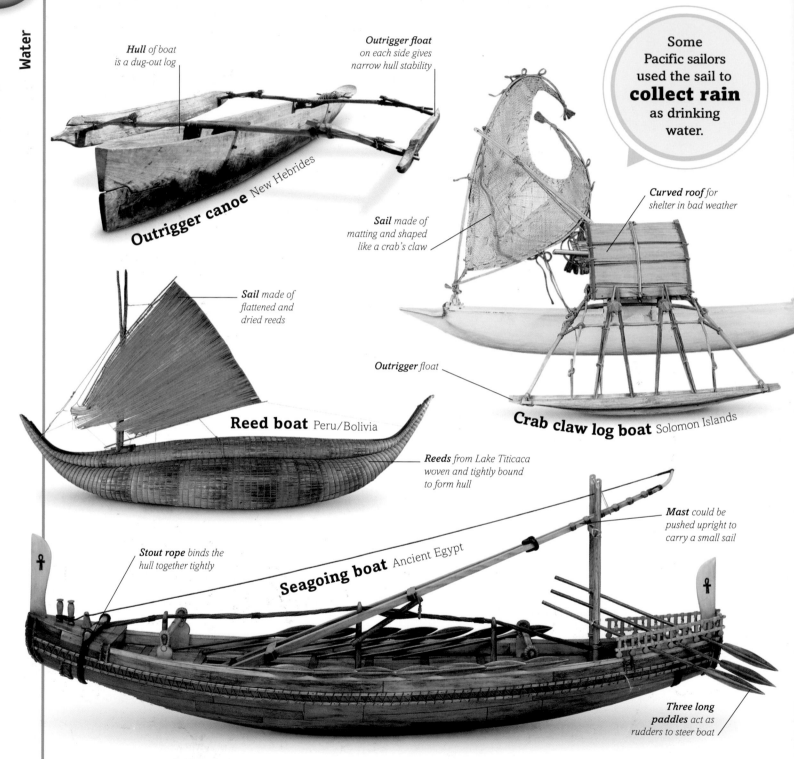

Hull of boat is a dug-out log

Outrigger float on each side gives narrow hull stability

Outrigger canoe New Hebrides

Some Pacific sailors used the sail to **collect rain** as drinking water.

Sail made of matting and shaped like a crab's claw

Curved roof for shelter in bad weather

Outrigger float

Crab claw log boat Solomon Islands

Sail made of flattened and dried reeds

Reed boat Peru/Bolivia

Reeds from Lake Titicaca woven and tightly bound to form hull

Stout rope binds the hull together tightly

Seagoing boat Ancient Egypt

Mast could be pushed upright to carry a small sail

Three long paddles act as rudders to steer boat

No one knows the name of the first sailor, or the craft that he or she used. They may have sat astride a log, or on bundles of reeds, lashed together. What we do know is that people have travelled or fished in boats for more than 10,000 years.

Some of the earliest boats were large tree trunks, hollowed out to form simple **dugout canoes**. Ancient people throughout the Pacific learned how to build **outrigger canoes**, with a second, smaller hull floating on the water to provide stability, while the Native American people built

154

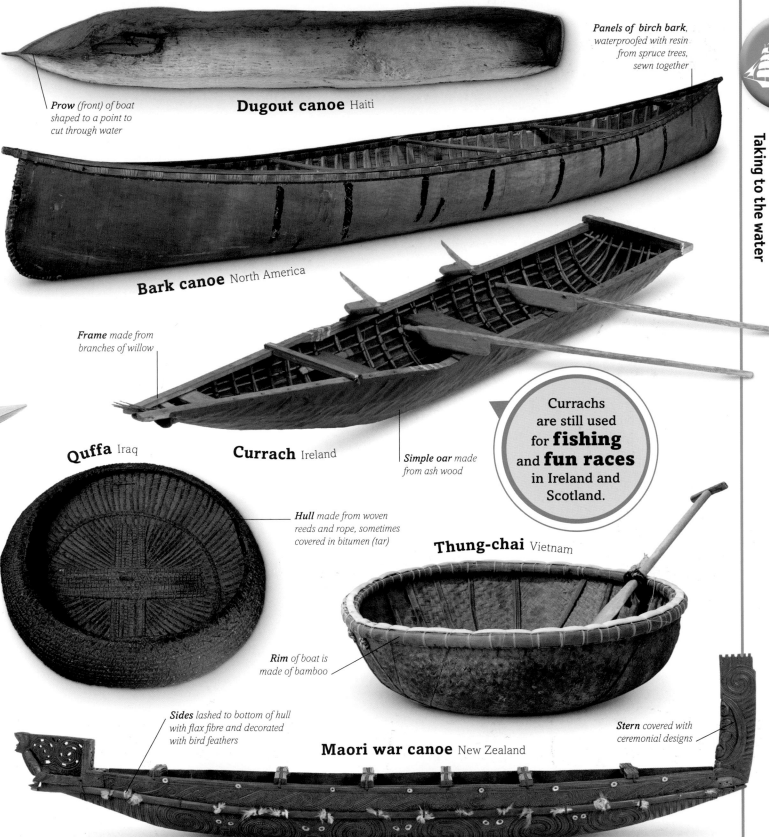

Dugout canoe Haiti

Prow (front) of boat shaped to a point to cut through water

Panels of birch bark, waterproofed with resin from spruce trees, sewn together

Bark canoe North America

Frame made from branches of willow

Quffa Iraq

Currach Ireland

Simple oar made from ash wood

Currachs are still used for **fishing** and **fun races** in Ireland and Scotland.

Hull made from woven reeds and rope, sometimes covered in bitumen (tar)

Thung-chai Vietnam

Rim of boat is made of bamboo

Sides lashed to bottom of hull with flax fibre and decorated with bird feathers

Stern covered with ceremonial designs

Maori war canoe New Zealand

bark canoes out of a wooden frame covered in tree bark. Reeds, which grow in abundance at the edges of many rivers and lakes, were dried, bound, and woven to form **reed boats**. Reeds could also be woven to form circular boats for fishing. Known as **Thung-chai** in Vietnam, and

coracles in UK, a similar form of boat called a **Quffa** existed in Iraq for at least 5,000 years. The ancient Egyptians built reed boats to sail the Nile River; around 5,500 years ago, they began to build larger, wooden **seagoing boats** to venture beyond the Nile into the Mediterranean Sea.

World of watercraft

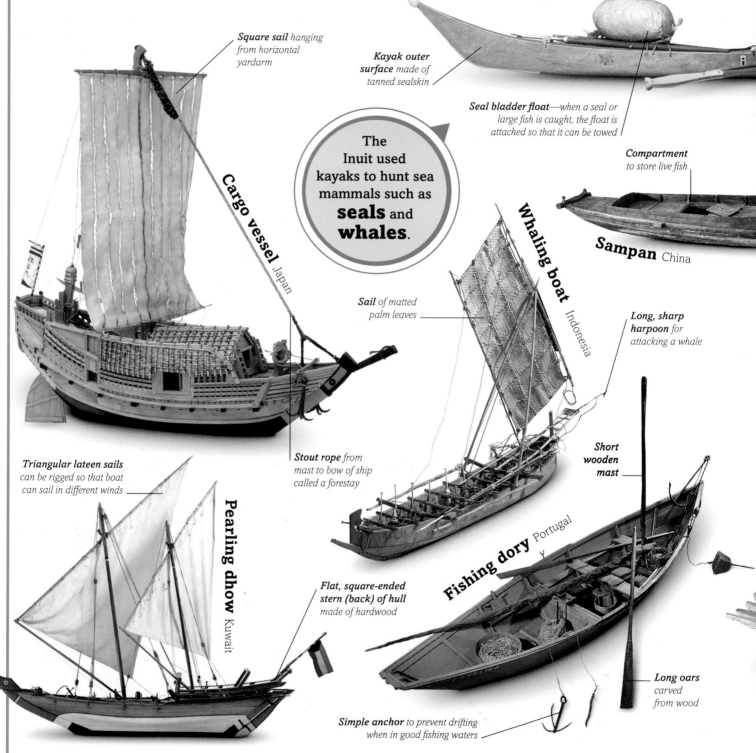

Square sail *hanging from horizontal yardarm*

Kayak outer surface *made of tanned sealskin*

Seal bladder float—*when a seal or large fish is caught, the float is attached so that it can be towed*

Compartment *to store live fish*

The Inuit used kayaks to hunt sea mammals such as **seals** and **whales**.

Cargo vessel Japan

Whaling boat Indonesia

Sampan China

Sail *of matted palm leaves*

Long, sharp harpoon *for attacking a whale*

Short wooden mast

Triangular lateen sails *can be rigged so that boat can sail in different winds*

Pearling dhow Kuwait

Stout rope *from mast to bow of ship called a forestay*

Fishing dory Portugal

Flat, square-ended stern (back) of hull *made of hardwood*

Long oars *carved from wood*

Simple anchor *to prevent drifting when in good fishing waters*

An amazing variety of vessels have been built to travel on water. Across the world, people have used ingenuity, and the local materials available, to build boats, rafts, canoes, and other watercraft, for fishing, transportation, war, and pleasure.

Among the simplest boats are **fishing rafts**, often just a bundle of tree branches lashed together to form a platform. The raft-like **Jangada**, however, is able to sail over reefs on the Brazilian coast to fish for hake and mackerel, often spending 2 to 3 days at sea. Throughout

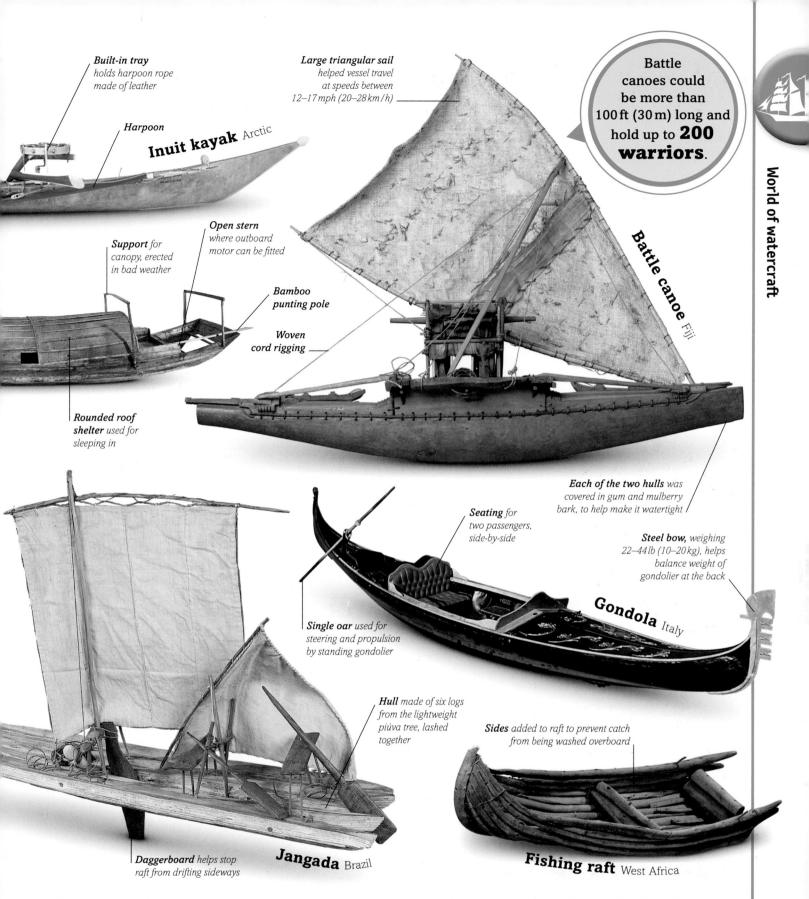

Built-in tray *holds harpoon rope made of leather*

Harpoon

Inuit kayak Arctic

Large triangular sail *helped vessel travel at speeds between 12–17 mph (20–28 km/h)*

Battle canoes could be more than 100 ft (30 m) long and hold up to **200 warriors**.

Battle canoe Fiji

Support *for canopy, erected in bad weather*

Open stern *where outboard motor can be fitted*

Bamboo punting pole

Woven cord rigging

Rounded roof shelter *used for sleeping in*

Each of the two hulls *was covered in gum and mulberry bark, to help make it watertight*

Seating *for two passengers, side-by-side*

Steel bow, *weighing 22–44 lb (10–20 kg), helps balance weight of gondolier at the back*

Gondola Italy

Single oar *used for steering and propulsion by standing gondolier*

Hull *made of six logs from the lightweight piúva tree, lashed together*

Sides *added to raft to prevent catch from being washed overboard*

Daggerboard *helps stop raft from drifting sideways*

Jangada Brazil

Fishing raft West Africa

Southeast Asia, another flat-bottomed boat, the **sampan**, is used by people to fish, travel, and even live in. In the Arctic, single- and two-person **Inuit kayaks** were used to hunt for mammals and fish, while in Indonesia, brave hunters chased after sperm whales, often two or three times longer than their flimsy **whaling boats**. On the Pacific island of Fiji, people built larger **battle canoes**, featuring a platform laid over a double hull. And in Italy, slender **gondolas** travel the canals that crisscross the city of Venice, acting as water taxis.

OVER THE TOP
A kayaker takes a terrifying plunge, hurtling over the highest of the five cascading waterfalls on the Agua Azul River in the Mexican state of Chiapas. He's one of six top professional kayakers who tackled the river and its waterfalls for the short adventure movie *Beyond The Drop*. For a safe landing, the kayaker must keep inside the flow of water, and land in the cushion of air and water at the foot of the waterfall.

It is likely that the first canoes and kayaks took to the water thousands of years ago, and that most were built of wood. But the appeal of paddling your own personal watercraft still holds today, even if modern canoes and kayaks are usually built from plastics, fibreglass, or, in the case of the most advanced, Kevlar and carbon fibre. Thousands of amateur kayakers enjoy paddling on rivers, lakes, or the sea, on weekends or on vacation. A handful of the best kayakers compete in competitions, either in speed races on flatwater, or on very technical whitewater slalom courses. Extreme kayaking is an adventure sport for the crazy few who enjoy paddling down racing rivers, including giant waterfalls!

Sailing ship

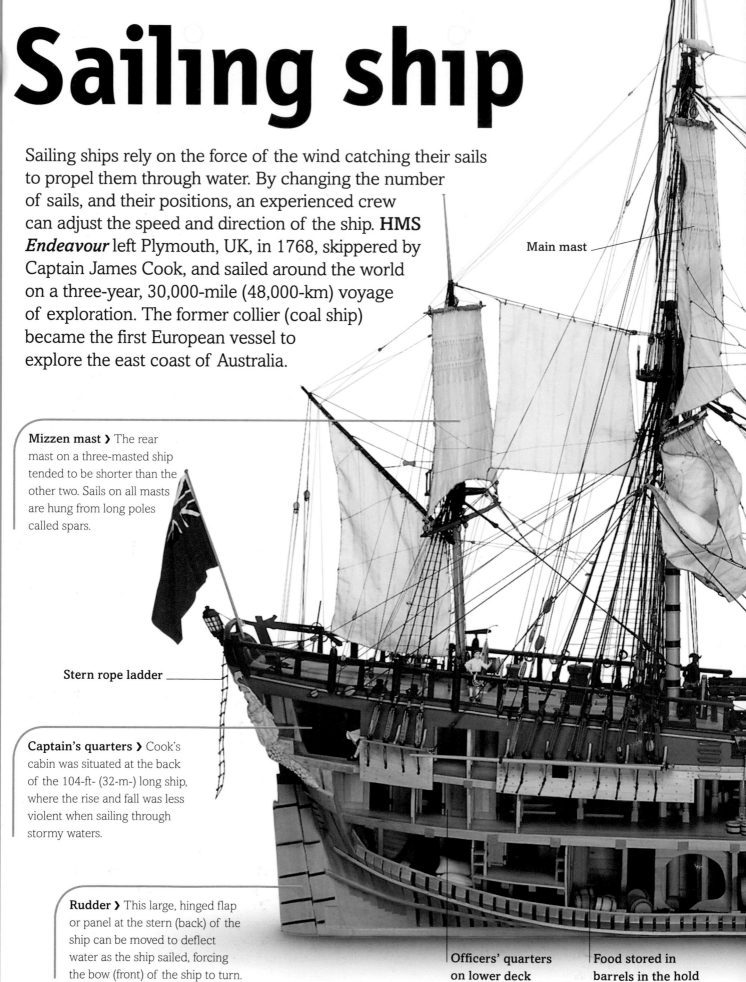

Sailing ships rely on the force of the wind catching their sails to propel them through water. By changing the number of sails, and their positions, an experienced crew can adjust the speed and direction of the ship. **HMS *Endeavour*** left Plymouth, UK, in 1768, skippered by Captain James Cook, and sailed around the world on a three-year, 30,000-mile (48,000-km) voyage of exploration. The former collier (coal ship) became the first European vessel to explore the east coast of Australia.

Main mast

Mizzen mast ❯ The rear mast on a three-masted ship tended to be shorter than the other two. Sails on all masts are hung from long poles called spars.

Stern rope ladder

Captain's quarters ❯ Cook's cabin was situated at the back of the 104-ft- (32-m-) long ship, where the rise and fall was less violent when sailing through stormy waters.

Rudder ❯ This large, hinged flap or panel at the stern (back) of the ship can be moved to deflect water as the ship sailed, forcing the bow (front) of the ship to turn.

Officers' quarters on lower deck

Food stored in barrels in the hold

Foremast ❯ This is the front mast on a three-masted ship. On the *Endeavour*, the foremast was built of pine and fir wood, and towered some 112 ft (34 m) above the ship's deck.

Jib sail ❯ Skilled sailors were able to use jib sails to steer the ship, by altering their positions. When fully rigged, with all of its sails on all its masts, the *Endeavour* had more than 29,000 square ft (2,700 square m) of sail.

HMS Endeavour

Bowsprit ❯ The long pole rising from the bow of the ship to which the rigging for the bottom of the jib sails was attached.

Hull ❯ For many centuries, the body of a sailing ship was crafted out of planks of wood. *Endeavour*'s hull was made mostly of white oak, and was flat-bottomed, for sailing in shallow waters. It was divided into different sections, including below-deck living quarters for 90 sailors.

One of 22 cannons protecting the ship

Rowboat

Sail power

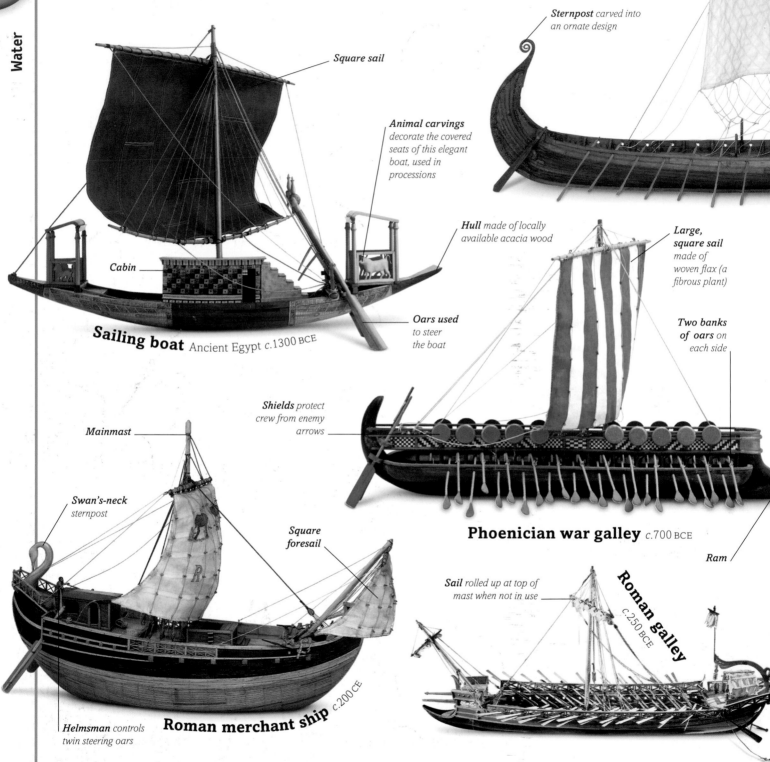

Sternpost *carved into an ornate design*

Square sail

Animal carvings *decorate the covered seats of this elegant boat, used in processions*

Hull *made of locally available acacia wood*

Cabin

Oars *used to steer the boat*

Sailing boat Ancient Egypt *c.*1300 BCE

Large, square sail *made of woven flax (a fibrous plant)*

Two banks of oars *on each side*

Shields *protect crew from enemy arrows*

Phoenician war galley *c.*700 BCE

Ram

Mainmast

Swan's-neck *sternpost*

Square foresail

Sail *rolled up at top of mast when not in use*

Roman galley *c.*250 BCE

Roman merchant ship *c.*200 CE

Helmsman *controls twin steering oars*

Thousands of years ago, people learned to harness the power of the wind to push their craft through the water. Sails made of cloth, reeds, or matting, and hung from a mast, caught the wind to move boats faster than people could row or paddle.

Some of the earliest-known **sailing boats** were found on the Nile River in Egypt, more than 5,000 years ago. They used a large, square sail made of cloth, which worked best when sailing downwind (with wind coming from behind the boat). Square sails were also invented independently in parts of

Large single sail
hung from a single spar,
called a yard, or yardarm

Hull built of
overlapping wooden
planks fixed to a frame

Viking longship
Norway *c.*800 CE

The
dragon head
on the prow of
this dromon fired
**burning
flames** at
the enemy.

Lookout position at the top
of the main mast, for spotting
approaching ships or land

Rigging enabled crew to
climb up and unfurl sails

Yardarm

Foresail

Oars for use
when there
is no wind

Oars manned by as many
as 100 crew members

Dromon Eastern Roman Empire *c.*650 CE

During
the Ming
Dynasty, China
had a navy with
more than **3,000
war junks**.

Junk China *c.*1840

Fighting junk
fitted with guns

Lantern

*Wooden
rudder*

Gunport

Cocca Italy *c.*1500

South America, and also in China, where they were often equipped to the **junks** that sailed the Pacific and Indian oceans. Many ancient sailing ships, such as **Phoenician war galleys**, **Roman galleys**, and **Viking longships**, were fitted with rows of oars, for when there was no wind.

Viking longships were designed with shallow hulls so they could sail right up to the shore to attack and raid settlements. The Vikings were skilled sailors who traveled all across Europe and, around 1000 CE, crossed the Atlantic reaching Newfoundland in Canada.

Trade and exploration

Wooden hull *is approximately 58 ft (17.7 m) long*

Main mast top castle *manned by crew member searching for land*

Santa Maria
Spain 1460

When the *Santa Maria* was finally **broken up**, the wood was used to build a **fort**.

Lateen sails *used when winds blew toward the side of the ship*

Caravel
Portugal 1490s

Hull *is approximately 90 ft (27.5 m) long*

Mayflower England 1600s

Short, deep wooden hull *could carry plenty of cargo below decks*

Mizzen mast *added to ship when it was converted from a warship to a survey vessel*

HMS Bounty England 1784

Hull *converted to transport breadfruit plants from Tahiti to the Caribbean*

HMS Beagle England 1820

Ship *carried 74 people on a five-year survey voyage*

From the 15th century onward, European sailing ships traveled the world. Many were trading vessels, carrying cargoes as varied as slaves, food, and spices. Others explored new lands, on epic voyages of discovery.

Portugal was a major sea trading nation in the 15th century, and **caravels** sailed along the coasts of Europe and Africa. Two accompanied the *Santa Maria* on Christopher Columbus' famous 1492 voyage across the Atlantic. Many European ships would later head west for trade, or to conquer, or

Masts carried sails, but ship was also powered by a diesel engine

Fram Norway 1892

Square hull to keep ship small, as ships were taxed based on their size

Square topsail

Fluyt Netherlands 1700s

Hull was specially strengthened against the pressure of ice freezing around it

The *Fram* had a **windmill** on board that ran a generator to power electric lights.

Bowsprit

Cutty Sark UK 1869

Skysail is the highest sail on the mast

Wooden hull 212 ft 7 in (64.8 m) long

Hull, made from iron plates riveted together, carried guano (animal dung), wheat, and coal

Wendur Scotland 1884

establish colonies, such as the ***Mayflower***, which carried pilgrims to settle in North America. As European explorers found new lands, more merchant ships engaged in trade. The ***fluyt*** was a common Dutch design with a very narrow deck. Fast ships called clippers, such as the ***Cutty Sark***, sailed between Asia and Europe. One of the most epic trips of all was made by ***Fram***, which sailed more than 60,000 miles (100,000 km) around the Arctic, before carrying Norwegian explorer Roald Amundsen to Antarctica, where he became the first person to reach the South Pole.

War at sea

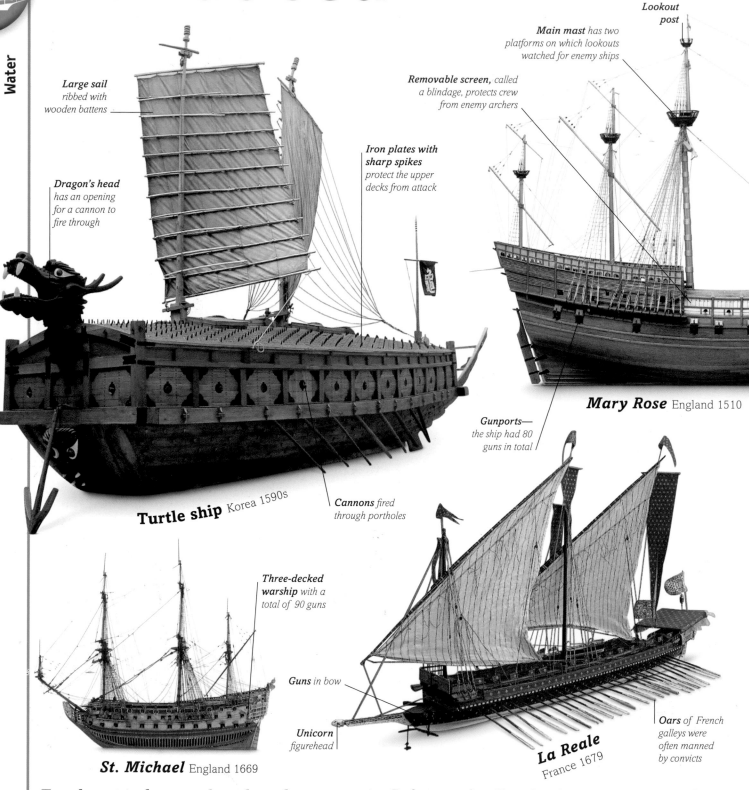

Large sail ribbed with wooden battens

Dragon's head has an opening for a cannon to fire through

Iron plates with sharp spikes protect the upper decks from attack

Lookout post

Main mast has two platforms on which lookouts watched for enemy ships

Removable screen, called a blindage, protects crew from enemy archers

Mary Rose England 1510

Gunports— the ship had 80 guns in total

Turtle ship Korea 1590s

Cannons fired through portholes

Three-decked warship with a total of 90 guns

St. Michael England 1669

Guns in bow

Unicorn figurehead

La Reale France 1679

Oars of French galleys were often manned by convicts

For almost as long as there have been ships, the sea has been a battlefield for rival nations planning invasion, or for control of shipping routes and trade. From the 16th century, warships bristled with guns and battles at sea became even more deadly.

Before naval artillery, battles at sea were mostly close combat, with fire, rams, or arrows used in attack. The Korean **turtle ship** protected itself against archers, and from being boarded, with its hefty, spiked deck armor. Big guns allowed ships to fight more at a distance. The *Mary Rose's* iron

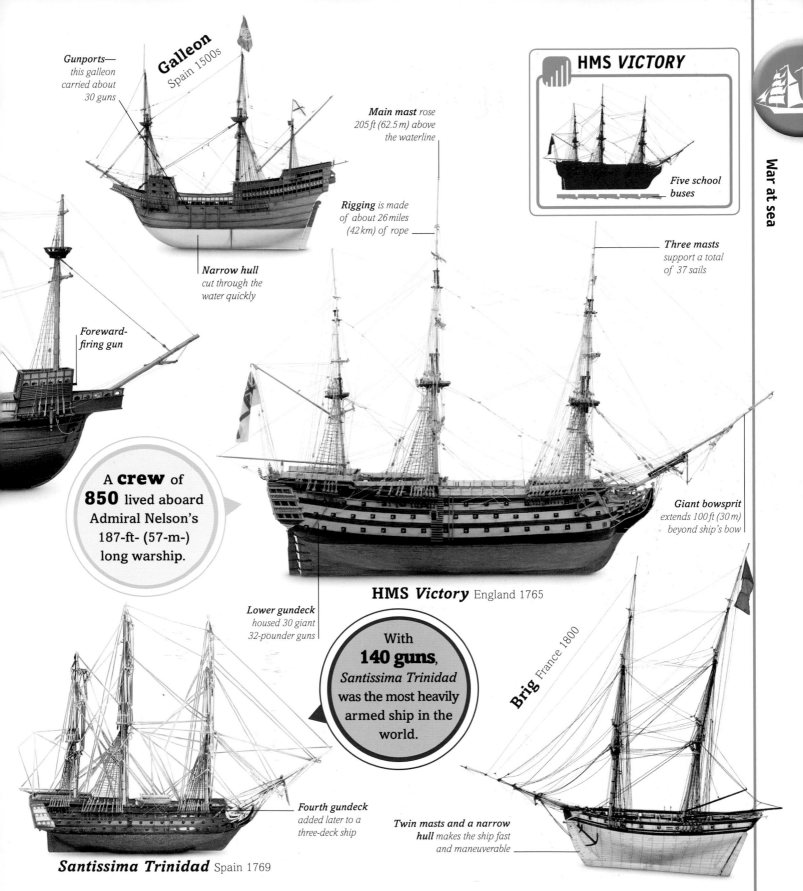

Gunports—
this galleon
carried about
30 guns

Galleon
Spain 1500s

Main mast rose
205 ft (62.5 m) above
the waterline

Rigging is made
of about 26 miles
(42 km) of rope

Narrow hull
cut through the
water quickly

**Foreward-
firing gun**

A **crew** of
850 lived aboard
Admiral Nelson's
187-ft- (57-m-)
long warship.

Lower gundeck
housed 30 giant
32-pounder guns

HMS *Victory* England 1765

With
140 guns,
Santissima Trinidad
was the most heavily
armed ship in the
world.

HMS VICTORY

**Five school
buses**

Three masts
support a total
of 37 sails

Giant bowsprit
extends 100 ft (30 m)
beyond ship's bow

Brig France 1800

Fourth gundeck
added later to a
three-deck ship

**Twin masts and a narrow
hull** makes the ship fast
and maneuverable

Santissima Trinidad Spain 1769

cannons fired through flaps called gunports, in
the hull. To boost firepower, some ships were built
with extra decks of guns. This led to three-decker
warships, such as the *St. Michael*, which fought
in the Caribbean, and the *Santissima Trinidad*,
which later received a fourth deck of heavy guns.

This made her menacing, but slow. Flagships,
such as the French navy's *La Reale*, were home
to a fleet's commander. **HMS** *Victory* was the
flagship under British admiral Lord Nelson at
the battle of Trafalgar. With 104 guns, she was
a formidable, as well as fast, fighting machine.

RIDING THE WIND
The BMW Oracle Racing Team 90 (BOR90) trimaran (three-hulled boat) lifts up into the air during a training run. The 113-ft- (34.5-m-) long, 90-ft- (27.4-m-) wide giant is about the same size as two basketball courts and was built to win the America's Cup, sailing's most prestigious competition, which it did in 2010. The picture shows how racing sailors better not be afraid of heights!

Trimaran BOR90 (later renamed USA–17) needed more than nine months of careful construction in the state of Washington before it could be let loose on the water for testing, crew training, and modifications. Its body is made mostly of carbon fiber and weighs 18 tons. The main sail is not made of fabric, but is solid and made of carbon fiber and Kevlar, a material found in bulletproof armor. The result was a 190-ft- (58-m-) tall monster sail. At 7,770 lb (3,524 kg), it was so heavy that powerful hydraulic systems were needed to move it, rather than regular rigging, but it boosted the trimaran's speed to more than 30 mph (50 km/h) during parts of its triumphant America's Cup run.

Steamship

Steamships burned coal or oil to heat water and create steam to power an engine. This either drove a paddle wheel or turned a screw propeller, as found on the **SS Great Britain**. When launched in 1843, SS *Great Britain* was the largest ship in the world, and the first iron-hulled steamship powered by a screw propeller. Two years later, it became the first propeller-powered steamship to cross the Atlantic Ocean, a journey that took 14 days.

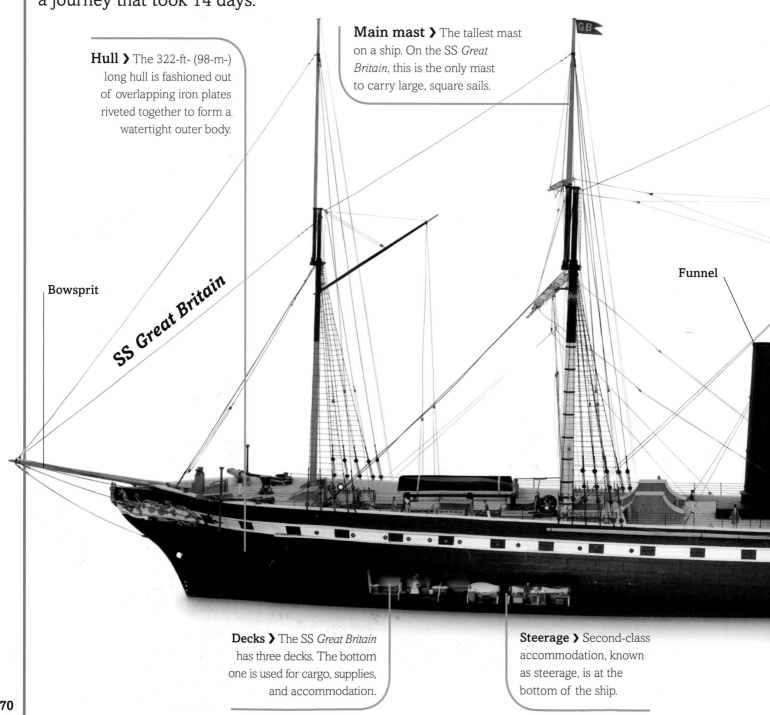

Hull › The 322-ft- (98-m-) long hull is fashioned out of overlapping iron plates riveted together to form a watertight outer body.

Main mast › The tallest mast on a ship. On the SS *Great Britain*, this is the only mast to carry large, square sails.

Bowsprit

SS Great Britain

Funnel

Decks › The SS *Great Britain* has three decks. The bottom one is used for cargo, supplies, and accommodation.

Steerage › Second-class accommodation, known as steerage, is at the bottom of the ship.

Rigging ❯ On the SS *Great Britain*, the rigging is made of iron cable rather than rope. This is to reduce drag.

Mast ❯ Five of the ship's masts can be folded down on deck to reduce air resistance when the ship is solely under steam power.

Spar ❯ Sails are hung from these long poles attached to masts.

Helm

Lifeboat ❯ There are seven lifeboats for 252 passengers and 130 crew.

First-class dining saloon and cabins

Propeller screw ❯ The giant propeller has six blades and measures 16 ft (4.9 m) in diameter. As it turns, the propeller pushes water back, moving the ship forward.

Steam meets steel

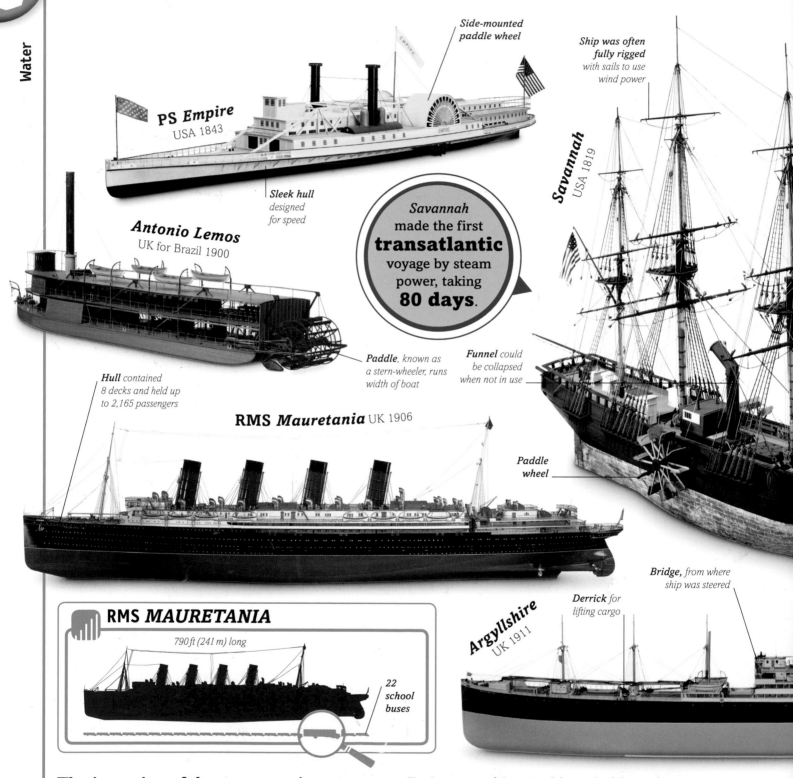

Side-mounted paddle wheel

PS Empire
USA 1843

Sleek hull designed for speed

Antonio Lemos
UK for Brazil 1900

Ship was often fully rigged with sails to use wind power

Savannah
USA 1819

Savannah made the first **transatlantic** voyage by steam power, taking **80 days**.

Paddle, known as a stern-wheeler, runs width of boat

Funnel could be collapsed when not in use

Hull contained 8 decks and held up to 2,165 passengers

Paddle wheel

RMS Mauretania UK 1906

Bridge, from where ship was steered

Derrick for lifting cargo

Argyllshire
UK 1911

RMS *MAURETANIA*

790 ft (241 m) long

22 school buses

The invention of the steam engine meant that ships no longer had to rely on the wind. When steam power was used to drive steel ships, the result was large, sturdy vessels that could travel greater distances faster than ever before.

Early steamships could not hold much cargo because of the vast amounts of coal they needed to carry as fuel. The **SS Agamemnon**, however, could run on just 22 tons of coal a day, allowing it to sail economically between Europe and the Far East. Powerful steam liners such as

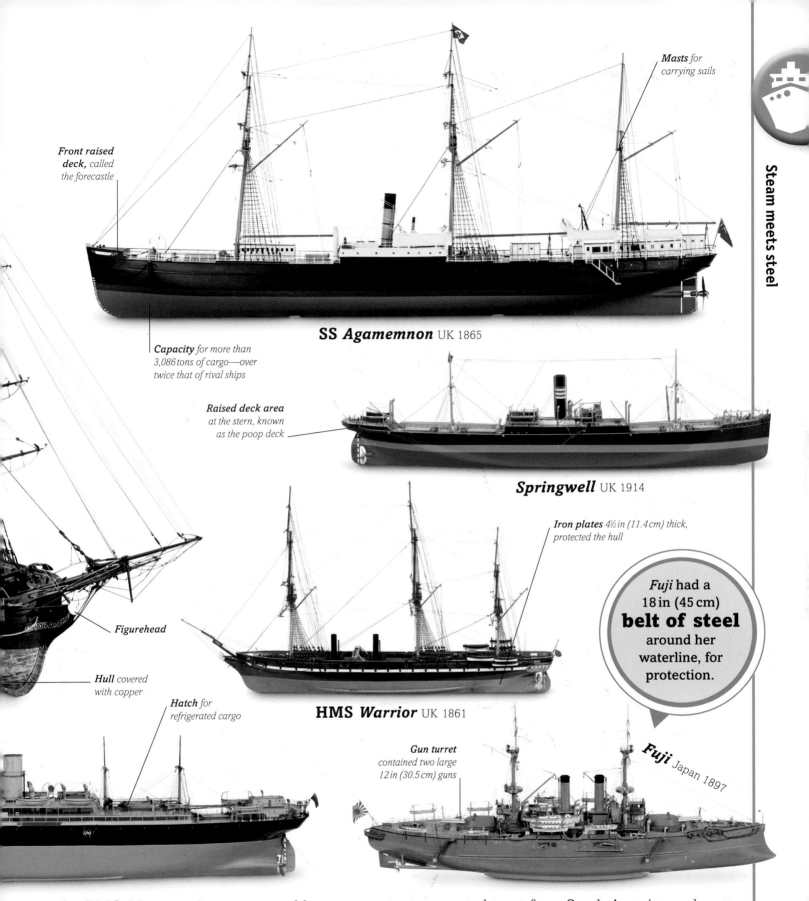

Masts for carrying sails

Front raised deck, called the forecastle

Capacity for more than 3,086 tons of cargo—over twice that of rival ships

SS *Agamemnon* UK 1865

Raised deck area at the stern, known as the poop deck

Springwell UK 1914

Iron plates 4½ in (11.4 cm) thick, protected the hull

Fuji had a 18 in (45 cm) **belt of steel** around her waterline, for protection.

Figurehead

Hull covered with copper

Hatch for refrigerated cargo

HMS *Warrior* UK 1861

Gun turret contained two large 12 in (30.5 cm) guns

Fuji Japan 1897

the **RMS *Mauretania***, were now able to cross the Atlantic in as little as four or five days. Early steamships, such as the **PS *Empire***, were mostly made of wood, but iron and steel hulls became more common. Steel made it possible to build refrigerated ships, such the ***Argyllshire***, which transported meat from South America and Australasia to Europe. Steel and steam were also adopted by navies. **HMS *Warrior*** was among the first Royal Navy ships to come with an iron hull and steel armor. It carried a crew of 706 as well as 40 giant artillery guns.

Working ships

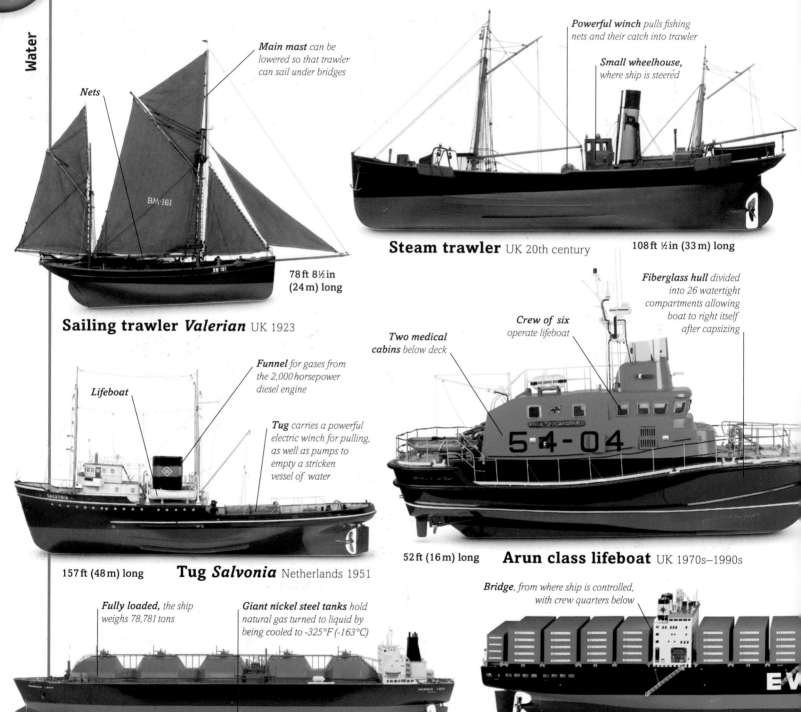

Main mast can be lowered so that trawler can sail under bridges

Nets

Sailing trawler *Valerian* UK 1923

78 ft 8½ in (24 m) long

Powerful winch pulls fishing nets and their catch into trawler

Small wheelhouse, where ship is steered

Steam trawler UK 20th century

108 ft ½ in (33 m) long

Funnel for gases from the 2,000 horsepower diesel engine

Lifeboat

Tug carries a powerful electric winch for pulling, as well as pumps to empty a stricken vessel of water

157 ft (48 m) long

Tug *Salvonia* Netherlands 1951

Fiberglass hull divided into 26 watertight compartments allowing boat to right itself after capsizing

Crew of six operate lifeboat

Two medical cabins below deck

5-4-04

52 ft (16 m) long

Arun class lifeboat UK 1970s–1990s

Fully loaded, the ship weighs 78,781 tons

Giant nickel steel tanks hold natural gas turned to liquid by being cooled to -325°F (-163°C)

Bridge, from where ship is controlled, with crew quarters below

Gas carrier *Norman Lady* Norway 1973

817 ft (249 m) long

965 ft (294 m) long

Every day, thousands of ships are at work in a variety of different ways. Many carry billions of tons of goods, fuel, and material across the waters of the world. Others save lives, assist other ships, and catch food from the seas and oceans.

Tankers carry liquids, such as oil or, in the case of *Norman Lady*, liquefied natural gas. The *Shin Aitoku Maru* is an oil tanker with a difference. Its computer-controlled sails help it save fuel, which is used to power its diesel engines. The *Ever Royal* carries goods and

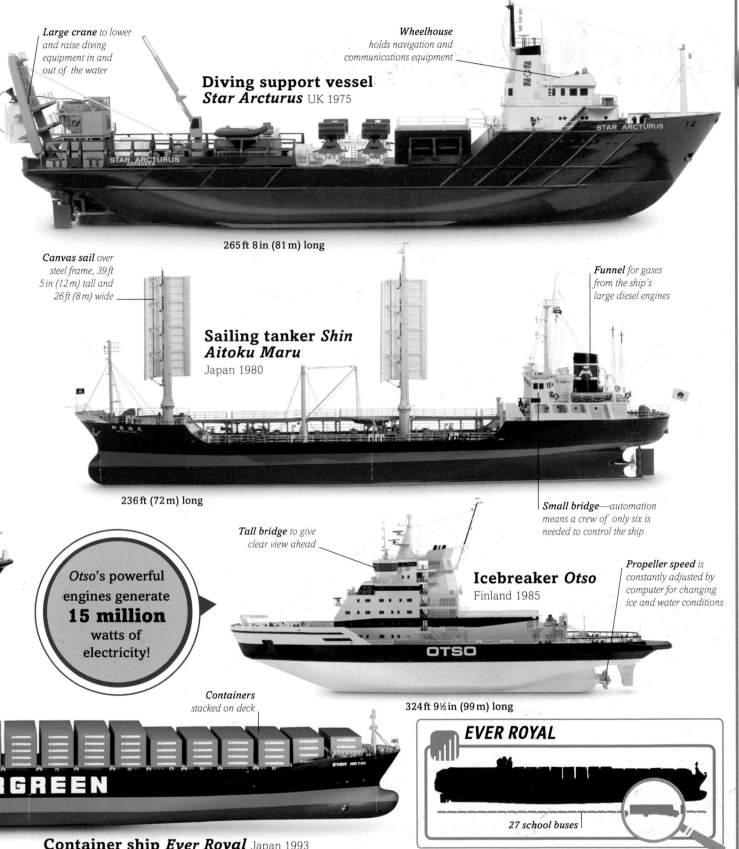

Large crane to lower and raise diving equipment in and out of the water

Wheelhouse holds navigation and communications equipment

Diving support vessel
Star Arcturus UK 1975

265 ft 8 in (81 m) long

Canvas sail over steel frame, 39 ft 5 in (12 m) tall and 26 ft (8 m) wide

Funnel for gases from the ship's large diesel engines

Sailing tanker *Shin Aitoku Maru*
Japan 1980

236 ft (72 m) long

Small bridge—automation means a crew of only six is needed to control the ship

Otso's powerful engines generate **15 million** watts of electricity!

Tall bridge to give clear view ahead

Icebreaker *Otso*
Finland 1985

Propeller speed is constantly adjusted by computer for changing ice and water conditions

OTSO

324 ft 9½ in (99 m) long

Containers stacked on deck

RGREEN

Container ship *Ever Royal* Japan 1993

EVER ROYAL

27 school buses

materials stored in up to 4,200 standard 20-ft-(6-m-) long containers, designed to be easily unloaded onto trucks. Some working ships help serve others. Icebreakers, such as *Otso*, can plow through ice many meters thick to clear a path to let ships through. Other vessels act as tugs, such as the oceangoing *Salvonia*, which can tow a stricken ship out of danger and home for repairs. Coastguards and other maritime rescue services operate boats like the **Arun class lifeboat**, which can travel through the stormiest of waters to rescue people at sea.

Passenger carriers

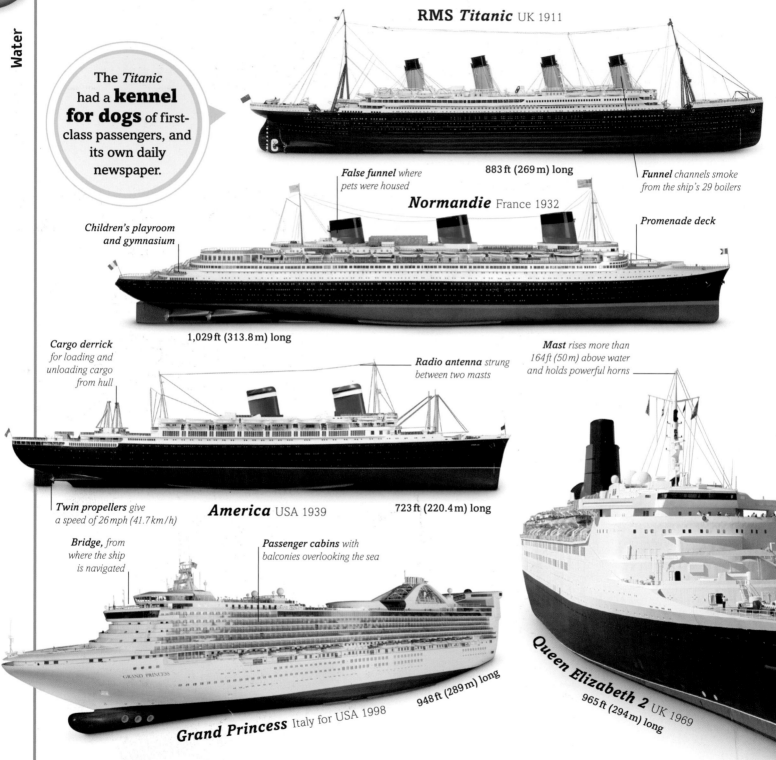

The *Titanic* had a **kennel for dogs** of first-class passengers, and its own daily newspaper.

RMS *Titanic* UK 1911

883 ft (269 m) long

Funnel channels smoke from the ship's 29 boilers

False funnel where pets were housed

Normandie France 1932

Children's playroom and gymnasium

Promenade deck

1,029 ft (313.8 m) long

Cargo derrick for loading and unloading cargo from hull

Radio antenna strung between two masts

Mast rises more than 164 ft (50 m) above water and holds powerful horns

Twin propellers give a speed of 26 mph (41.7 km/h)

America USA 1939

723 ft (220.4 m) long

Bridge, from where the ship is navigated

Passenger cabins with balconies overlooking the sea

Grand Princess Italy for USA 1998

948 ft (289 m) long

Queen Elizabeth 2 UK 1969

965 ft (294 m) long

Every year, hundreds of millions of people travel on ships for work or pleasure. Many use ferry services, linking places separated by water. Others cruise aboard large passenger liners, traveling the seas and oceans of the world.

Water taxis, such as Tokyo's *Himiko* water bus, transport people short distances, while larger ferries like the *Arcturus* move people and their vehicles across lakes and seas. The **MDV 1200 Class ferry** has capacity for 175 cars and more than 600 passengers. The *America* liner held

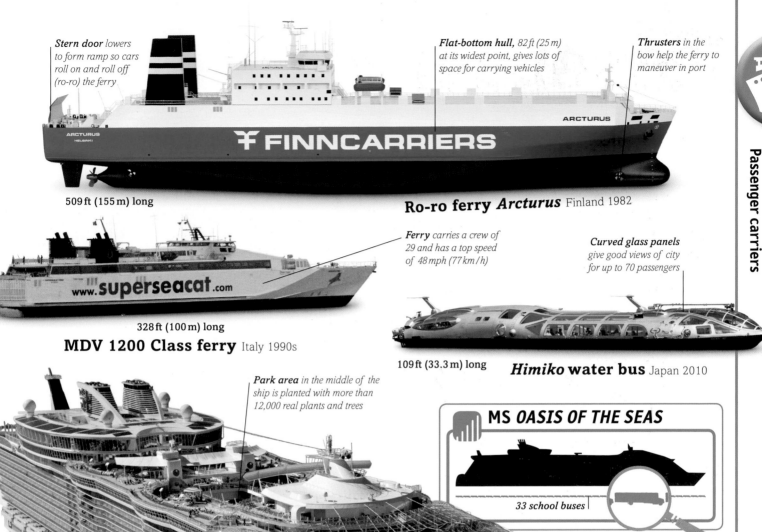

Stern door lowers to form ramp so cars roll on and roll off (ro-ro) the ferry

Flat-bottom hull, 82 ft (25 m) at its widest point, gives lots of space for carrying vehicles

Thrusters in the bow help the ferry to maneuver in port

509 ft (155 m) long

Ro-ro ferry *Arcturus* Finland 1982

Ferry carries a crew of 29 and has a top speed of 48 mph (77 km/h)

Curved glass panels give good views of city for up to 70 passengers

328 ft (100 m) long

MDV 1200 Class ferry Italy 1990s

109 ft (33.3 m) long

***Himiko* water bus** Japan 2010

Park area in the middle of the ship is planted with more than 12,000 real plants and trees

MS *OASIS OF THE SEAS*

33 school buses

Helipad, in case emergency transport by helicopter is needed

18 lifeboats, each holding 370 people

From 1969–2004, the *QE2* crossed the Atlantic Ocean a record **806 times**.

MS Oasis of the Seas USA 2008
1,188 ft (362 m) long

1,202 passengers, but during World War II was converted into a troop ship carrying 7,678 soldiers. Over the years, even bigger passenger liners were launched, including the **RMS Titanic**, which sank on its maiden voyage in 1912, and the **Normandie**, which could carry

1,972 passengers at a rapid 34 mph (54 km/h). With 17 decks carrying up to 3,600 passengers, the **Grand Princess** became the world's largest liner, until overtaken by the gigantic **MS Oasis of the Seas**, which, at 248,330 tons, weighs almost five times as much as the *Titanic*.

CITY ON THE SEA
The world's biggest cruise ship, Royal Caribbean International's *Allure of the Seas,* enters her home harbor of Port Everglades, Florida, in 2010. This gigantic, 16-deck floating hotel is almost as long as four football fields, and houses up to 6,318 guests who are looked after by a crew of 2,384 people. It's almost as if a small floating city has taken to the water.

Built in Finland between 2008 and 2010, this gigantic vessel is 1,188 ft (362 m) long. She rises to 236 ft (72 m) above the waterline, but her funnels can telescope down for passing under low bridges. The liner's many attractions include 25 restaurants, a 1,380-seat theater, a full-size basketball court, a rock climbing wall, 21 swimming pools and jacuzzis, and wave machines that pump out more than 58,000 gallons (220,000 liters) of water a minute, so people can surf as they cruise! There's even a 2,230-ft- (680-m-) long running track, and a park area with thousands of real plants and trees. The 248,330-ton ship cruises the Caribbean or Mediterranean Sea at the stately speed of 26 mph (42 km/h).

World War ships

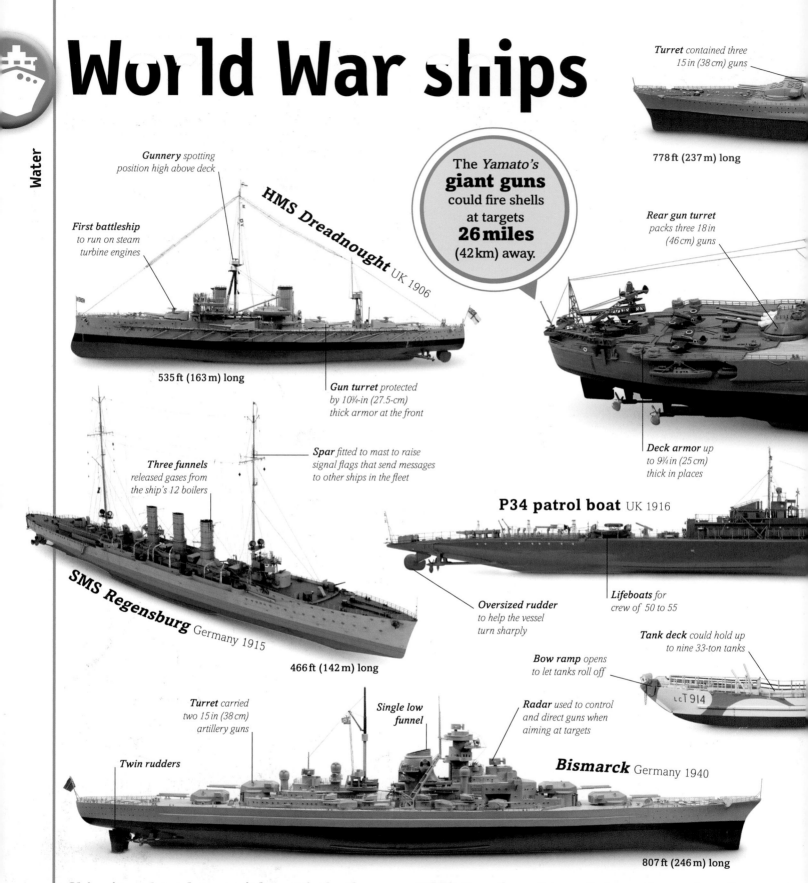

Turret contained three 15 in (38 cm) guns

778 ft (237 m) long

Gunnery spotting position high above deck

HMS Dreadnought UK 1906

First battleship to run on steam turbine engines

The *Yamato's* **giant guns** could fire shells at targets **26 miles** (42 km) away.

Rear gun turret packs three 18 in (46 cm) guns

535 ft (163 m) long

Gun turret protected by 10¾-in (27.5-cm) thick armor at the front

Spar fitted to mast to raise signal flags that send messages to other ships in the fleet

Three funnels released gases from the ship's 12 boilers

Deck armor up to 9¾ in (25 cm) thick in places

P34 patrol boat UK 1916

SMS Regensburg Germany 1915

Oversized rudder to help the vessel turn sharply

Lifeboats for crew of 50 to 55

466 ft (142 m) long

Tank deck could hold up to nine 33-ton tanks

Bow ramp opens to let tanks roll off

Turret carried two 15 in (38 cm) artillery guns

Single low funnel

Radar used to control and direct guns when aiming at targets

Twin rudders

LCT 914

Bismarck Germany 1940

807 ft (246 m) long

Shipping played a crucial part in both World War I and World War II. As well as fighting in battles, warships were used to disrupt enemy supply convoys, protect their own navies, and transport troops and equipment to invade enemy territory.

HMS *Dreadnought* was faster and more heavily armed than previous battleships and started an arms race between the major naval powers before World War I. Smaller ships, such as the cruiser **SMS** *Regensburg*, and the **P34 patrol boat**, saw active service during WWI. P34 was

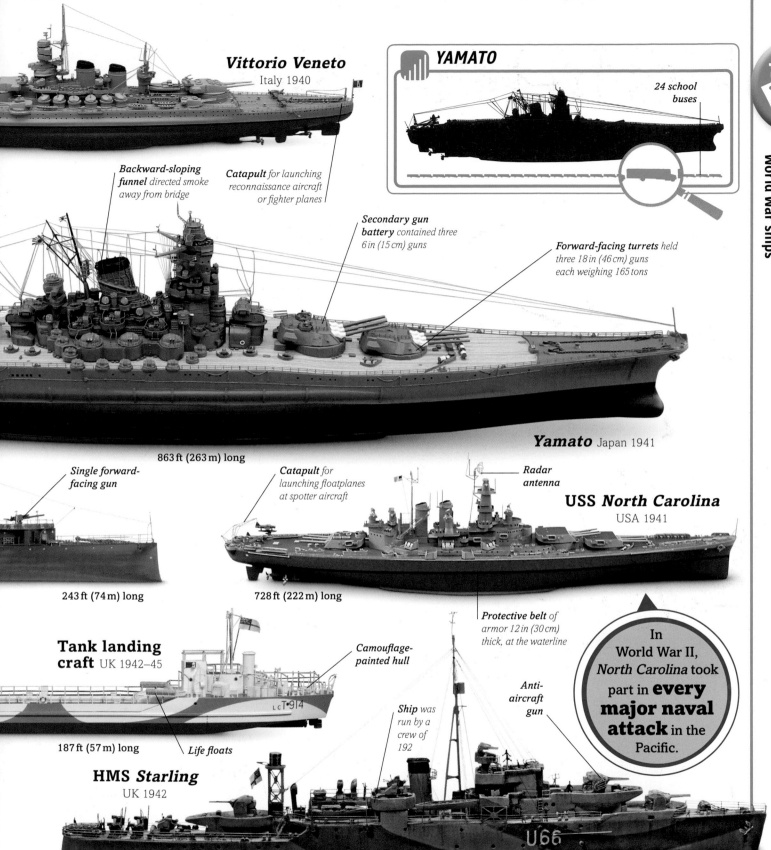

Vittorio Veneto
Italy 1940

YAMATO

24 school buses

Backward-sloping funnel directed smoke away from bridge

Catapult for launching reconnaissance aircraft or fighter planes

Secondary gun battery contained three 6 in (15 cm) guns

Forward-facing turrets held three 18 in (46 cm) guns each weighing 165 tons

Yamato Japan 1941

863 ft (263 m) long

Single forward-facing gun

Catapult for launching floatplanes at spotter aircraft

Radar antenna

USS North Carolina
USA 1941

243 ft (74 m) long

728 ft (222 m) long

Tank landing craft UK 1942–45

Camouflage-painted hull

Protective belt of armor 12 in (30 cm) thick, at the waterline

Anti-aircraft gun

In World War II, *North Carolina* took part in **every major naval attack** in the Pacific.

187 ft (57 m) long — **Life floats**

Ship was run by a crew of 192

HMS Starling
UK 1942

U66

299 ft (91 m) long

one of the first dedicated antisubmarine vessels. **HMS Starling** performed a similar role during World War II, sinking 14 German U-boats. The *Bismarck* was Germany's biggest battleship, until it was sunk in 1941. Biggest of all was the *Yamato*, at over 77,161 tons. It was heavily armed, with nine giant guns, dozens of smaller artillery weapons, and 162 antiaircraft guns. It cruised the Pacific with a range of 8,264 miles (13,300 km). **Tank landing craft** had a tenth of that range, but were crucial in ferrying tanks during the Normandy landings.

Aircraft carriers

Gases from funnel could create difficult air currents for landing aircraft

Up to 36 biplanes could be carried

Elevator raises planes stored below onto flight deck

Nuclear reactors can keep USS *George Washington* running for **18 years**, with no need to refuel!

786 ft 5 in (239.7 m) long

HMS Furious UK 1917

Hangar for aircraft storage

Missile launcher

Akagi Japan 1927

855 ft 4 in (260.7 m) long

Hangar deck on two levels

Bulges in hull makes the ship more stable and adds protection against torpedoes

Quick-firing antiaircraft guns

Four propellers move the carrier at speeds up to 35 mph (56 km/h)

Twin 8 in (20 cm) guns in turret can aim shells at targets more than 17 miles (27 km) away

Ship can hold more than 2,700 personnel

USS Saratoga USA 1927

888 ft (270.7 m) long

Antiaircraft guns

Radio masts for communication between ship and aircraft

Hangers could hold more than 60 aircraft

Aircraft parked on armored flight deck

HMS Illustrious UK 1940

800 ft (243.8 m) long

HMS Ark Royal UK 1938

Flight deck ended in "round down" to reduce air turbulence for planes taking off

751 ft (229 m) long

As aircraft became important military weapons, ships that could act as floating airbases were designed. These aircraft carriers are huge vessels with a large, flat flight deck, from which helicopters and planes can take off and land.

Many early aircraft carriers, including the **USS Saratoga**, **HMS Furious**, and the **Akagi**, were initially designed as battle cruisers before being converted. The *Akagi* carried up to 66 aircraft, which took off from three flight decks, while the *Saratoga* could carry up to 78 planes. Specially

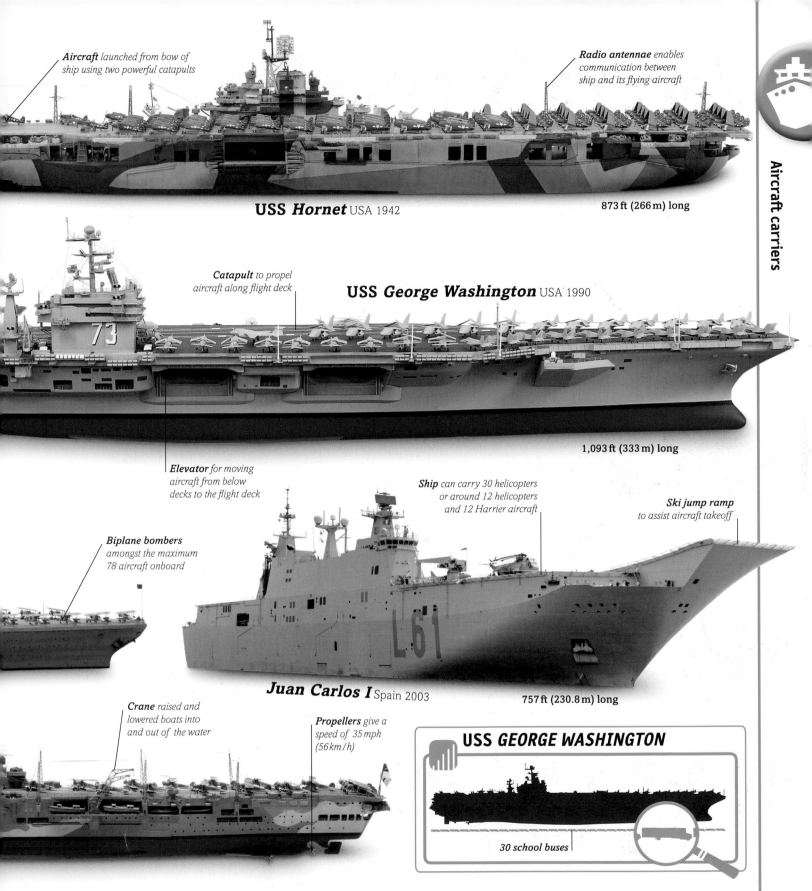

Aircraft launched from bow of ship using two powerful catapults

Radio antennae enables communication between ship and its flying aircraft

USS *Hornet* USA 1942

873 ft (266 m) long

Catapult to propel aircraft along flight deck

USS *George Washington* USA 1990

73

1,093 ft (333 m) long

Elevator for moving aircraft from below decks to the flight deck

Ship can carry 30 helicopters or around 12 helicopters and 12 Harrier aircraft

Ski jump ramp to assist aircraft takeoff

Biplane bombers amongst the maximum 78 aircraft onboard

L61

Juan Carlos I Spain 2003

757 ft (230.8 m) long

Crane raised and lowered boats into and out of the water

Propellers give a speed of 35 mph (56 km/h)

USS *GEORGE WASHINGTON*

30 school buses

built aircraft carriers, such as **HMS *Illustrious*** and the **USS *Hornet*,** featured catapults powered by hydraulics or steam to propel the aircraft on takeoff, as well as hangers below the flight deck to store inactive planes. Aircraft carriers have large crews—1,580 in the case of

HMS *Ark Royal*. However, this figure is dwarfed by the more than 6,000 who serve aboard the Nimitz Class carrier, **USS *George Washington*.** This 97,003-ton ship holds up to 90 aircraft of varying types, from reconnaissance planes and helicopters to fighters and bombers.

Modern warships

Merlin helicopter

Turret with two 4.5 in (113 mm) guns with a range of 11 miles (18 km)

Twin propellers

HMS *Diamond* UK 1952

D 35

390 ft (119 m) long

Crane for deploying equipment or recovering mines

151 ft (46 m) long

Tracking antenna can receive data sent from satellites or rockets

Ship manned by a crew of 120 as well as up to 100 technical experts

M1157

Twin propellers powered by diesel engine

HMS *Kirkliston*
UK 1954

The ship's Tomahawk missiles have a range of more than **800 miles** (1,300 km).

Monge A601 France 1990   738 ft (225 m) long

USS *Arleigh Burke*
USA 1991

Tomahawk cruise missiles can launch vertically from this launch grid

Sikorsky SH-60 Seahawk helicopter on helipad

51

505 ft (154 m) long

Aircraft carriers and nuclear submarines have taken over from battleships as the biggest and most lethal craft in a navy's fleet. Yet there remains plenty of work for smaller ships, which are built to perform a wide variety of important roles.

Frigates like **HMS *Lancaster*** and **HMCS *Vancouver*** are multipurpose—able to protect and escort other ships, perform coastal patrols, intercept suspicious ships, and engage in antisubmarine warfare. The **USS *Arleigh Burke*** destroyer also tackles submarines, as well as

Funnel

Radar and electronics mast

Antiaircraft missile system—ship is also armed with antiship missiles and antisubmarine torpedoes

F229

HMS *Lancaster* UK 1992   436 ft (133 m) long

Sea King helicopter carried on the stern

Radar antenna

440 ft (134 m) long

HMCS *Vancouver* Canada 1993

Helipad on stern can bring in doctors or evacuate injured personnel

Crane for loading and unloading a maximum of 24 containers of supplies

A 511

331 ft (101 m) long   **Elbe class** Germany 1993

495 ft (151 m) long

Murasame class destroyers Japan 1994

Landing craft well can hold 40 amphibious assault vehicles

Flight deck supports 6–8 Harrier II jet aircraft

843 ft (257 m) long

USS *Iwo Jima* USA 2000

Camouflaged hull

Twin diesel engines power four waterjets, to propel the boat forward

USS *IWO JIMA*

23 school buses

Type 022 missile boat China 2004   138 ft (42 m) long

attacking other targets at sea or on land, using guided missiles. Some warships have highly specialized roles. **HMS *Kirkliston*** swept for mines laid in shallow coastal waters. The ***Monge* A601** monitors the skies, using its 14 antennae and other electronic systems to track missiles

and space missions. The **Type 022 missile boat** can creep under enemy warning systems to launch attacks on shipping, while the **USS *Iwo Jima*** supports missions onshore, carrying just short of 1,900 marines, up to 30 helicopters, and large numbers of amphibious landing craft.

Modern warships

185

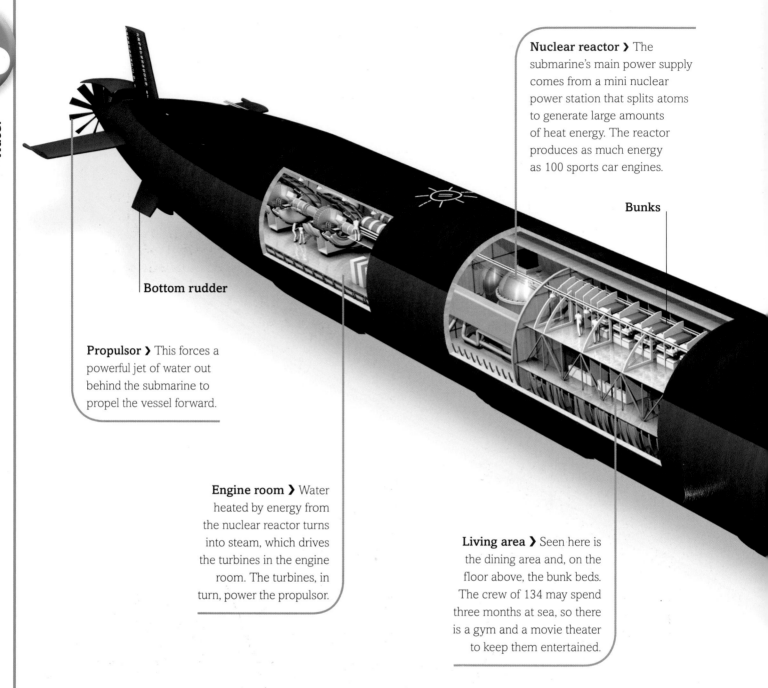

Nuclear reactor ❯ The submarine's main power supply comes from a mini nuclear power station that splits atoms to generate large amounts of heat energy. The reactor produces as much energy as 100 sports car engines.

Bunks

Bottom rudder

Propulsor ❯ This forces a powerful jet of water out behind the submarine to propel the vessel forward.

Engine room ❯ Water heated by energy from the nuclear reactor turns into steam, which drives the turbines in the engine room. The turbines, in turn, power the propulsor.

Living area ❯ Seen here is the dining area and, on the floor above, the bunk beds. The crew of 134 may spend three months at sea, so there is a gym and a movie theater to keep them entertained.

Submarine

Submarines can adjust their buoyancy (how much they can float or sink) using large ballast tanks that can be filled with air or seawater. These tanks allow submarines to dive deep below sea level, cruise stealthily underwater, or rise to the surface. The 377-ft- (115-m-) long **Virginia class submarine** serves in the US Navy. Packed with advanced systems, each submarine took around nine million working hours to build.

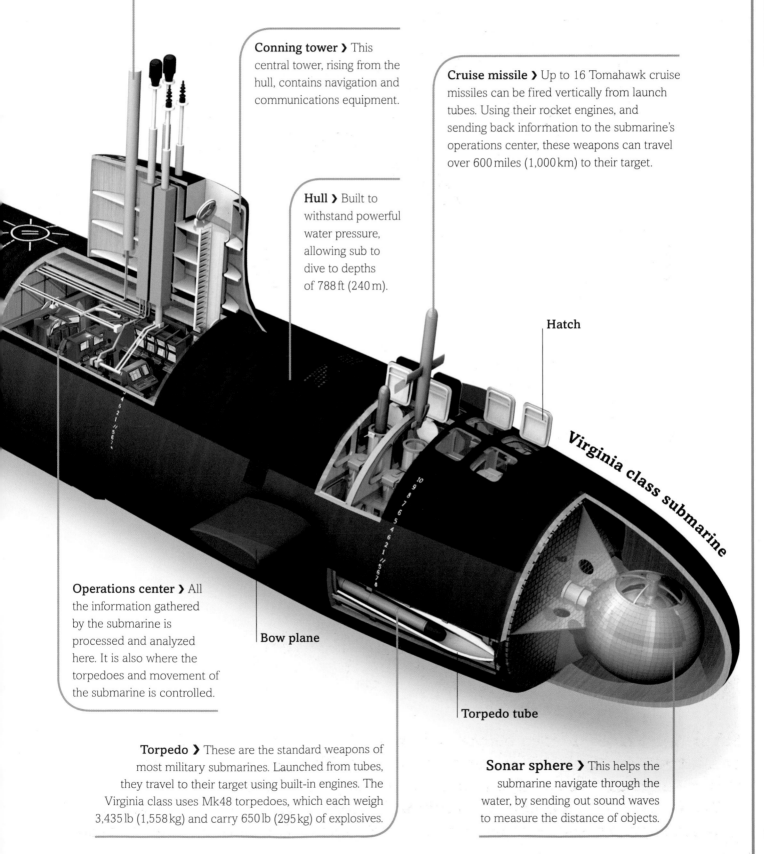

Masts > These carry radio and global positioning antennae, and a mast that allows the crew to see above the surface using night vision and a zoom lens.

Conning tower > This central tower, rising from the hull, contains navigation and communications equipment.

Cruise missile > Up to 16 Tomahawk cruise missiles can be fired vertically from launch tubes. Using their rocket engines, and sending back information to the submarine's operations center, these weapons can travel over 600 miles (1,000 km) to their target.

Hull > Built to withstand powerful water pressure, allowing sub to dive to depths of 788 ft (240 m).

Hatch

Virginia class submarine

Operations center > All the information gathered by the submarine is processed and analyzed here. It is also where the torpedoes and movement of the submarine is controlled.

Bow plane

Torpedo tube

Torpedo > These are the standard weapons of most military submarines. Launched from tubes, they travel to their target using built-in engines. The Virginia class uses Mk48 torpedoes, which each weigh 3,435 lb (1,558 kg) and carry 650 lb (295 kg) of explosives.

Sonar sphere > This helps the submarine navigate through the water, by sending out sound waves to measure the distance of objects.

Dive, dive, dive

Three Aichi M6A were stored in, and launched, from this submarine

Access hatch

64 ft (19.5 m) long

Turtle USA 1776

HMS Holland No. 1 UK 1901

Propeller gives a top speed of 9 mph (15 km/h) when submerged

U-9 Germany 1910

188 ft 3 in (57.4 m) long

Foot pedals used to turn the propeller

6 ft (1.8 m) tall

3/4 in (2 cm) cannon

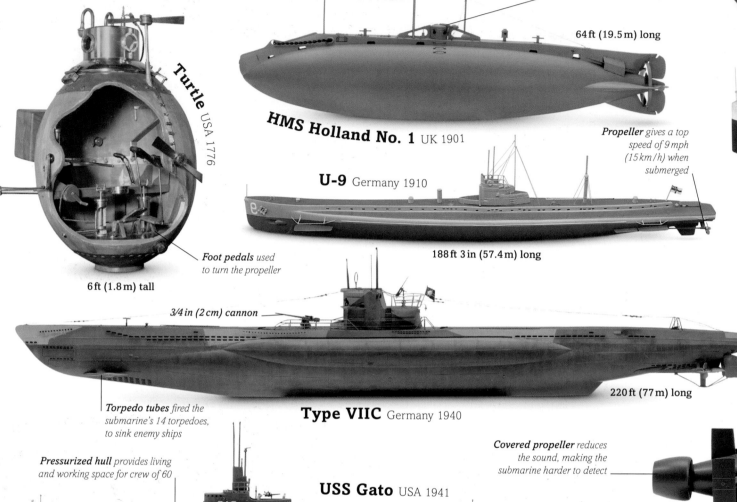

220 ft (77 m) long

Type VIIC Germany 1940

Torpedo tubes fired the submarine's 14 torpedoes, to sink enemy ships

Covered propeller reduces the sound, making the submarine harder to detect

Pressurized hull provides living and working space for crew of 60

USS Gato USA 1941

Bow torpedo tubes

311 ft 7 in (95 m) long

Stern torpedo tubes

Top rudder helps steer the submarine

YURI DOLGORUKI

15.4 school buses

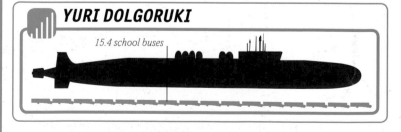

558 ft (170 m) long

With their ability to lurk beneath the waves for weeks at a time, submarines are a potentially deadly underwater weapon. Submersibles are much smaller vessels, used for underwater scientific research, and rescue and salvage work.

The **Turtle** was the first sub to see action, when it attempted to place explosives on the hulls of enemy ships during the Civil War. It was not until World War I that subs became effective in warfare. The German **U-9** sank 16 ships, and the **Type VIIC** U-boat reached depths of 500 ft

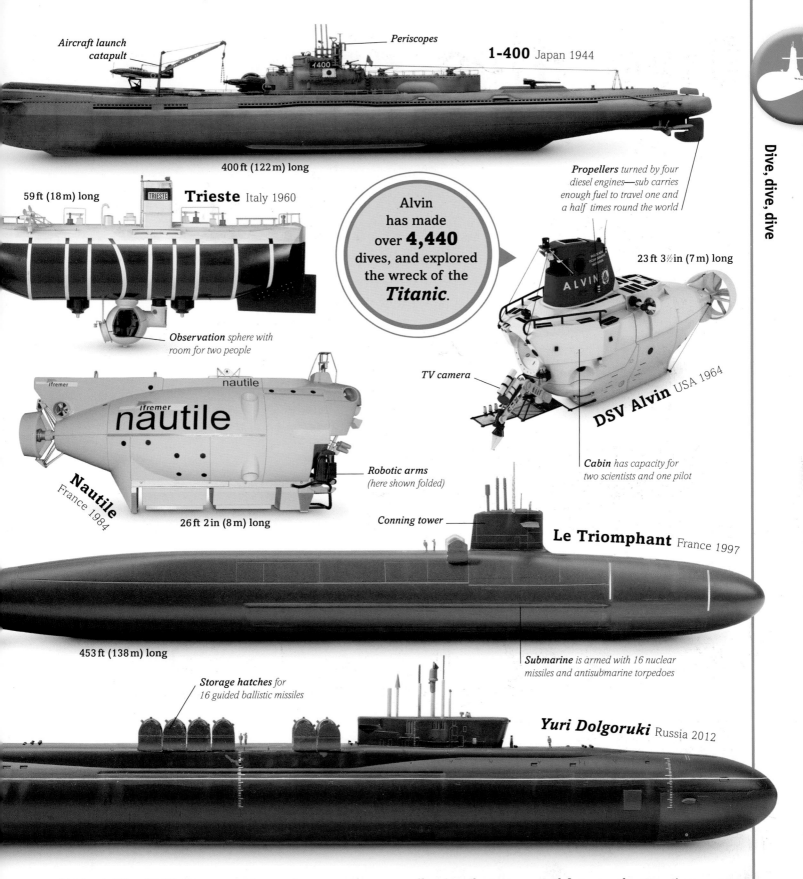

Aircraft launch catapult

Periscopes

1-400 Japan 1944

400 ft (122 m) long

Propellers turned by four diesel engines—sub carries enough fuel to travel one and a half times round the world

59 ft (18 m) long

Trieste Italy 1960

Alvin has made over **4,440** dives, and explored the wreck of the ***Titanic***.

23 ft 3½ in (7 m) long

Observation sphere with room for two people

TV camera

DSV Alvin USA 1964

Cabin has capacity for two scientists and one pilot

Nautile France 1984

Robotic arms (here shown folded)

26 ft 2 in (8 m) long

Conning tower

Le Triomphant France 1997

453 ft (138 m) long

Submarine is armed with 16 nuclear missiles and antisubmarine torpedoes

Storage hatches for 16 guided ballistic missiles

Yuri Dolgoruki Russia 2012

(150 m). The **USS Gato** could travel up to 12,500 miles (20,000 km) on patrols, while **1-400** class submarines, the largest of World War II, could launch aircraft from their decks. Nuclear energy gave modern submarines like **Le Triomphant** and *Yuri Dolgoruki* limitless power,

allowing them to patrol for months at a time. Small research submersibles have limited range, but can perform amazing feats. **DSV Alvin** can dive to 21,000 ft (6,400 m), while **Trieste** carried people to the deepest part of the Pacific Ocean, 35,797 ft (10,911 m) below sea level.

Need for speed

Navigation and communications antennae

BHC AP1-88 Hovercraft
UK 1990s

Large cabin can hold 190–243 passengers

Rubber skirt is filled with air by fans under the body of the hovercraft

This craft is used by the Canadian Coastguard

Capacity for up to 30 cars, which enter craft using a ramp at the back

Railings for observers on the roof of the cabin

Voskhod 352 Eurofoil
Russia 1973

SR.N4 Mk.I Hovercraft UK 1968

Six-bladed fan propels craft at speeds up to 43 mph (70 km/h)

Skirt, made up of 68 sections, keeps the craft on a cushion of air

Windshield of cockpit, which seats 3 to 4

Military *Zubr*-class hovercraft are the world's **biggest** and can carry up to **500 troops**.

BHC Coastal Pro Hovercraft UK 2015

Some vessels don't travel through water, they skim the surface, so that most of their hull, or body, rides above it. This means they can travel faster. Surface-skimming craft, such as hovercrafts and hydrofoils, are definitely fast movers!

A hovercraft rides on a cushion of air generated by lift fans under their bodies, which enables it to travel over both land and water. The **SR.N4 Mk.I Hovercraft** could hold 254 passengers and cruise at over 60 mph (100 km/h), while the **BHC AP1-88 Hovercraft** was used by the

Handlebars contain
levers for throttle
and brake

Bridge from where
the craft is controlled
and steered

Sea-Doo® Spark™ Canada 2013

Boeing 929 Jetfoil USA 1974

Perspex canopy
covers cockpit

**Smooth aluminum
body** fitted over
a steel frame

The K7 set
a world water
speed record of
276 mph
(444 km/h)
in 1964.

Handlebars
contain sound
system and speakers

Bluebird K7 UK 1955

**Rearview
mirror**

S. SUTTIPUN

7

Singha Drinking Water

Kawasaki Ultra 310LX Japan 2015

V-shaped hull allows craft
to travel smoothly through
choppy water

**Sleek,
streamlined
body design**
fashioned out of
light but strong
carbon fiber

F1 Powerboat USA 2014

**Catamaran
hull** design with
two floating hulls

Canadian Coastguard for rescue missions.
Hydrofoils, such as the **Voskhod 352 Eurofoil**,
use wing-like foils under the hull to lift the boat
out of the water as it travels forward. Jetfoils are
hydrofoils that use water jets to provide their
forward thrust, such as the **Boeing 929 Jetfoil**,
which has a top speed of 50 mph (80 km/h).
Personal watercraft, like the **Sea-Doo® Spark™**
and the **Kawasaki Ultra 310LX,** also use water
thrusters, while the fastest boats of all, **F1
Powerboats**, use propellers driven by powerful
engines to race at over 125 mph (200 km/h).

Fun and games

Inboard motor *at the back of the boat spins propeller to move boat forward*

Motorboat USA 1950s

Inflatable body, *7 ft 2½ in (2.2 m) long, takes less than 90 seconds to inflate*

Wilderness raft USA

Safety helmets *must be worn as well as life jackets*

Whitewater dinghy USA

Mooring ring

1,200 inflatable dinghies paddled down the Aar River in Switzerland in 2011.

Twin hulls *make this a catamaran-style cabin cruiser*

Flexible cover *can be removed in good weather*

Cabin cruiser USA

Chimney stack

Old tires *cushion sides of boat when moored*

Narrowboat UK 1960s

There is nothing like having fun on the water! Plenty of different boats and watercraft of all shapes and sizes allow people to have fun on rivers, lakes, and seas, to explore wildernesses, and to take part in races and competitions.

A **wilderness raft** is a type of inflatable dinghy that is small and light enough to be carried in a backpack—before it is filled with air. Rugged **whitewater dinghies** are larger and ride down rapids and fast-flowing water. Paddles are used in **canoes** and **kayaks**, while a **rowboat** has

Large fan, inside a safety cage, is spun by the engine to push the boat forward

In 2013, an airboat reached **102 mph** (163.5 km/h)—a top speed!

Large sail made of cotton rigged to mast

Sailing dinghy RNSA 14 UK 1920s

Shallow hull for traveling through swamplands

Airboat USA 2010s

Hull made of overlapping wood panels over a wood frame

Tiller

Rowboat Boy Albert UK 1920s

Oars fitted into oarlocks

Metal rudder is controlled by turning tiller

Boom is gripped for stability and to adjust sail angle to wind

Twin-bladed paddle allows kayaker to paddle continuously without switching sides

Kayaker sits in an enclosed seat

Kayak UK 1980s

Rope handles for lifting boat out of water

Single-bladed paddle used to push the water backward

Mast fits into joint on the board

Windsurfer USA 1990s

Canoe UK 1980s

oars, which pivot in fixtures called oarlocks as they are rowed back and forth. **Sailing dinghies** are used to teach people how to sail, while **airboats** offer thrilling rides, speeding along with the help of large fans spun by car or aircraft engines. **Narrowboats** were once used to haul coal, cotton, and other goods along canals before there were train and road networks; today, they are equipped with beds and kitchens, and used for pleasure cruising. You can live aboard **cabin cruisers**, too, which travel on open water as well as canals.

A FLYING SUCCESS
Guido Cappellini's F1 Powerboat flies across the surface of Doha Bay during the Qatar F1 Powerboat Grand Prix in 2009. This racing catamaran is tearing along at over 125 mph (200 km/h) around a course marked by floating buoys. As many as 24 F1 powerboats take part in each race, battling for position, because points earned count toward the coveted World Championship title.

F1 Powerboats are the ultimate speed machines on water. Equipped with monstrous 425 horsepower engines, they weigh around 1,102 lb (500 kg) and can accelerate from a standing start to 100 mph (160 km/h) in only four seconds, quickly hitting top speeds of around 140 mph (225 km/h). Inside its sleek carbon fiber body, the driver is firmly strapped in, and protected by a crash cabin, as he pushes his powerboat to the limit. There are no gears and no brakes. It is edge-of-your-seat racing, with boats taking tight corners at 62–93 mph (100–150 km/h). Cappellini won this and four other races in the 2009 season, earning him the world-championship crown for a record tenth time.

AIR

Airplane

Airplanes are heavier than air, so they need to overcome the force of gravity, which pulls them toward the ground. They do this with the help of curved wings, which produce an upward force, called lift, as the plane moves through the air. Most aircraft today are monoplanes, which means they have a single set of wings. This **de Havilland DH60 Gipsy Moth** is a biplane, with two pairs of wings and an open cockpit with two seats.

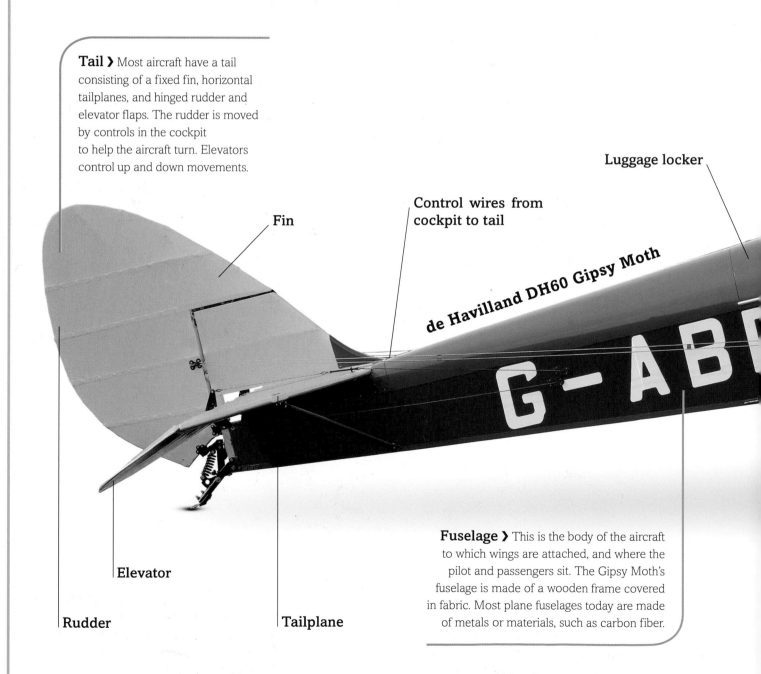

Tail ❯ Most aircraft have a tail consisting of a fixed fin, horizontal tailplanes, and hinged rudder and elevator flaps. The rudder is moved by controls in the cockpit to help the aircraft turn. Elevators control up and down movements.

Fin

Control wires from cockpit to tail

Luggage locker

de Havilland DH60 Gipsy Moth

G-AB

Elevator

Rudder

Tailplane

Fuselage ❯ This is the body of the aircraft to which wings are attached, and where the pilot and passengers sit. The Gipsy Moth's fuselage is made of a wooden frame covered in fabric. Most plane fuselages today are made of metals or materials, such as carbon fiber.

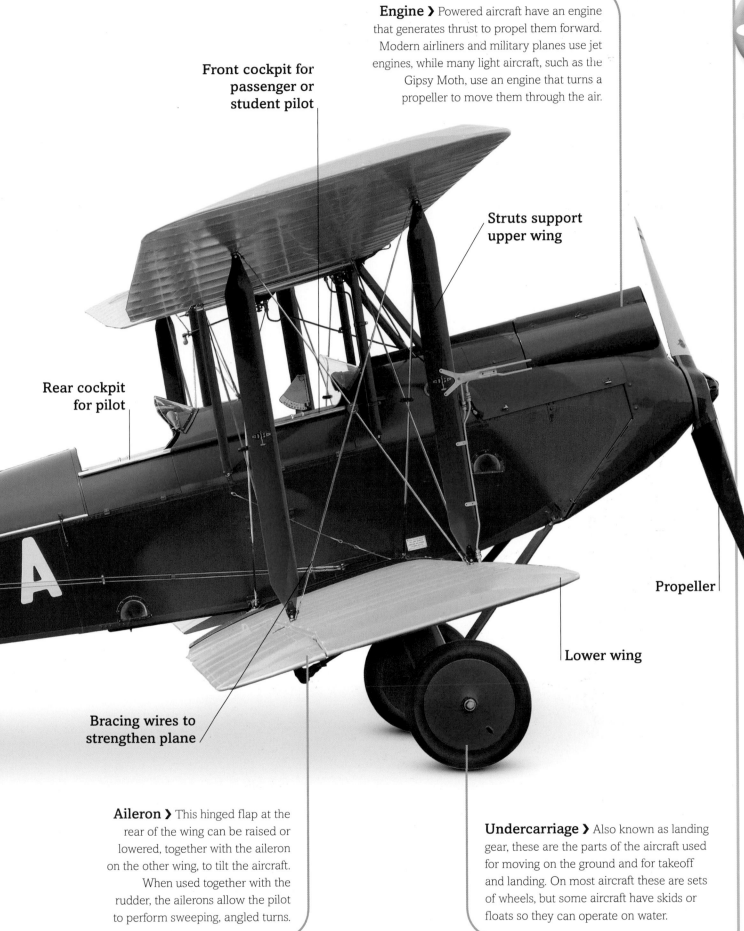

Front cockpit for passenger or student pilot

Engine > Powered aircraft have an engine that generates thrust to propel them forward. Modern airliners and military planes use jet engines, while many light aircraft, such as the Gipsy Moth, use an engine that turns a propeller to move them through the air.

Struts support upper wing

Rear cockpit for pilot

Propeller

Lower wing

Bracing wires to strengthen plane

Aileron > This hinged flap at the rear of the wing can be raised or lowered, together with the aileron on the other wing, to tilt the aircraft. When used together with the rudder, the ailerons allow the pilot to perform sweeping, angled turns.

Undercarriage > Also known as landing gear, these are the parts of the aircraft used for moving on the ground and for takeoff and landing. On most aircraft these are sets of wheels, but some aircraft have skids or floats so they can operate on water.

Taking to the skies

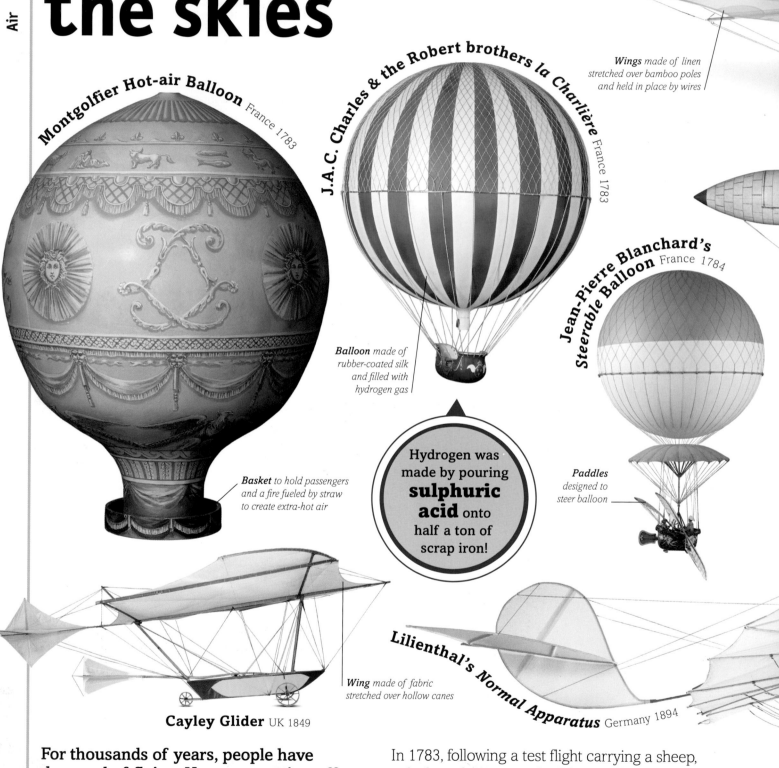

Montgolfier Hot-air Balloon France 1783

J.A.C. Charles & the Robert brothers la Charlière France 1783

Wings made of linen stretched over bamboo poles and held in place by wires

Balloon made of rubber-coated silk and filled with hydrogen gas

Jean-Pierre Blanchard's Steerable Balloon France 1784

Basket to hold passengers and a fire fueled by straw to create extra-hot air

Hydrogen was made by pouring **sulphuric acid** onto half a ton of scrap iron!

Paddles designed to steer balloon

Wing made of fabric stretched over hollow canes

Cayley Glider UK 1849

Lilienthal's Normal Apparatus Germany 1894

For thousands of years, people have dreamed of flying. However, getting off the ground successfully proved impossible until the invention of lighter-than-air craft, such as balloons and airships, and research into the principles of flight using gliders.

In 1783, following a test flight carrying a sheep, a duck, and a rooster, the **Montgolfier Hot-air Balloon** took off in Paris, France, with two human passengers. Paris was the center of the new balloon age. Just 10 days later the city saw the launch of the first hydrogen-filled balloon, the

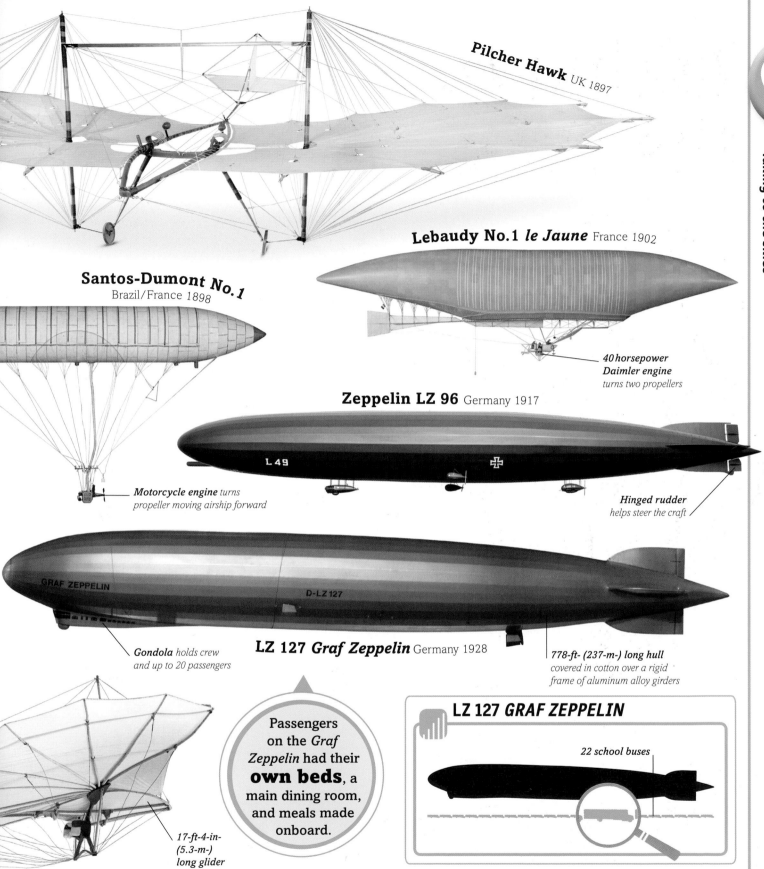

Pilcher Hawk UK 1897

Lebaudy No.1 *le Jaune* France 1902

Santos-Dumont No.1
Brazil/France 1898

*40 horsepower
Daimler engine*
turns two propellers

Zeppelin LZ 96 Germany 1917

L 49

Motorcycle engine turns
propeller moving airship forward

Hinged rudder
helps steer the craft

GRAF ZEPPELIN

D-LZ 127

LZ 127 *Graf Zeppelin* Germany 1928

Gondola holds crew
and up to 20 passengers

*778-ft- (237-m-) long hull
covered in cotton over a rigid
frame of aluminum alloy girders*

*17-ft-4-in-
(5.3-m-)
long glider*

Passengers
on the *Graf
Zeppelin* had their
own beds, a
main dining room,
and meals made
onboard.

LZ 127 *GRAF ZEPPELIN*

22 school buses

la Charlière, and, in 1898, the first flight of the airship **Santos-Dumont No.1**. In Germany, large airships, such as the **Zeppelin LZ 96**, scouted and bombed during World War I, while postwar airships, such as the *Graf Zeppelin*, offered long-distance transportation to the wealthy. Other inventors believed that winged gliders were the way up. In the 1890s, German engineer Otto Lilienthal made many successful flights in gliders such as the *Normal Apparatus*. His work inspired other glider designs, as well as the Wright Brothers' work on a powered aircraft.

First planes

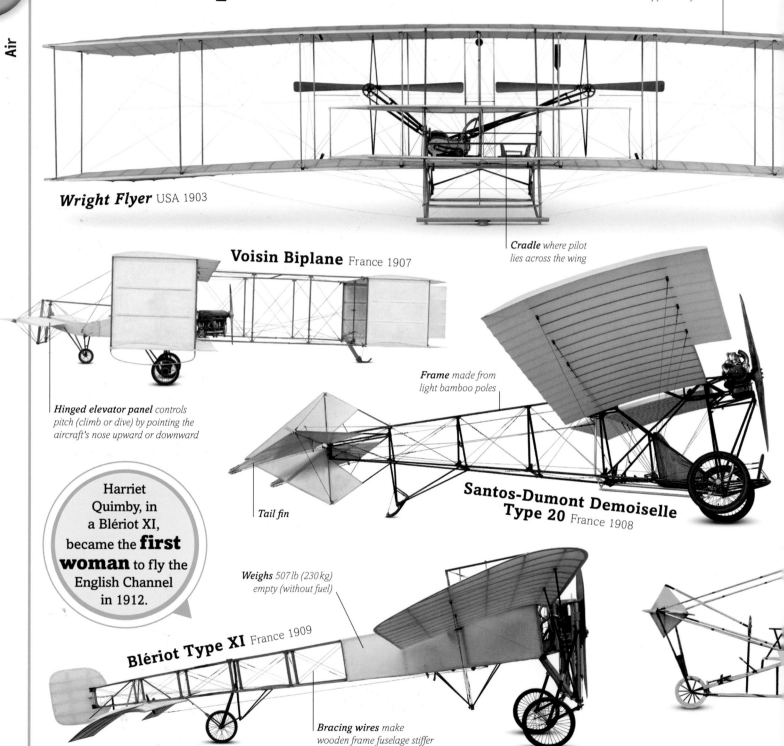

Wings stretch to 40 ft 4 in (12.3 m) and are supported by struts

Wright Flyer USA 1903

Cradle where pilot lies across the wing

Voisin Biplane France 1907

Frame made from light bamboo poles

Hinged elevator panel controls pitch (climb or dive) by pointing the aircraft's nose upward or downward

Tail fin

Santos-Dumont Demoiselle Type 20 France 1908

Harriet Quimby, in a Blériot XI, became the **first woman** to fly the English Channel in 1912.

Weighs 507 lb (230 kg) empty (without fuel)

Blériot Type XI France 1909

Bracing wires make wooden frame fuselage stiffer

On December 17, 1903, bicycle-maker Orville Wright lifted off into the air in a powered aircraft. This first flight lasted only 12 seconds and covered less than the length of a modern airliner, but it marked the beginning of a new age.

Built by two brothers, the *Wright Flyer* was a biplane, with two sets of wings, and two propellers spinning behind them. The **Voisin Biplane** and **Shorts S27** copied this pusher-propeller design, but other aircraft, such as the **Santos-Dumont Demoiselle**, mounted their

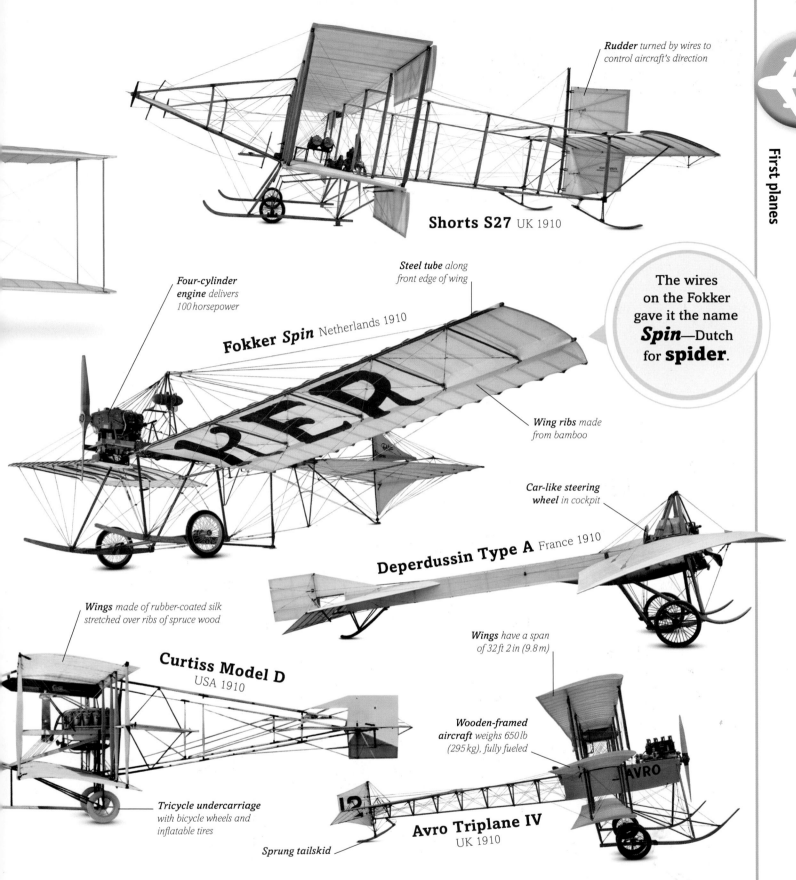

Rudder *turned by wires to control aircraft's direction*

Shorts S27 UK 1910

Steel tube along front edge of wing

Four-cylinder engine delivers 100 horsepower

Fokker *Spin* Netherlands 1910

The wires on the Fokker gave it the name *Spin*—Dutch for **spider**.

Wing ribs made from bamboo

Car-like steering wheel in cockpit

Deperdussin Type A France 1910

Wings made of rubber-coated silk stretched over ribs of spruce wood

Curtiss Model D
USA 1910

Wings have a span of 32 ft 2 in (9.8 m)

Wooden-framed aircraft weighs 650 lb (295 kg), fully fueled

Tricycle undercarriage with bicycle wheels and inflatable tires

Avro Triplane IV
UK 1910

Sprung tailskid

engine and propeller at the front, or were monoplanes, with a single pair of wings. Early aircraft were built light, using wood, cloth-covered wings, and wires to brace and stiffen their structures. The **Blériot XI** carried French aviator Louis Blériot on the successful first flight from France to England across the English Channel in 1909. The **Deperdussin Type A** flew 60 miles (100 km) at a record speed of 60 mph (100 km/h) in 1911, carrying two people. This, and other record breakers, helped to prove that planes could be a practical form of transportation.

THE GIRL OF NERVE
Daredevil wingwalker Lilian Boyer hangs from the wingtip of a Curtiss JN-4 Jenny biplane without a safety harness. Flying was new to the public in the 1920s and a ride in a biplane could be an unnerving experience for some, even when safely strapped into their seat. So, large crowds were thrilled by the exploits of barnstormers who performed amazing feats of daring in the sky.

In 1921, Boyer, a 20-year-old restaurant waitress, proved fearless when on her second flight in an aircraft, she stepped out of her seat and onto the wing. Later that year, she teamed up with former World War I pilot Billy Brock. The pair performed 352 shows across North America throughout the 1920s, dazzling crowds with their exploits. Boyer would stand on the wing of the aircraft as it performed a loop-the-loop, or dangle from the wing hanging by one hand, or even by a cord she gripped with her teeth! She also mastered jumping from a speeding car to a plane—a stunt she pulled on 143 occasions before bans on low flying came into place in 1929. Miraculously, Boyer lived to the grand age of 88.

Fighter planes

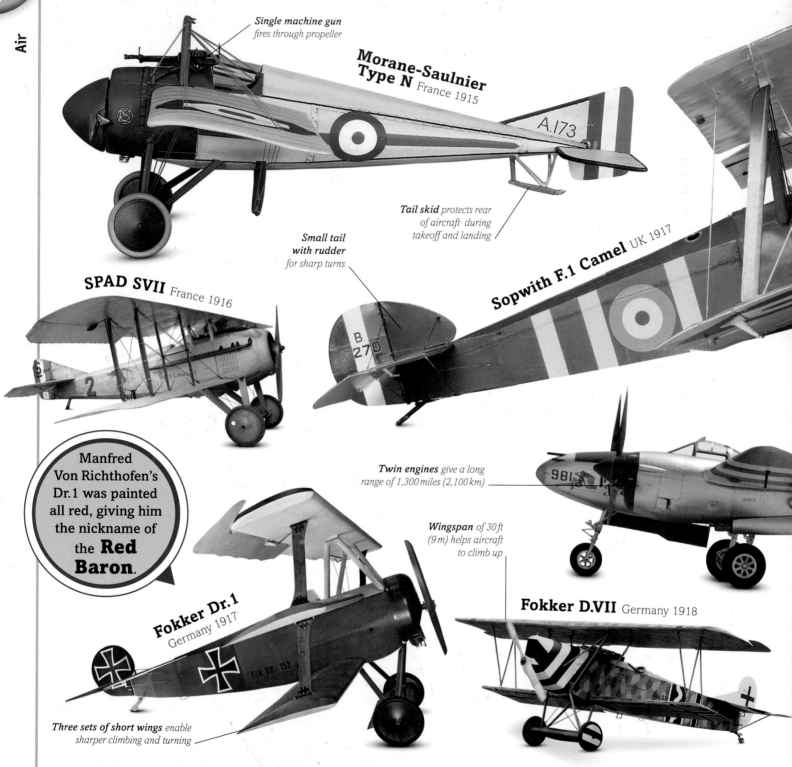

Single machine gun *fires through propeller*

Morane-Saulnier Type N France 1915

A.173

Tail skid *protects rear of aircraft during takeoff and landing*

Small tail with rudder *for sharp turns*

SPAD SVII France 1916

Sopwith F.1 Camel UK 1917

B 270

Manfred Von Richthofen's Dr.1 was painted all red, giving him the nickname of the **Red Baron**.

Twin engines *give a long range of 1,300 miles (2,100 km)*

981

Wingspan *of 30 ft (9 m) helps aircraft to climb up*

Fokker D.VII Germany 1918

Fokker Dr.1 Germany 1917

Fok DR. 152

Three sets of short wings *enable sharper climbing and turning*

Fast and maneuverable, fighter planes were an air force's hunter-killers during World Wars I and II. Their forward-firing weapons, such as cannons and machine guns, were mounted on the nose or the wings to shoot down other aircraft.

Early World War I fighters, such as the **Morane-Saulnier Type N**, preyed on slow, often unarmed, bombers and reconnaissance aircraft. They were soon outpaced by faster fliers, such as the **Sopwith Camel** and **Fokker D.VII**, which engaged in furious dogfights against each other.

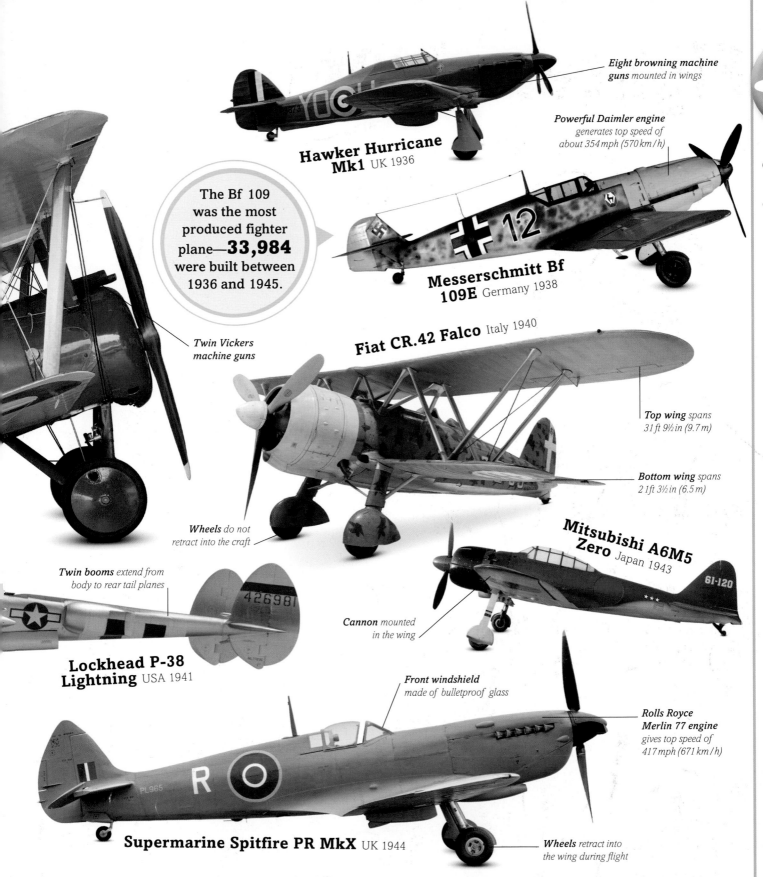

Eight browning machine guns mounted in wings

Hawker Hurricane Mk1 UK 1936

Powerful Daimler engine generates top speed of about 354 mph (570 km/h)

The Bf 109 was the most produced fighter plane—**33,984** were built between 1936 and 1945.

Messerschmitt Bf 109E Germany 1938

Twin Vickers machine guns

Fiat CR.42 Falco Italy 1940

Top wing spans 31 ft 9½ in (9.7 m)

Bottom wing spans 21 ft 3½ in (6.5 m)

Wheels do not retract into the craft

Mitsubishi A6M5 Zero Japan 1943

Twin booms extend from body to rear tail planes

Lockhead P-38 Lightning USA 1941

Cannon mounted in the wing

Front windshield made of bulletproof glass

Rolls Royce Merlin 77 engine gives top speed of 417 mph (671 km/h)

Supermarine Spitfire PR MkX UK 1944

Wheels retract into the wing during flight

The famous German fighter ace, Baron Manfred von Richthofen, made 19 of his 80 "kills" in his **Fokker Dr.1** triplane. Fighter designs mostly moved from biplanes (with two pairs of wings) to monoplanes (with a single pair of wings) after World War I, and aircraft such as the **Hawker Hurricane Mk1** and the **Messerschmitt Bf 109E** battled in the sky. Some fighters, such as the **Mitsubishi A6M5 Zero**, also served as bombers, while the **Supermarine Spitfire PR MkX** relied on its speed to avoid other fighters as it took photos over enemy lines.

Strike force

Wooden wing frame *covered in canvas*

Avro 504 UK 1913

H1968

Tail skid helps *slow aircraft down while landing*

Three-bladed propeller

Junkers Ju87 Stuka Germany 1935

Tail with rudder

Electronics in tail to *confuse enemy radar and detect incoming missiles*

LA 058

Chin turret manned *by bombardier who also aims the bombs*

124485

Heinkel He111
Germany 1940

Boeing B-17G Flying Fortress USA 1935

Top speed of 270 mph (434 km/h)

83 BK

Exhausts to release gases from *the Rolls Royce Merlin engine*

Fuel tanks in *wings and body*

de Havilland DH98 Mosquito UK 1940

The **B-2** *Spirit* is the world's most expensive aircraft, costing **$2.1 billion** each!

Strike aircraft attack ground targets using bombs or missiles. The first bombers were regular planes from which small bombs were dropped by hand. Special bombers were developed at the end of World War I and saw major action in World War II.

Some World War II bombers, such as the **Junkers Ju87 Stuka**, would dive low to bomb enemy forces on the ground. Others operated from high altitude, as much as 29,528 ft (9,000 m) in the case of the **Boeing B-17G Flying Fortress**. The **Avro Lancaster** had over double the bomb-carrying

Cockpit seats four of the seven-man crew with fifth in the nose

Mid gun turret armed with twin machine guns

Avro Lancaster UK 1941

Rolls Royce Merlin engines give top speed of 282 mph (454 km/h)

B-29A Superfortress USA 1944

Boeing B-52H Stratofortress USA 1961

Twin turbofan engines give top speed of 1,429 mph (2,300 km/h)

Tupolev Tu-22M3 Russia 1978

Could carry up to 69,446 lb (31,500 kg) of weapons

Could carry 10 missiles or 33,069 lb (15,000 kg) of bombs

Nose houses radar system to detect enemy fighters from up to 60 miles (100 km) away

Mikoyan-Gurevich MiG-29 Russia 1982

Northrop Grumman B-2 Spirit USA 1990

Rocket pods make this a multi-role aircraft

Elevons help aircraft turn, climb, and descend

BOEING B-52H STRATOFORTRESS

159 ft (48.5 m) long, equivalent to four school buses

capacity of the B-17G and more than 7,000 were built. Both were heavily armed, with machine gunners in turrets. Made out of wood, the **de Havilland DH98** *Mosquito* relied on its speed and agility to evade enemies. Fifty years later, the **Northrop Grumman B-2** *Spirit* uses stealth technology to strike its targets undetected. Some jet-powered bombers could travel long distances, such as the **Tupolev Tu-22M3**, with a range of 4,200 miles (6,800 km), and the eight-engine **Boeing B-52H Stratofortress**, which could fly more than 10,000 miles (16,000 km).

Racers and record-breakers

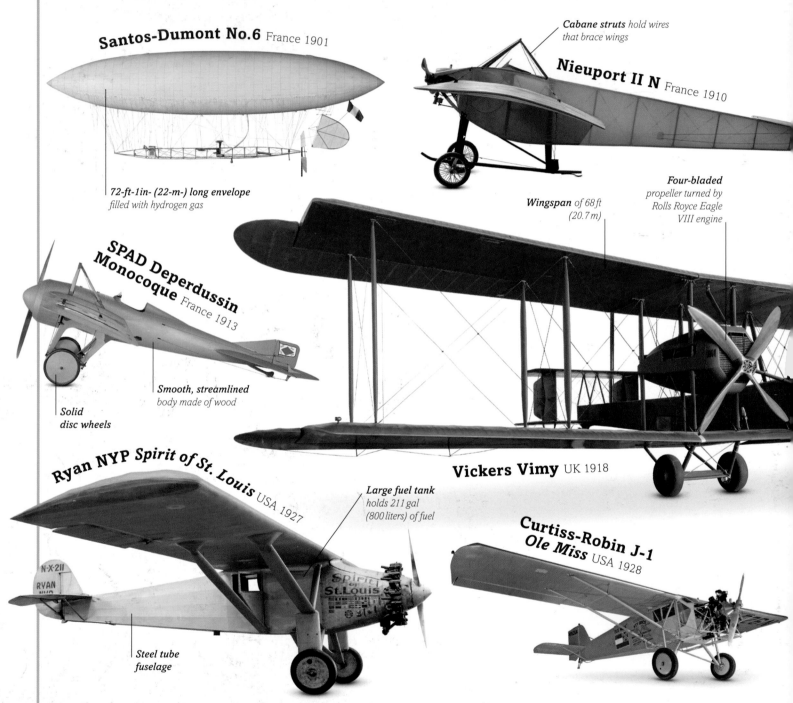

Santos-Dumont No.6 France 1901

72-ft-1in- (22-m-) long envelope filled with hydrogen gas

Cabane struts hold wires that brace wings

Nieuport II N France 1910

Four-bladed propeller turned by Rolls Royce Eagle VIII engine

Wingspan of 68 ft (20.7 m)

SPAD Deperdussin Monocoque France 1913

Smooth, streamlined body made of wood

Solid disc wheels

Vickers Vimy UK 1918

Ryan NYP Spirit of St. Louis USA 1927

Large fuel tank holds 211 gal (800 liters) of fuel

Curtiss-Robin J-1 Ole Miss USA 1928

Steel tube fuselage

Getting into the air wasn't enough for some pilots and engineers. They wanted to push their planes to the limit and fly higher, faster, longer than others. Races were held, records set and broken, as aircraft became stronger, more powerful, and reliable.

In 1901, the **Santos-Dumont No.6** airship won one of the first aviation prizes—100,000 French francs in 1901 for a flight around the Eiffel Tower. In 1919, the **Vickers Vimy** made the first nonstop flight across the Atlantic. American aviator Charles Lindbergh completed a 33½ hour

Supermarine S6B UK 1930

Macchi Castoldi M.C.72 Italy 1931

Floats designed
to give off heat to
cool engine fluids

Gee Bee Model Z Super Sportster USA 1931

*Streamlined
wheel coverings*

*Hinged rudder
on tail for turning*

The fastest
propeller-driven
seaplane is the
M.C.72, with a speed
of **441 mph**
(709 km/h).

Smooth wings of
39 ft 4 in (12 m) span
to cut through air

Percival P10 Vega Gull UK 1935

Engine gives top
speed of 137 mph
(220 km/h)

Aircraft only has 7.5
minutes of rocket power
to climb into air

Sliding glass canopy
reveals seating for pilot
and three passengers

Bücker Bü133C Jungmeister Germany 1936

Skid for landing as
wheels were discarded
after take off

**Messerschmitt Me163
Komet** Germany 1944

nonstop solo flight from New York to Paris in 1927
in the *Spirit of St. Louis*. In 1935, a **Curtiss-
Robin J-1** called *Ole Miss*, aided by inflight
refuelling, stayed aloft for 27 days. As aircraft
design developed, speed records were frequently
broken. The **SPAD Deperdussin Monocoque**

set a record of 130 mph (210 km/h), while the
Supermarine S6B and the **Macchi Castoldi
M.C.72** broke the 373 mph (600 km/h) and the
435 mph (700 km/h) barriers. Even faster was the
rocket-powered **Messerschmitt Me163 Komet**,
which reached 624 mph (1,005 km/h) in 1941.

Jet fighters

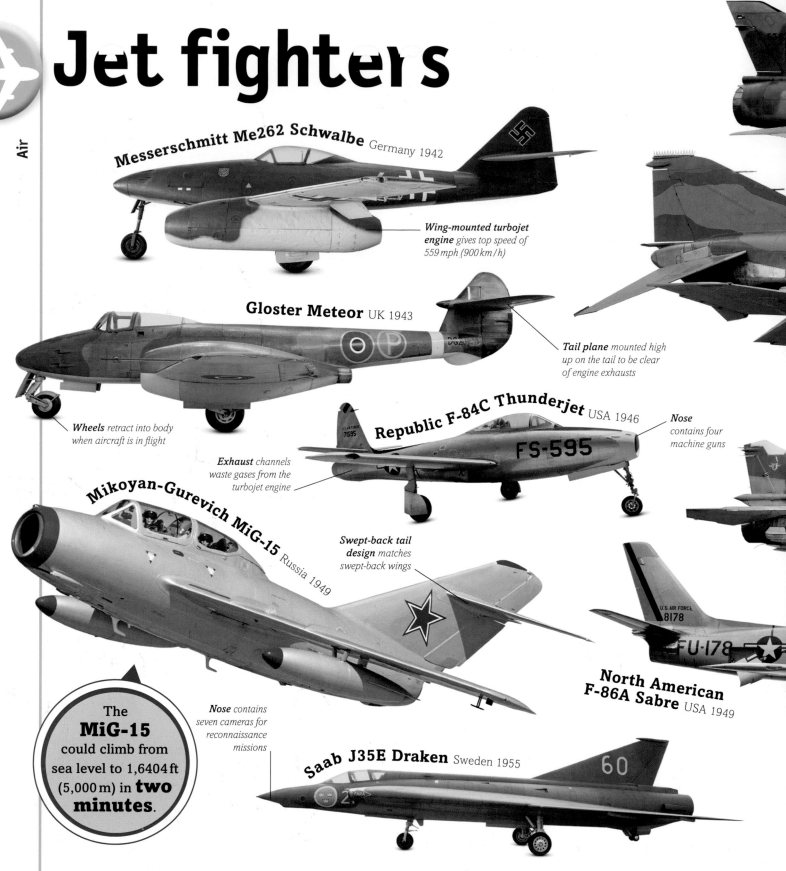

Messerschmitt Me262 Schwalbe Germany 1942

Wing-mounted turbojet engine gives top speed of 559 mph (900 km/h)

Gloster Meteor UK 1943

Tail plane mounted high up on the tail to be clear of engine exhausts

Wheels retract into body when aircraft is in flight

Exhaust channels waste gases from the turbojet engine

Republic F-84C Thunderjet USA 1946

FS-595

Nose contains four machine guns

Mikoyan-Gurevich MiG-15 Russia 1949

Swept-back tail design matches swept-back wings

North American F-86A Sabre USA 1949

The **MiG-15** could climb from sea level to 1,6404 ft (5,000 m) in **two minutes**.

Nose contains seven cameras for reconnaissance missions

Saab J35E Draken Sweden 1955

Developed during World War II, jet fighters are mostly fast, nimble single-seaters that carry a wide range of weaponry, from cannons to missiles. They attack and chase off enemy fighters to establish air superiority over a region.

North American F-86A Sabres and Mikoyan-Gurevich MiG-15s fought each other during the Korean War of 1950. The **Republic F-84C Thunderjet** flew 86,408 missions during the same war, and was the first mass-production jet fighter that could refuel

Dassault Mirage III France 1960

Cockpit seats two people

Delta wing has maximum span of 27 ft (8.2 m)

More F-4 Phantoms were built than any other US supersonic jet—**5,195** in total.

Front seat where pilot sits

McDonnell Douglas F-4 Phantom II USA 1960

Large external fuel tank

English Electric Lightning F53 UK 1970

53-686

Mikoyan-Gurevich MiG-23 Russia 1970

20-01

External fuel tank holds more than 263.9 gal (1,037 liters)

Lockheed Martin F-22 Raptor USA 2005

Nose contains six Browning M3 machine guns

Cockpit with ejection seat

Eurofighter Typhoon FGR4 Multinational 2007

midair from a tanker aircraft. The **Mikoyan-Gurevich MiG-23** and the **Dassault Mirage III** could operate as fighter-bombers, carrying ground attack weapons under their bodies and wings. Designed for quick operations, the **Saab J35E Draken**, could be re-armed in just 10 minutes. It could take off from roads as well as runways. Modern warbirds, such as the **Lockheed Martin F-22 Raptor** and the **Eurofighter Typhoon FGR4**, are versatile. They can attack air and ground targets, as well as perform reconnaissance missions.

SUPER SPEED An extraordinary sight greets the eyes as a United States Navy Grumman F-14 Tomcat accelerates just 500 ft (150 m) above the Pacific Ocean. A cloud of condensed water vapor forms around the aircraft, known as a shock collar, or vapor cone. The aircraft will shortly go supersonic and travel faster than the speed of sound, an event often accompanied by a loud noise, known as a sonic boom.

When a fast aircraft travels, it generates a series of pressure waves in the air. These waves travel at the speed of sound, approximately 761 mph (1,225 km/h) at sea level, and a little lower at higher altitudes. As the aircraft's speed increases, the waves are forced together to form a single shock wave, which makes a thunder-like boom when released. Most sonic booms last between 0.1 and 0.5 seconds. The first supersonic flight was in 1947. Today, many military jet aircraft regularly travel at supersonic speeds. The F-14 has a top speed of more than 1,500 mph (2,400 km/h) at high altitude. Only two passenger airliners have ever operated at supersonic speeds: the Russian Tupolev Tu-144 and the British/French Concorde.

Seaplanes

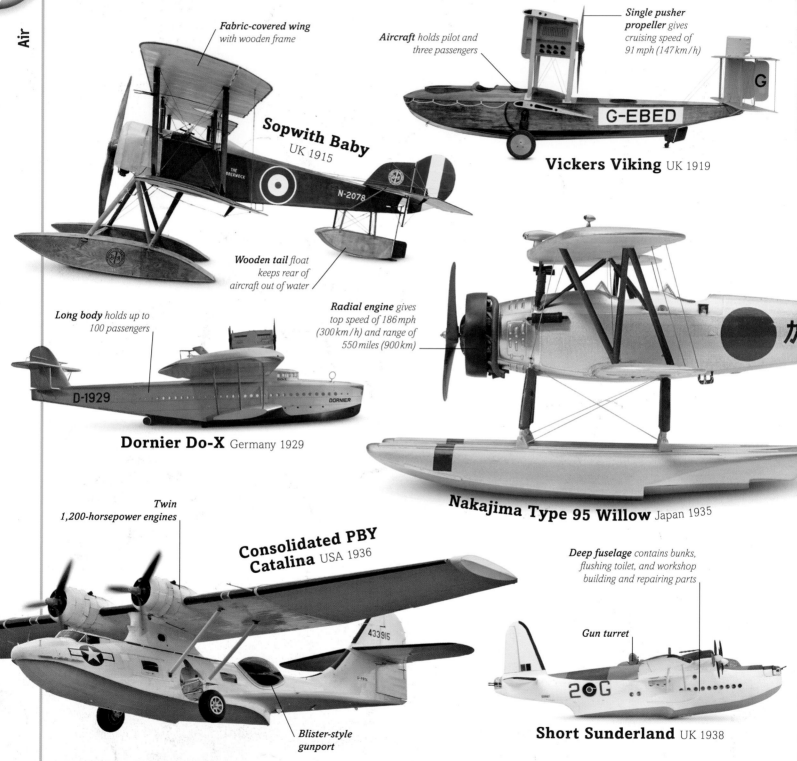

Fabric-covered wing with wooden frame

Sopwith Baby
UK 1915

Single pusher propeller gives cruising speed of 91 mph (147 km/h)

Aircraft holds pilot and three passengers

Vickers Viking UK 1919

Wooden tail float keeps rear of aircraft out of water

Long body holds up to 100 passengers

Radial engine gives top speed of 186 mph (300 km/h) and range of 550 miles (900 km)

Dornier Do-X Germany 1929

Nakajima Type 95 Willow Japan 1935

Twin 1,200-horsepower engines

Consolidated PBY Catalina USA 1936

Deep fuselage contains bunks, flushing toilet, and workshop building and repairing parts

Gun turret

Blister-style gunport

Short Sunderland UK 1938

Planes that can land and take off from water are known as seaplanes. There are two types of these versatile machines—floatplanes, which sit on water using pontoons (buoyant floats), and flying boats with a watertight body, like a boat.

Floatplanes saw service in both the World Wars. The **Sopwith Baby** patrolled coasts and spotted airships in WWI. The **Nakajima Type 95 Willow** flew as a light bomber during WWII, while military flying boats, such as the **Short Sunderland** and **Consolidated PBY Catalina**,

Wings with 46 ft (14 m) span could fold back for storage on a ship

Supermarine Walrus UK 1939

Front deck where crew stand to moor aircraft

Tail rudder

Wheels retract into body while flying or cruising on water

Cabin holds 10 passengers

de Havilland DHC-3 Otter Canada 1953

Wingspan of 57 ft 8 in (17.6 m) enables aircraft to take off over short distances

Turboprop engine gives top speed of 330 mph (530 km/h)

Nose cone contains radar system

Beriev Be-12 *Chaika*
Russia 1960

This plane can scoop **1,320 gallons** (5,000 liters) of water from a lake in **10 seconds**.

Pusher propeller forces air back to move aircraft forward

Lake LA-4
USA 1967

Large float underneath wing

Wing

Retractable tricycle undercarriage

Canadair CL-215
Canada 1967

performed patrols, hunted submarines, and escorted ships. Other flying boats, such as the 12-engined **Dornier Do-X**, carried passengers across long distances. Some seaplanes are amphibious and can operate from land or water. The **Supermarine Walrus** would take off from a warship and land on water, and was then returned to the ship by crane. It was used in Canada along with other seaplanes, such as the **de Havilland Otter** and the **Canadair CL-215**. The Canadair is designed to skim a lake or river scooping up large quantities of water to drop on forest fires.

Light aircraft

Boeing-Stearman PT-17/N2S Kaydet USA 1940

Wings *made of wood and covered in fabric*

Wing *carries 38.8 gal (147 liters) of fuel*

Cessna 172 USA 1964

Beagle Pup Series 2 UK 1969

Two-blade metal propeller *driven by 150 horsepower engine*

Cabin *holds eight passengers and has single door*

Wings *have a span of 20 ft (6.1 m)*

Cessna 421B USA 1973

Pitts Special S-2A USA 1973

Ailerons *on upper and lower wings help plane perform complete 360° roll in two seconds*

A **S-2A** set a world record in 2014, performing **81 spins** in a row.

Light aircraft are small civilian craft with one or two engines and a fully loaded weight of less than 12,500 lb (5,670 kg). They are used for travel, learning to fly, aerobatics, and racing, and some as airmail carriers, ambulances, or cropdusters.

Some light aircraft are very light, such as the **Bede BD-5J**, which weighs 358½ lb (162.7 kg) empty, making it the lightest jet aircraft in the world, and the **Flight Design CTSW**, which weighs 702 lb (318.4 kg) empty and has a parachute system that can carry the entire

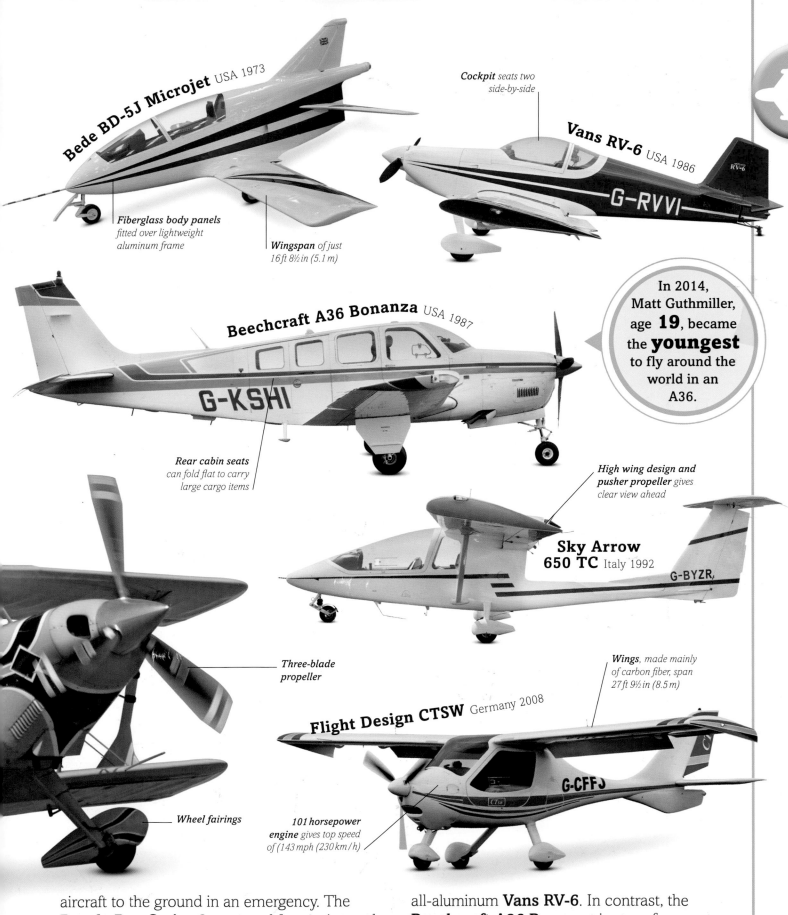

Bede BD-5J Microjet USA 1973

Fiberglass body panels fitted over lightweight aluminum frame

Wingspan of just 16 ft 8½ in (5.1 m)

Cockpit seats two side-by-side

Vans RV-6 USA 1986

G-RVVI

Beechcraft A36 Bonanza USA 1987

G-KSHI

Rear cabin seats can fold flat to carry large cargo items

In 2014, Matt Guthmiller, age **19**, became the **youngest** to fly around the world in an A36.

High wing design and pusher propeller gives clear view ahead

Sky Arrow 650 TC Italy 1992

G-BYZR

Three-blade propeller

Wings, made mainly of carbon fiber, span 27 ft 9½ in (8.5 m)

Flight Design CTSW Germany 2008

Wheel fairings

101 horsepower engine gives top speed of (143 mph (230 km/h)

G-CFFJ

aircraft to the ground in an emergency. The **Beagle Pup Series 2** was used for touring and aerobatics, while the two-seater **Pitts Special S-2A**, which can spin, roll, and climb sharply, is just used for tricks. Early Pitts planes were offered as kits to be built at home, as was the all-aluminum **Vans RV-6**. In contrast, the **Beechcraft A36 Bonanza** is one of more than 17,000 Bonanzas built in factories. The most manufactured light aircraft of all is the four-seater **Cessna 172**, of which more than 43,000 were produced.

Plane spotting

Open cockpit for pilot

Closed cabin for passengers

Fokker F.II
Netherlands 1920

H·NABC

**Ford 5-AT
Trimotor** USA 1928

Body panels made
of corrugated
(ridged) aluminum

F.IIs were
flown by **KLM**,
the world's
oldest airline
still flying under
its original
name.

Plywood body keeps
weight down to 3,219 lb
(1,460 kg) when empty

Douglas DC-2 USA 1934

44
PH-AJU

Undercarriage folds
up into the aircraft to
cut drag when flying

Giant wings
have span of
262 ft (80 m)

**de Havilland DH89
Dragon Rapide** UK 1934

G-AGTM

**Sud-Aviation
Caravelle** France 1955

AIR INTER

*Rear-mounted turbojet
engine* gives top speed
of 500 mph (805 km/h)

**de Havilland DH106
Comet 4C** UK 1960

DAN-AIR LONDON
DAN-AIR

Tailplanes contain elevator panels
to help the plane climb or descend

Early passenger planes were converted bombers and other military aircraft. Planes specially built for air travel truly arrived in the 1920s and 1930s. Today, flying has become a fast, convenient, and common form of transportation.

The **Fokker F.II** carried just four passengers, while the **Ford 5-AT Trimotor** could hold 13, plus two crew members. The **Douglas DC-2** could carry one passenger more and was flown by more than 30 airlines all around the world, as was the simple but rugged **de Havilland DH89**

Swept-back wings have span of 123 ft (37.5 m)

Turbojet engine, one of three, gives aircraft top speed of 559 mph (900 km/h)

Tupolev Tu-154 Russia 1969

CCCP-85020

Large tail contains hinged rudder to aid turning

Cockpit contains seats for the pilot and copilot

D-CALM

Dornier Do228-101 Germany 1985

Upturned wingtips, called winglets

Airbus A320-214 Multinational 1995

Sharklets - hunting down fuel burn

A320 AIRBUS

F-WWIQ 5098

Airbus A380-800 Multinational 2005

SINGAPORE AIRLINES

Today, 25,000 passenger planes carry more than **3.4 billion passengers** every year.

Tail rises 80 ft (24.5 m) above the ground

Powerful jet engines give top cruising speed of 587 mph (945 km/h)

AIRBUS A380-800

The Airbus A380-800 is as long as 6.6 school buses

238.7 ft (72.7 m) long

Boeing 787-8 Dreamliner USA 2009

QATAR

DREAMLINER N1018

Clear cabin windows can be tinted to filter out sunlight

Dragon Rapide. Larger airliners powered by jet engines emerged after World War II. The first short-haul jet airliner, the **Sud-Aviation Caravelle**, carried 80 passengers, while the **Tupolev Tu-154** could carry up to 180. Today, the biggest of all is the **Airbus A380-800**, which can carry up to 853 people on two passenger decks. Some modern airliners can travel long distances without landing to refuel. The **Boeing 787-8 Dreamliner** can fly up to 8,000 miles (13,000 km) nonstop—enough to make it from the USA to China.

221

COMING IN LOW
Vacationers sunning themselves on the Caribbean island of Saint Martin get their cameras out as an Air Caraibes Airbus A330 airliner comes in to land at Princess Juliana International Airport. The stunning sight is repeated over the sands of Maho Beach several times day, as the Caribbean island airport receives more than 58,000 aircraft movements (takeoffs or landings) every year.

The airport's 7,545 ft- (2,300 m-) long runway is relatively short by modern standards, and it stretches close to the airport's boundary with the beach. An Airbus A330, which can carry more than 200 passengers, needs at least 3,280 ft (1,000 m)—preferably more—to come to a halt once it has touched down. As a result, pilots make their approach over the shimmering waters of the Caribbean as low as they can, in order to get their plane's wheels on the tarmac as quickly as possible. Planes can be just 65 to 100 ft (20 to 30 m) above the ground by the time they fly over the beach. Maho may not be the best beach on the island, but it draws large crowds of plane-spotters, eager to get close to big airliners in flight.

Straight up and supersonic

Bell X-1 USA 1946

Nose shaped like a bullet

Probe measures the distance the plane moves sideways

The Bell X-1 was nicknamed *Glamorous Glennis* after the pilot's wife.

Fairey Delta 2 UK 1954

WG777

Two-seater version used as training aircraft

Tail fin contains radio antenna

McDonnell F-101 Voodoo USA 1957

60312

Happy Hooligans

U.S. AIR FORCE

Internal fuel tanks hold up to 2,053 gal (7,771 liters)

NASA/ARMY

703

N703NA

BELL X

Lockheed F-104G Starfighter USA 1958

Narrow, circular body with short wings cuts through the air

Fuel tanks mounted on wing tips

The quest for speed led to supersonic aircraft—planes able to fly faster than the speed of sound, 767 mph (1,235 km/h) at sea level. Engineers have also created aircraft that can take off and land vertically, like a helicopter—VTOL planes.

The first supersonic aircraft was the rocket-powered **Bell X-1** piloted by American Charles "Chuck" Yeager. Improvements in jet engines saw startling increases in speeds. The **Fairey Delta 2** was the first to fly faster than 1,000 mph (1,609 km/h), the **Lockheed F-104G Starfighter**

Mikoyan-Gurevich MiG-21 Russia 1959

External fuel tank

Exhaust for gases from turbojet engine

BAe/Aerospatiale Concorde Type 1 UK/France 1976

British airways

Fuselage is 9 ft 6 in (2.9 m) wide, 203 ft (62 m) long, and holds 100 passengers

Lockheed SR71 Blackbird USA 1964

Pilot sits in ejection seat

Outer cockpit windshield made of quartz can heat up to 572°F (300°C) when flying fast

In 1990, an SR71 flew **coast-to-coast** across the entire USA in under **68 minutes**.

46

Yakovlev Yak-38 Russia 1971

Nosewheel supports the front of the aircraft

Nose contains laser range finder to measure distances

3D

Hawker Siddeley Harrier GR 3 UK 1973

Blades nearly 25 ft (7.6 m) in length spun by turboshaft engine

Engine nozzle moves to direct thrust down or back

Engines tilt upward for takeoff and forward for level flight

Bell Boeing MV-22B Osprey USA 2007

Tail fin

Instrument boom

Bell XV-15 Tiltrotor USA 1977

03

Fuselage can hold 32 armed troops

the first to reach 1,242 mph (2,000 km/h), and the **MiG-21** topped 1,479 mph (2,380 km/h). Then, in 1976, the **Lockheed SR71 Blackbird**, a jet spy plane, set a record of 2,193 mph (3,529 km/h), which has not been broken since. VTOL aircraft are used in places without long runways. Some,

such as the **Hawker Siddeley Harrier GR 3** and **Yakovlev Yak-38**, have engine nozzles that move to direct thrust downward or behind. Tilt-rotor planes, such as the **Bell XV-15**, swivel their entire propeller-spinning engines upward for takeoff and forward for regular flight.

Eyes in the sky

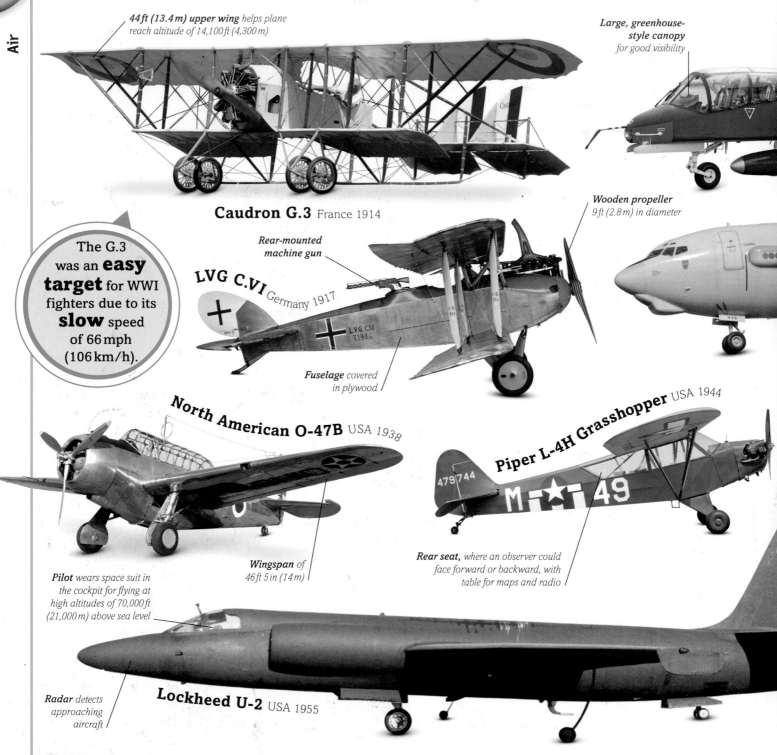

44 ft (13.4 m) upper wing helps plane reach altitude of 14,100 ft (4,300 m)

Large, greenhouse-style canopy for good visibility

Caudron G.3 France 1914

Wooden propeller 9 ft (2.8 m) in diameter

The G.3 was an **easy target** for WWI fighters due to its **slow** speed of 66 mph (106 km/h).

Rear-mounted machine gun

LVG C.VI Germany 1917

Fuselage covered in plywood

North American O-47B USA 1938

Piper L-4H Grasshopper USA 1944

479 744

M ★ 49

Wingspan of 46 ft 5 in (14 m)

Rear seat, where an observer could face forward or backward, with table for maps and radio

Pilot wears space suit in the cockpit for flying at high altitudes of 70,000 ft (21,000 m) above sea level

Radar detects approaching aircraft

Lockheed U-2 USA 1955

Reconnaissance planes scout the land and sea from above. Some go further, acting as spies in the sky using telephoto lenses and other tools to spot troop positions and detect enemy weapons, facilities, or other crucial activity on the ground.

The first spotter planes, such as the **Caudron G.3** and the **LVG C.VI**, were used to detect enemy artillery and troop movements. Later observation aircraft, such as the **OV-10 Bronco**, could scout territory and carry weapons. It could also take off from roads or makeshift runways,

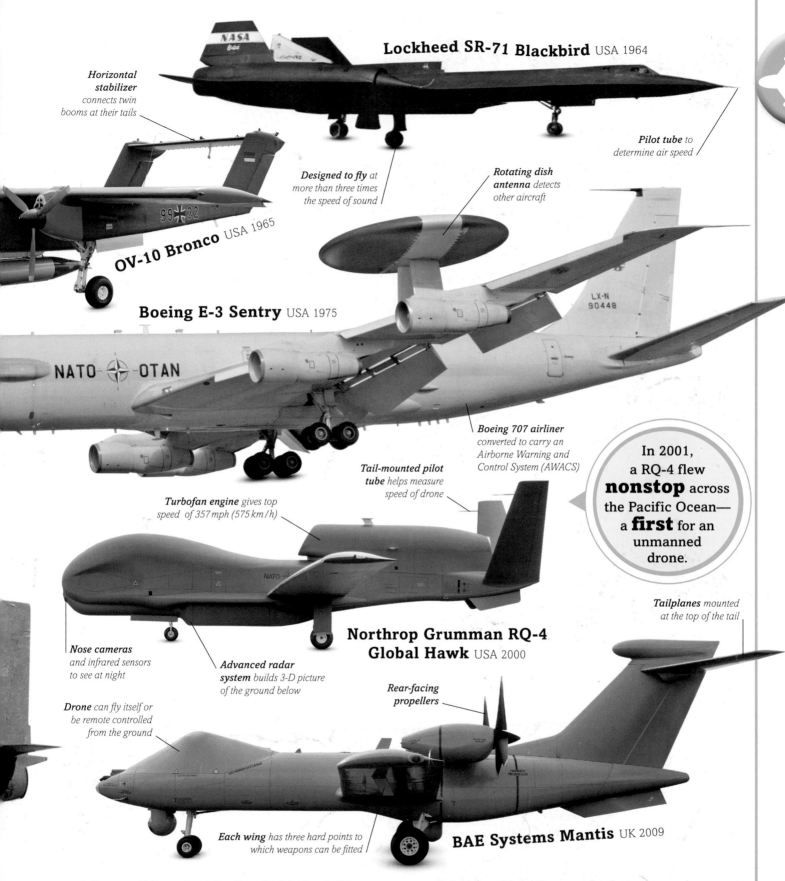

Lockheed SR-71 Blackbird USA 1964

Horizontal stabilizer connects twin booms at their tails

Pilot tube to determine air speed

Designed to fly at more than three times the speed of sound

Rotating dish antenna detects other aircraft

OV-10 Bronco USA 1965

Boeing E-3 Sentry USA 1975

NATO ✦ OTAN

LX-N 90448

Boeing 707 airliner converted to carry an Airborne Warning and Control System (AWACS)

Tail-mounted pilot tube helps measure speed of drone

Turbofan engine gives top speed of 357 mph (575 km/h)

In 2001, a RQ-4 flew **nonstop** across the Pacific Ocean— a **first** for an unmanned drone.

Nose cameras and infrared sensors to see at night

Advanced radar system builds 3-D picture of the ground below

Northrop Grumman RQ-4 Global Hawk USA 2000

Tailplanes mounted at the top of the tail

Rear-facing propellers

Drone can fly itself or be remote controlled from the ground

Each wing has three hard points to which weapons can be fitted

BAE Systems Mantis UK 2009

and fly more than 1,400 miles (2,200 km). The **SR-71 Blackbird** was a dedicated spy plane that operated at high speed and altitude, out of the range of enemy ground-to-air missiles. No Blackbird was ever shot down by enemy forces. Advanced fighters feature stealth technology that confuses enemy radars and other sensors, in order to spy undetected. Unmanned aerial vehicles (UAVs), or drones, such as the **BAE Systems Mantis**, can fly long missions gathering information without risking pilots' lives. The Mantis can fly up to 30 hours.

Helicopter

A helicopter's long, thin rotor blades have a curved shape, similar to that of an aircraft's wing. When these blades are spun quickly by the engine, they travel through the air and, like an aircraft wing, create lift. Their ability to take off and land vertically, and to hover midair, make helicopters incredibly useful for military and police work, and search-and-rescue missions, as performed by this **Sea King**.

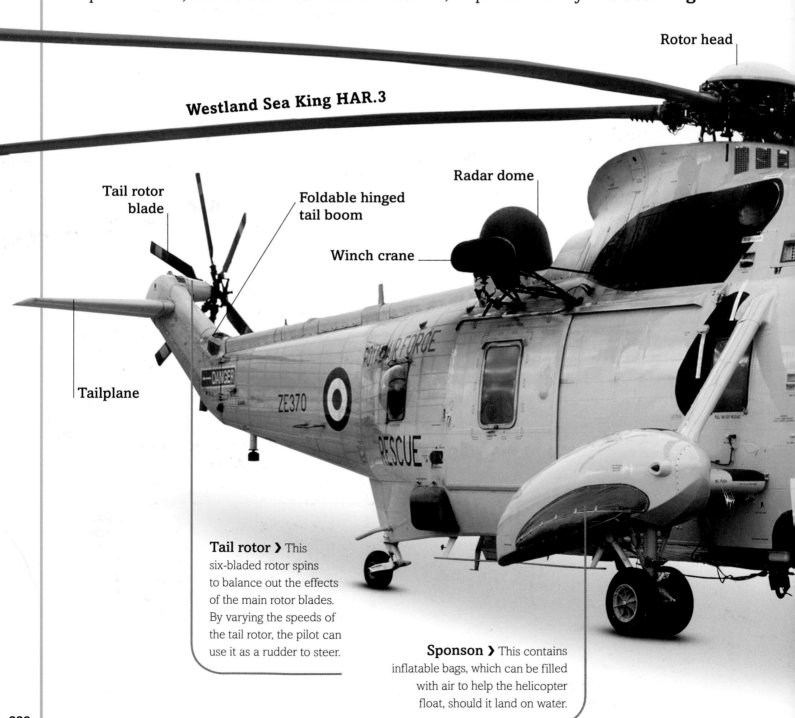

Westland Sea King HAR.3

Rotor head

Tail rotor blade

Foldable hinged tail boom

Radar dome

Winch crane

Tailplane

ZE370

ROYAL AIR FORCE

RESCUE

Tail rotor › This six-bladed rotor spins to balance out the effects of the main rotor blades. By varying the speeds of the tail rotor, the pilot can use it as a rudder to steer.

Sponson › This contains inflatable bags, which can be filled with air to help the helicopter float, should it land on water.

Turbine engine > The helicopter's two Rolls Royce Gnome turboshaft engines spin the rotor head, which can be angled to change the helicopter's direction. The Sea King has a cruising speed of 129 mph (208 km/h), and a maximum range of 764 miles (1,230 km).

Rotor blade > The rotor blades are fitted to the rotor head, which is spun by the engine to generate lift. The Sea King can rise up at speeds of 33 ft (10 m) per second. When the helicopter is stored on a ship, or in a hangar, the blades can be folded up.

Interior > The pilot and the copilot fly the helicopter from the cockpit, while two crew members operate the radio and winch system, which can lift people out of the water and into the helicopter. The Sea King can hold up to 18 rescued people or 6 stretchers.

Powerful forward-facing headlight

Hull and avionics > The Sea King's hull-shaped body enables it to float on water. Stored inside its nose are radio and navigation electronics that enable the helicopter to find stricken boats and people at sea.

Undercarriage wheels

Whirlybirds

Focke-Wulf Fa61 Germany 1936

de Havilland/Cierva C24 Autogiro UK 1931

Body is 20 ft (6.1 m) in length

In 1939, when few helicopters had taken off, an Fa61 climbed to **11,240 ft** (2,436 m).

SNCASE Liore et Oliver LeO C302 France 1939

Radial engine powers propeller to move autogiro forward

Drive shaft connects engine to tail rotor

One of two fuel tanks, each of which can hold 21.4 gal (81 liters)

Tail rotor guard prevents blades from striking the ground and snapping

Three-bladed main rotor with diameter of 37 ft 8 in (11.5 m)

Tail rotor

Sikorsky R-4 USA 1942

Landing skids could be replaced with floats for landing on water

With long, thin, wing-shaped blades whizzing around, it is no surprise that the first autogiros and helicopters got the nickname *whirlybirds*. These versatile craft first came into their own in the 1930s and 1940s.

Autogiros, such as the **Cierva C24**, use a main rotor for lift, but also have a propeller at the front to provide thrust. This gave the C24 a top speed of 110 mph (177 km/h). The experimental **Focke-Wulf Fa61** came with two sets of rotors, to increase lift, but only two were ever made.

Bubble canopy encloses two-seat cockpit

Hiller UH-12B (Hiller 360) USA 1947

Sikorsky S51/H-5 USA 1945

Landing skids

Cockpit seats four, with pilot in front and three passengers behind

Westland Dragonfly HR3 UK 1947

Body from a Focke-Wulf Fw44 biplane

Folding rotor blades for storage onboard ship

Twin rotor blades with overall diameter of 35 ft (10.7 m)

Tail rotor blade made of wood

Mil Mi-1M Soviet Union 1948

CCCP-D2299

Bell 47G USA 1953

Body houses a 63.4-gal (240-liter) fuel tank

Two sets of rotor blades spin in opposite directions

Rotorless tail

Breguet GIII France 1949

A Bell 47D was the **first helicopter** to fly over the **Alps** in 1950.

F-WFKC L.BREGUET

Goldfish bowl–style bubble canopy gives crew an all-around view

Cabin seats five

In contrast, more than 5,600 Bell 47 helicopters were built between 1946 and 1974. These included the **Bell 47G**, which became famous for medical evacuation, a task also performed by the **Westland Dragonfly HR3,** which flew the world's first scheduled helicopter service from 1950 onward. The **Sikorsky R-4** was the first helicopter used by the American and the British militaries, rescuing injured air crash survivors in Asia as early as 1944. The Soviet Union's first production helicopter was the **Mil Mi-1M**, of which more than 2,500 were eventually built.

Working choppers

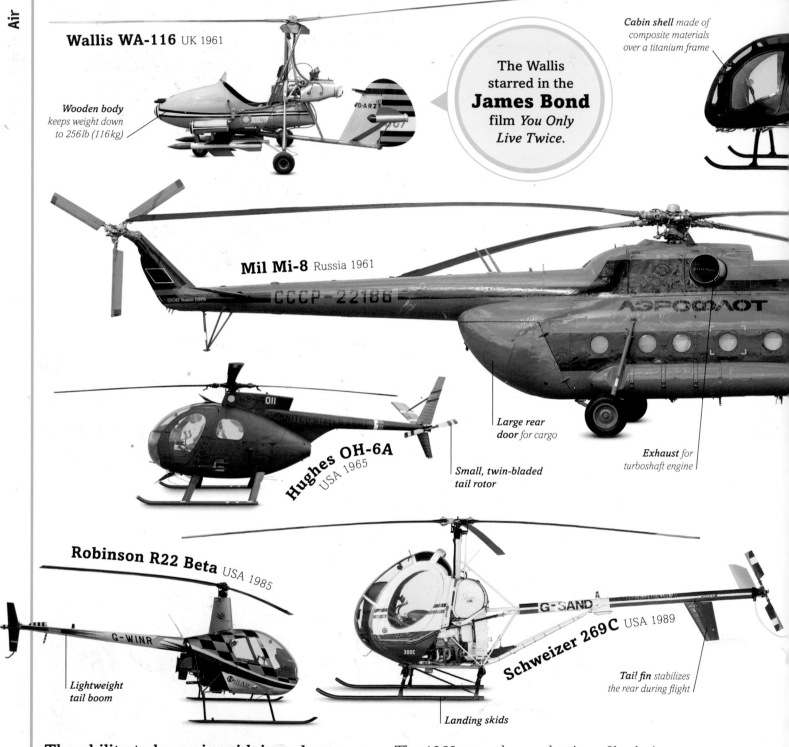

Wallis WA-116 UK 1961

Wooden body keeps weight down to 256 lb (116 kg)

The Wallis starred in the **James Bond** film *You Only Live Twice*.

Cabin shell made of composite materials over a titanium frame

Mil Mi-8 Russia 1961

CCCP-22186

АЭРОФЛОТ

Large rear door for cargo

Exhaust for turboshaft engine

Hughes OH-6A USA 1965

Small, twin-bladed tail rotor

Robinson R22 Beta USA 1985

G-WINR

Lightweight tail boom

G-SAND

Schweizer 269C USA 1989

Tail fin stabilizes the rear during flight

Landing skids

The ability to hover in midair makes helicopters ideal platforms for aerial photography, search and rescue, and reconnaissance missions. They can also operate from isolated areas and city helipads, ferrying people and supplies.

The 1960s saw the production of both tiny autogiros and giant helicopters. The single-seater **Wallis WA-116** was just 11 ft 2 in (3.4 m) long, but could fly more than 125 miles (200 km), while the **Mil Mi-8** was 60 ft (18.2 m) long and could carry 27 people or 6,614 lb (3,000 kg) of cargo. Biggest

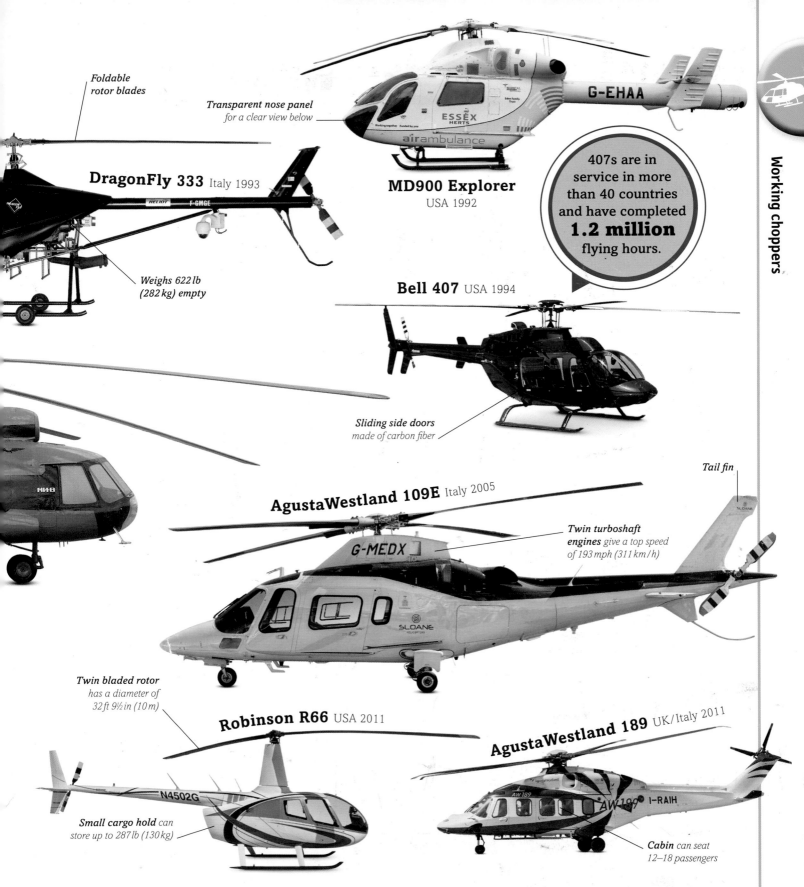

Foldable rotor blades

DragonFly 333 Italy 1993

Transparent nose panel for a clear view below

MD900 Explorer USA 1992

407s are in service in more than 40 countries and have completed **1.2 million** flying hours.

Weighs 622 lb (282 kg) empty

Bell 407 USA 1994

Sliding side doors made of carbon fiber

Tail fin

AgustaWestland 109E Italy 2005

Twin turboshaft engines give a top speed of 193 mph (311 km/h)

Twin bladed rotor has a diameter of 32 ft 9½ in (10 m)

Robinson R66 USA 2011

AgustaWestland 189 UK/Italy 2011

Small cargo hold can store up to 287 lb (130 kg)

Cabin can seat 12–18 passengers

of all is the 131-ft- (40-m-) long Mil Mi-26. The **DragonFly 333** was developed for filmmakers and archaeologists to perform aerial surveys, while the **Robinson R22 Beta** was used to patrol pipelines and to get around large farms or ranches. The **MD900 Explorer** is used by coastguards and

the police forces, and also serves as an air ambulance, a task some **Bell 407** seven-seater helicopters also perform. Other 407s transport workers to and from offshore oil rigs, while variants of the **Schweizer 269C** have been used to train more than 60,000 army helicopter pilots.

Air support

Bell AH-1 Cobra USA 1965

Twin-bladed tail rotor

Movable turret holds either twin machine guns, or grenade launchers

Kamov Ka-25PL Russia 1965

Mil Mi-24A Hind-A Russia 1971

Tough titanium rotor blades

Short wing provides mounting points for weapons, such as cannons

Cockpit seats pilot and copilot

SA Gazelle France 1973

Enclosed fenestron (fan in tailfin)

Mil Mi-14 BT Russia 1973

Rotor blades have a diameter of 70 ft (21.3 m)

Sponson (storage area)

Rear wheels retract up into sponson allowing helicopter to land on water

Radar equipment housed in fuselage fairing

Military helicopters serve armies, navies, and air forces all over the world. Their ability to land in small spaces, hover in midair, and drop supplies accurately make them invaluable on the battlefield, as well as behind the lines.

Many military helicopters, such as the **Sikorsky S-70i** *Black Hawk*, are multi-purpose, able to move troops and equipment, or scout land or sea for threats. Some, such as the **Bell AH-1 Cobra** and the **Kamov Ka-52** *Alligator*, are designed to attack mostly ground targets, using weapons such

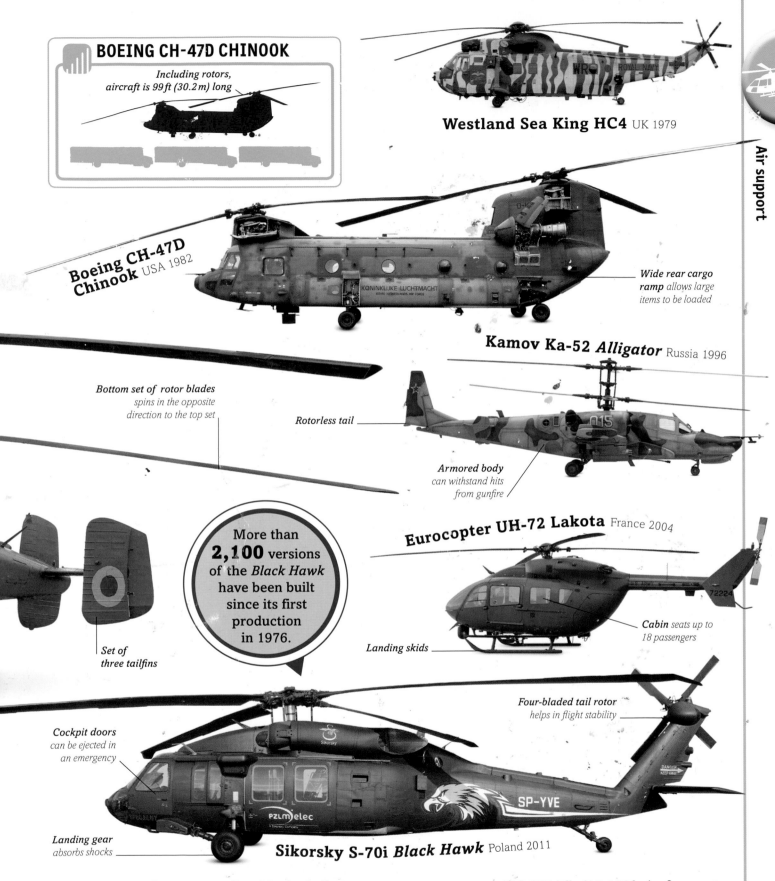

BOEING CH-47D CHINOOK

Including rotors, aircraft is 99 ft (30.2 m) long

Westland Sea King HC4 UK 1979

Boeing CH-47D Chinook USA 1982

Wide rear cargo ramp *allows large items to be loaded*

Kamov Ka-52 *Alligator* Russia 1996

Bottom set of rotor blades spins in the opposite direction to the top set

Rotorless tail

Armored body can withstand hits from gunfire

More than **2,100** versions of the *Black Hawk* have been built since its first production in 1976.

Eurocopter UH-72 Lakota France 2004

Cabin seats up to 18 passengers

Landing skids

Set of three tailfins

Four-bladed tail rotor helps in flight stability

Cockpit doors can be ejected in an emergency

Landing gear absorbs shocks

Sikorsky S-70i *Black Hawk* Poland 2011

as cannons, rockets, or small guided missiles. Larger choppers can deploy troops, supplies, or equipment, or evacuate the wounded or civilians out of a warzone. The **Westland Sea King HC4** can carry up to 28 commandos in its cabin, while the **Boeing CH-47D Chinook** can seat nearly 55 troops, or carry 26,455.5 lb (12,000 kg) of cargo. The **Kamov Ka-25PL**, with two sets of rotors, one above the other, is designed to hunt and attack enemy submarines. The same role is performed by the **Mil Mi-14 BT**, which can carry one torpedo or eight depth charges.

Spacecraft

Spacecraft are machines that are launched by rocket engines out into space. Many of them are unmanned probes, sent out to explore parts of the solar system. A small number have been manned, and have carried more than 500 people into space. In 1969, an American **Apollo 11 spacecraft** was launched by a Saturn V rocket and carried three astronauts into orbit around the moon. Two of them descended in the Lunar Module onto the moon's surface.

Apollo 11 spacecraft

Engine nozzle

Service Module ›
This module provided life-support systems and power for the crew, and housed the spacecraft's main engine.

Fuel tanks › Tanks within the Service Module supplied fuel to the main engine.

Thrusters › Small thrusters made fine adjustments to the spacecraft's movements.

Command Module ›
The 10-ft-6-in- (3.2-m-) tall Command Module was the only part of the Apollo spacecraft to return to Earth. It orbited the Moon, while the astronauts completed a return journey to its surface in the Lunar Module, then separated from the Service Module and traveled back to Earth.

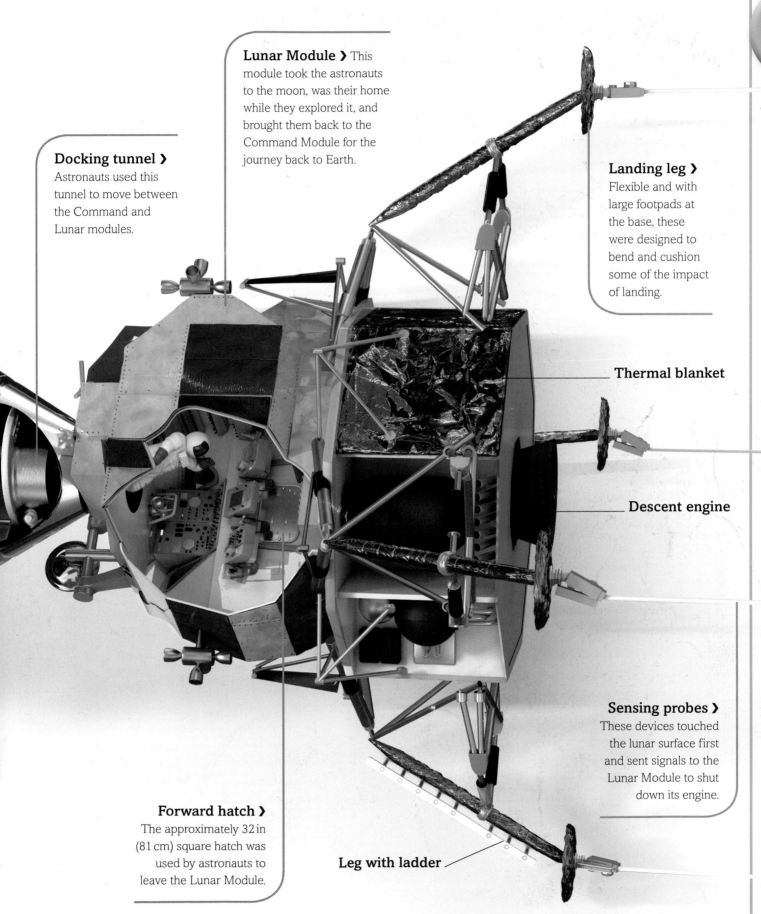

Lunar Module ❯ This module took the astronauts to the moon, was their home while they explored it, and brought them back to the Command Module for the journey back to Earth.

Docking tunnel ❯
Astronauts used this tunnel to move between the Command and Lunar modules.

Landing leg ❯
Flexible and with large footpads at the base, these were designed to bend and cushion some of the impact of landing.

Thermal blanket

Descent engine

Sensing probes ❯
These devices touched the lunar surface first and sent signals to the Lunar Module to shut down its engine.

Forward hatch ❯
The approximately 32 in (81 cm) square hatch was used by astronauts to leave the Lunar Module.

Leg with ladder

Launch vehicles

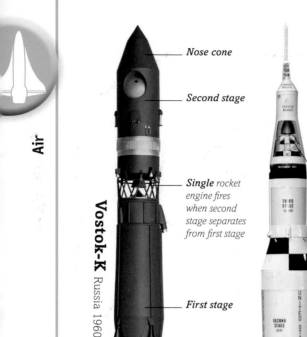

Vostok-K Russia 1960

- Nose cone
- Second stage
- **Single** rocket engine fires when second stage separates from first stage
- First stage

Saturn V USA 1966

- **Lunar module** of the Apollo spacecraft
- **Third stage** separates from second, nine minutes after liftoff
- **Launch vehicle** weighs 6.2 million lb (2.8 million kg)

Cabin holds five to seven astronauts

Space Shuttle Discovery USA 1990

Shuttle's three rocket engines propel it to speeds of more than 16,777 mph (27,000 km/h)

Payloads can weigh up to 9.5 tons

Long March 2F China 1999

Saturn V's five rocket engines burned **3,358 gal** (12,710 liters) of fuel per second.

Twin-bodied White Knight plane carries SpaceShipTwo to launch altitude

SpaceShipTwo is released at 49,213 ft (15,000 m)

LENGTH Short to long

Vehicle	Length
Soyuz FG	162 ft (49.5 m)
Ariane 5	151–171 ft (46–52 m)
Saturn V	363 ft (110.6 m)

Enormous power is needed to overcome gravity and travel into space—so satellites and spacecraft are propelled by launch vehicles, with rocket engines and their own fuel supply. While rockets can only be used once, space shuttles are reusable.

To carry heavy cargos into space multistage launch vehicles are used, such as the two-stage **Long March 2F**, which carried the Shenzhou spacecraft in 2003, and the **Ariane 5s**, which have made more than 75 successful launches. Each stage of a launch vehicle has its own

Nose *holds Soyuz or Progress spacecraft*

Soyuz FG Russia 2001

Four booster rockets *64-ft- (19.6-m-) tall fire at launch*

Fairing *covers payload during launch, but opens to release craft or satellite once in orbit*

Atlas V USA 2002

Powerful boosters *fall away four minutes after launch*

Spacecraft's emergency crew escape system

A Delta IV Heavy weighs more than **200** female **elephants!**

Delta IV Heavy USA 2004

Ariane 5 Multinational 2005

Each rocket booster weighs 305 tons, when full of fuel

Rocket boosters *fire for under 90 seconds at launch*

Virgin Galactic SpaceShipTwo USA 2010

Dream Chaser USA
under development

Upturned wing for gliding back down to Earth

rocket engines, and falls away after its fuel is exhausted, leaving the remaining smaller, lighter vehicle to continue. The biggest lifter among current launch vehicles is the **Delta IV Heavy**, which can carry 31-ton loads into Earth orbit. This is just a quarter of the load carried by the three-stage **Saturn V**, used for the Apollo Moon landings. Space planes, such as the **Space Shuttle** *Discovery* and the **SpaceShipTwo**, are powered by rocket engines but use their wings to glide back to the Earth after their mission.

Space probes

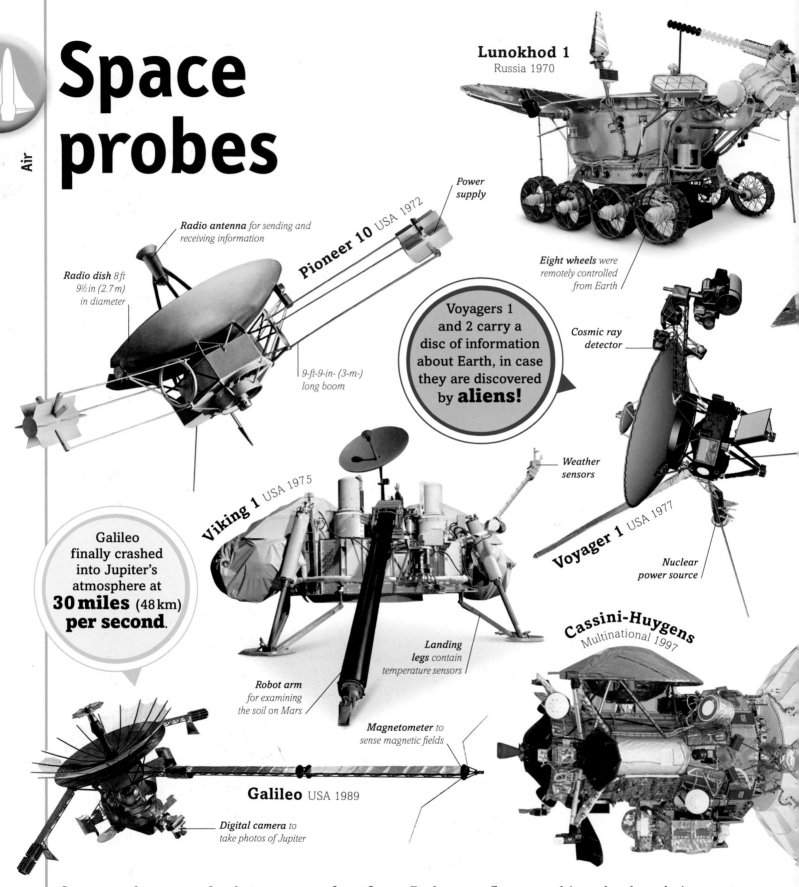

Lunokhod 1
Russia 1970

Radio antenna *for sending and receiving information*

Pioneer 10 USA 1972

Power supply

Radio dish *8 ft 9½ in (2.7 m) in diameter*

9-ft-9-in- (3-m-) long boom

Voyagers 1 and 2 carry a disc of information about Earth, in case they are discovered by **aliens!**

Eight wheels *were remotely controlled from Earth*

Cosmic ray detector

Viking 1 USA 1975

Galileo finally crashed into Jupiter's atmosphere at **30 miles** (48 km) **per second**.

Weather sensors

Voyager 1 USA 1977

Nuclear power source

Landing legs *contain temperature sensors*

Cassini-Huygens
Multinational 1997

Robot arm *for examining the soil on Mars*

Magnetometer *to sense magnetic fields*

Galileo USA 1989

Digital camera *to take photos of Jupiter*

Space probes are robotic, unmanned craft that explore planets, moons, asteroids, and comets, and send information and images back to Earth using radio waves. The work of these probes has helped us to understand our solar system.

Probes can fly past, orbit, or land on their target. **Viking 1** was the first long-term probe to land on Mars, sending back data until 1982. **Lunokhod 1** was the first successful rover, traveling 6.5 miles (10.5 km) around the moon, while the **Curiosity Rover** continues to analyze

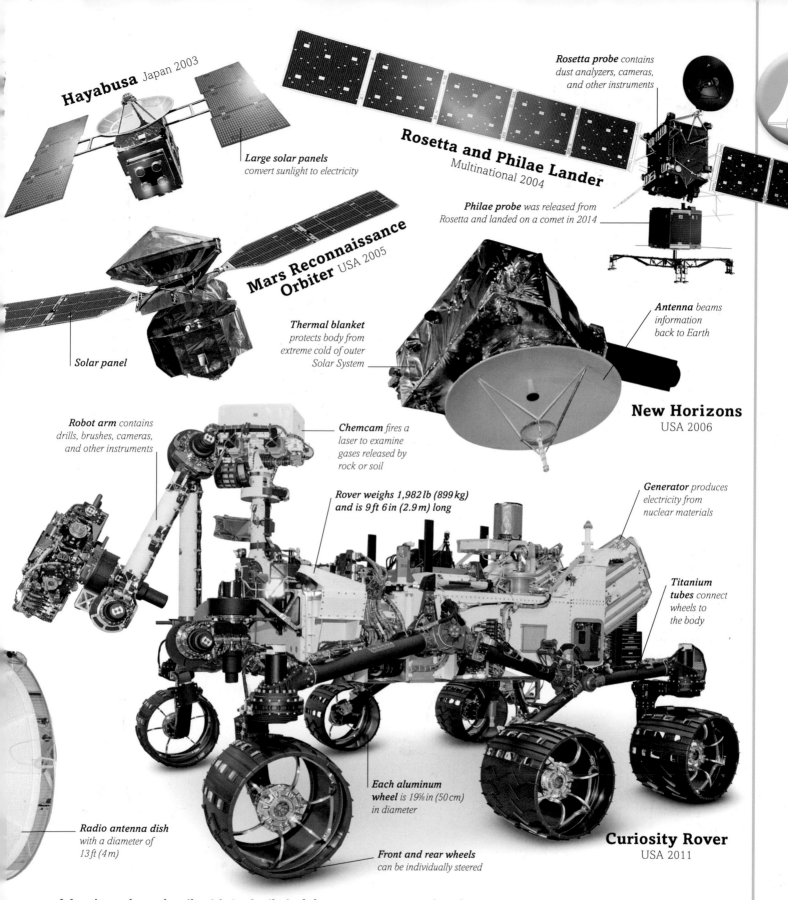

Hayabusa Japan 2003

Large solar panels convert sunlight to electricity

Rosetta probe contains dust analyzers, cameras, and other instruments

Rosetta and Philae Lander
Multinational 2004

Philae probe was released from Rosetta and landed on a comet in 2014

Mars Reconnaissance Orbiter USA 2005

Solar panel

Thermal blanket protects body from extreme cold of outer Solar System

Antenna beams information back to Earth

New Horizons
USA 2006

Robot arm contains drills, brushes, cameras, and other instruments

Chemcam fires a laser to examine gases released by rock or soil

Rover weighs 1,982 lb (899 kg) and is 9 ft 6 in (2.9 m) long

Generator produces electricity from nuclear materials

Titanium tubes connect wheels to the body

Radio antenna dish with a diameter of 13 ft (4 m)

Each aluminum wheel is 19⅝ in (50 cm) in diameter

Front and rear wheels can be individually steered

Curiosity Rover
USA 2011

Mars's rock and soil with its built-in laboratory. **Pioneer 10** became the first probe to travel beyond the asteroid belt, when it flew toward Jupiter. Later, however, **Galileo** orbited the planet 34 times sending back many photos and measurements during its 14-year mission. Some probes have traveled even farther. **New Horizons** reached Pluto in 2015, after a 9½ year journey, while **Voyager 1**, launched in 1977, is now more than 11.8 billion miles (19 billion km) away from the Earth and, with Voyager 2 and Pioneers 10 and 11, has left our solar system.

Out of this world

Door *opens to release parachute during Earth reentry*

Radio antenna *sends signals back to Earth*

Spacecraft *measures 9 ft 9½ in (3 m) in diameter and holds two astronauts*

Mercury USA 1961

Vostok 1 Russia 1961

Gemini USA 196

Spherical descent capsule *holds a single cosmonaut in an ejection seat*

Recovery compartment *releases main and reserve parachutes to bring capsule safely back to Earth*

ISS is 336 ft (108.5 m) wide

Solar panels *attached to solar observatory with cameras taking pictures of the Sun*

Main capsule *is 6 ft 7 in (2 m) wide and 11 ft 6 in (3.5 m) tall*

Skylab
USA 1973

Orbital module, *where the cosmonauts live during the mission*

Soyuz Russia 1967

After losing one of its solar panels, astronauts erected a large **sunshade** to keep Skylab cool.

Descent module *carries cosmonauts back to Earth*

Orbital workshop *contains crew beds, a shower, and a toilet*

Fewer than 600 people have traveled into space. The first astronauts, known as cosmonauts in Russia, orbited Earth in tiny, one-person space capsules. Later astronauts traveled to the Moon, and to orbiting space stations, where they could live and work.

In 1961, Yuri Gagarin became the first spaceman, with a 108-minute flight in the cramped 7-ft 6-in (2.3-m) capsule of a **Vostok 1** spacecraft. A month later, the USA sent Alan Shepard into space on board **Mercury**. Until space stations were built, early manned missions were short.

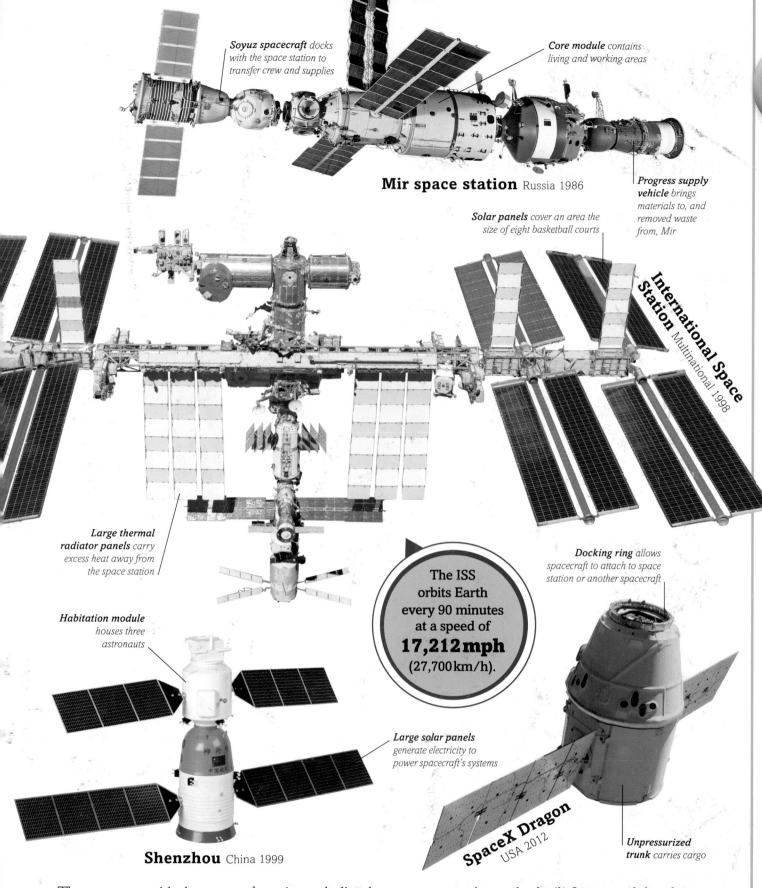

Soyuz spacecraft *docks with the space station to transfer crew and supplies*

Core module *contains living and working areas*

Mir space station Russia 1986

Progress supply vehicle *brings materials to, and removed waste from, Mir*

Solar panels *cover an area the size of eight basketball courts*

International Space Station *Multinational 1998*

Large thermal radiator panels *carry excess heat away from the space station*

Docking ring *allows spacecraft to attach to space station or another spacecraft*

The ISS orbits Earth every 90 minutes at a speed of **17,212 mph** (27,700 km/h).

Habitation module *houses three astronauts*

Shenzhou China 1999

Large solar panels *generate electricity to power spacecraft's systems*

SpaceX Dragon USA 2012

Unpressurized trunk *carries cargo*

Three crews, with three members in each, lived in the **Skylab** space station for a total of 171½ days, performing 300 experiments. Cosmonauts inhabited the **Mir Space Station** for 12½ years, with Valeri Polyakov spending a record-breaking 437 days, 18 hours in a row. Mir was the first space station to be built from modules that were put together in space. The biggest space station to date is the **International Space Station** (ISS), which needed more than 100 spaceflights, and 1,000 hours of space walks, to assemble. It has been manned since 2000.

LIFTOFF!

More than two thousand tons of spacecraft and fuel head into space as space shuttle *Endeavour* thunders out of the launch pad in 2009 at the Kennedy Space Center in Florida. From 1982 to 2011, shuttles made more than 130 successful spaceflights.

Each of a shuttle's two large, solid rocket boosters holds 100,000 lb (450,000 kg) of fuel, which is used up in the first two minutes. The shuttle's main engines continue burning, using all of the 530,000 gal (two million liters) of fuel held in the 157-ft- (48-m-) long orange, external fuel tank by eight minutes after launch, when the shuttle is traveling more than 16,800 mph (27,000 km/h). This mission carried seven astronauts to the International Space Station, returning to Earth 17 days later.

GLOSSARY

Accelerate
To speed up and go faster.

Aerobatics
Acrobatics in the air, performed by aircraft for entertainment as well as in competitions.

Ailerons
Hinged surfaces, usually on an aircraft's wing, that can be raised or lowered to help an aircraft roll or turn.

Alloy
A mixture of two or more elements, at least one of which is a metal. Alloys often have useful properties that differ from those of the elements from which they are made.

Amphibious
A vehicle that can travel both on land and in water.

Articulated train
A train with cars linked together by a single, pivoting joint.

Autogiro
An aircraft with both a main rotor, for lift, and a propeller, to give forward thrust.

Battery
A store of chemicals in a case that, when connected to a circuit, supplies electricity.

Boiler
The part of a steam engine in which steam is produced.

Bow
The forward part of a vessel.

Bowsprit
A spar (pole) that extends forward from a ship's bow.

Bridge
The part of a ship from where the captain controls the vessel.

Buffer
A shock-absorbing pad that cushions the impact of rail vehicles as they come together.

Bumper
A metal, rubber, or plastic bar fitted along the front and, sometimes, the back of a vehicle to limit damage if it bumps into something.

Cab
The part of a train or truck

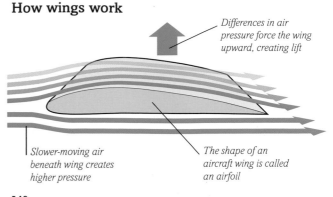

How wings work

Differences in air pressure force the wing upward, creating lift

Slower-moving air beneath wing creates higher pressure

The shape of an aircraft wing is called an airfoil

Lift
As the curved wing moves through the air, the air passing over the wing moves faster than the air passing beneath. Fast-moving air has a lower pressure. It is the slower, high-pressure air beneath the wing that forces it upward.

where the driver sits and controls the vehicle.

Class
A group of locomotives built to a common design.

Convoy
A group of ships or vehicles travelling in formation.

Coupling
The parts, or mechanism, that allow railroad locomotives to be joined together.

Derailleur
The part of a bike that moves the bicycle chain from one gear wheel to another when the rider changes gear.

Destroyer
A small, fast warship armed with guns, torpedoes, or guided missiles.

Diesel
A type of fuel made from oil used in many vehicle engines.

Disk brakes
A type of brake that uses pads to press against a turning disk, creating friction to slow the vehicle down.

Drag
A force of resistance on a vehicle as it moves through air or water, slowing it down.

Drone
Also known as an Unmanned Aerial Vehicle (UAV), a flying machine that either controls itself or is controlled remotely by a human operator.

Electromagnets
Magnets that are powered by electricity and can be switched on or off.

Elevator
A control surface on an aircraft that causes the plane to raise or lower its nose and climb or dive.

Excavator
A vehicle used at building sites to dig holes using a

John Deere 6150 RH

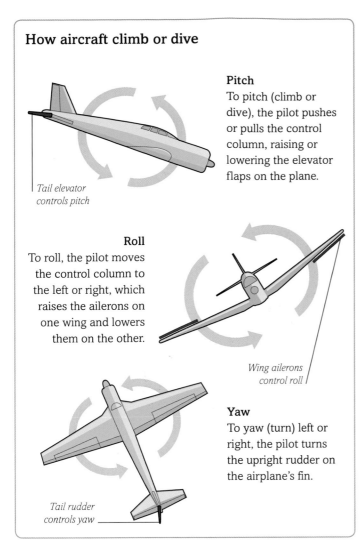

How aircraft climb or dive

Pitch
To pitch (climb or dive), the pilot pushes or pulls the control column, raising or lowering the elevator flaps on the plane.

Tail elevator controls pitch

Roll
To roll, the pilot moves the control column to the left or right, which raises the ailerons on one wing and lowers them on the other.

Wing ailerons control roll

Yaw
To yaw (turn) left or right, the pilot turns the upright rudder on the airplane's fin.

Tail rudder controls yaw

steel bucket attached to a long arm.

Exhaust
A tube that channels waste gases away from a vehicle's engine and out into the open air.

Firebox
The section at the rear of a steam locomotive boiler where the fuel is burned to heat the water in the boiler.

Flaps
Moveable parts of the rear edge of a wing that are used to increase lift at slower air speeds.

Fly-by-wire
An electronic flight control system used in aircraft instead of mechanical or machine-operated controls.

Foremast
The mast nearest the front of a ship.

Four-wheel drive (4WD)
Where power from the engine is used to turn both the front and back wheels of a vehicle.

Freight
Goods transported in bulk by truck, train, ship, or aircraft.

Friction
The force that slows movement between two objects that rub together. Brakes create lots of friction to slow down a vehicle.

Fuselage
The main body of an aircraft, to which the wings and tail are attached.

Galley (ship)
A fighting ship propelled by oars, and sometimes sails, used in the past in the Mediterranean Sea.

Gear
Toothed wheels that are used in trucks and cars to change the amount of speed or force used to turn wheels.

Generator
A machine that creates electricity.

GPS
Short for global positioning system, this refers to a navigation system that uses signals from a group of space satellites to determine a vehicle's position on Earth's surface.

Hatchback
A small car with a rear door and window covering the trunk area.

Hood
A body panel, usually made of metal, that can open to reveal the vehicle's engine.

Horsepower (hp)
A commonly used measure of the power of a vehicle's engine.

Hull
The main body of a boat or a ship.

Hybrid
A vehicle that has both a gas engine and a second

source of power, such as an electric motor.

Hydraulics
A system that uses liquid to transfer force from one place to another, to operate a vehicle's brakes, for example.

Internal combustion engine
A type of engine in which fuel and air are mixed and burned (combusted) inside cylinders to produce power.

Lift
The force created by air moving over a wing or rotor blade to keep an aircraft rising through the air.

Locomotive
A wheeled vehicle used for pulling trains. Electric locomotives rely on electricity provided by an external source, while steam and diesel locomotives generate their own power.

Maglev train
Short for magnetic levitation, a train that works by being raised above special tracks and moved forward by the power of electromagnets.

Motocross
A type of motorcycle sport where riders race around laps of a cross-country course full of bumps and dips.

Ducati 916SPS

Inside a car

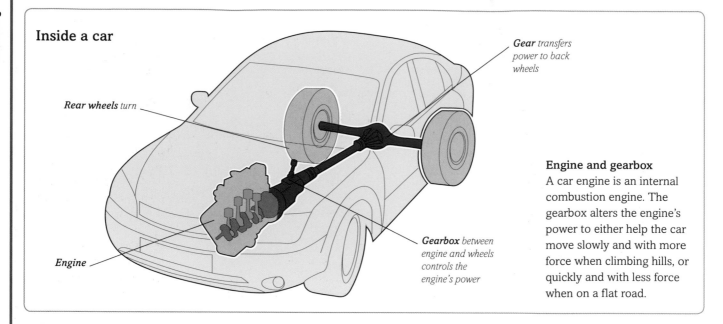

Gear transfers power to back wheels

Rear wheels turn

Engine

Gearbox between engine and wheels controls the engine's power

Engine and gearbox
A car engine is an internal combustion engine. The gearbox alters the engine's power to either help the car move slowly and with more force when climbing hills, or quickly and with less force when on a flat road.

NASCAR
Short for National Association for Stock Car Auto Racing, a popular type of car- and truck-racing competition on tracks in North America.

Off-road
To travel in a vehicle away from roads and over tracks, trails, or open ground.

Orbit
The path of one object around a larger one under the influence of its gravity, such as that of a space probe around a planet.

Outboard motor
A detachable engine mounted on a boat's stern.

Outriggers
Bars that extend out from the side of vehicles, such as cranes or canoes, to provide support and help the vehicle balance.

Payload
The load carried by an aircraft or space launch vehicle, which can include both passengers and cargo.

Pollution
Waste products that reach the air, water, or land and can do damage to the environment or the health of living things.

Probe
An unmanned vehicle travelling into space to a planet, moon, comet, or other body in order to collect information.

Propeller
A set of blades spun by an engine to power a vehicle.

Radar
The system of bouncing radio waves off objects to measure their distance, or to reveal objects that cannot be seen.

Roll bar
A strong frame or tube above the head of a driver or passenger that protects them should the vehicle roll over during an accident.

Roll cage
A strong frame inside a vehicle that protects the people sitting inside.

Rocket engine
An engine that burns fuel along with oxygen or oxidiser (oxygen-producing chemicals) to produce a stream of gases. The rocket engine carries its own supply of oxygen or oxidiser.

Rotor blades
Long, thin airfoils that are spun by a helicopter, or other rotorcraft, to produce lift.

Rudder
A vertical plate or board that can be moved to steer a vessel or help turn an aircraft.

Saddle
The seat on a bicycle, motorcycle, or horse where the rider sits.

Solar panel
A device that converts energy from sunlight into electricity.

Sonar
A system for detecting and locating objects, particularly underwater, using sound waves.

DHR B Class No. 19

Japanese cargo vessel

Spoiler
A device on a car or aircraft, often shaped like a wing, that alters the airflow around the vehicle to generate more drag or downforce. Often found on race cars, to keep them gripping the ground.

Spokes
The rods or bars that connect the center, or hub, of a wheel with its rim.

Stern
The rear part of a boat or a vessel.

Streamlined
A streamlined object has smooth curves so that air or water flows easily, increasing movement.

Street-legal
A car, motorcycle, or truck equipped with all the features required to make it suitable for use on public roads.

Suspension
A system of springs and shock absorbers on a vehicle to help give a smooth ride over bumps and dips.

Supersonic
To fly faster than the speed of sound. The speed of sound is about 768mph (1,236km/h) at sea level.

Switcher
A small locomotive used for moving wagons or train cars around a railroad yard. Also known as a shunter.

Thrust
The force that pushes a powered aircraft through the air, usually generated by an engine.

Tiller
A horizontal bar or handle attached to the rudder of a boat to allow a sailor to steer it.

Ton
A unit of measurement equal to 2,000lb (907.2kg).

Torpedo
A self-propelled underwater weapon with an explosive warhead that is launched from a ship or submarine and travels toward a set target.

Trunk
A space for storage in a car.

Turbocharger
A device that uses waste gases to boost an engine's power.

Waterline
The level normally reached by the water on the side of a ship.

Wheelhouse
The part of a ship or boat that holds the ship's wheel, which is used for steering the vessel. In larger ships, the wheelhouse is part of the structure known as the bridge.

VTOL aircraft
Short for vertical takeoff and landing, VTOL refers to aircraft that can use their thrust to head straight up into the air like a helicopter, and so do not require a long runway.

Yard
A long pole, or spar, attached to a ship's mast to which the top of a square sail is fixed.

How a submarine dives

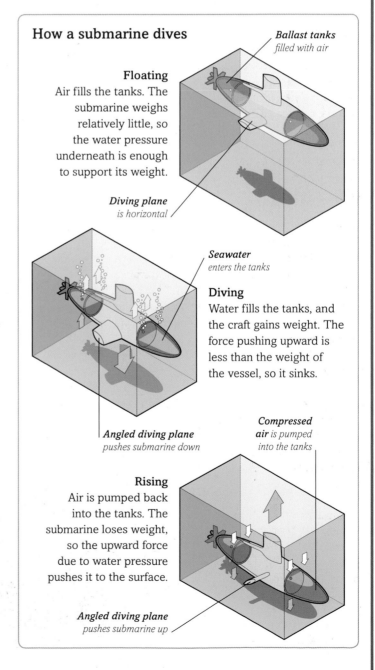

Ballast tanks filled with air

Floating
Air fills the tanks. The submarine weighs relatively little, so the water pressure underneath is enough to support its weight.

Diving plane is horizontal

Seawater enters the tanks

Diving
Water fills the tanks, and the craft gains weight. The force pushing upward is less than the weight of the vessel, so it sinks.

Angled diving plane pushes submarine down

Compressed air is pumped into the tanks

Rising
Air is pumped back into the tanks. The submarine loses weight, so the upward force due to water pressure pushes it to the surface.

Angled diving plane pushes submarine up

Index

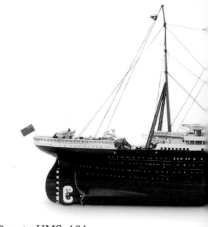

Mark V

RMS Titanic

Kenworth C540

Pearling dhow

JCB 3CX

Piper L-4h Grasshopper

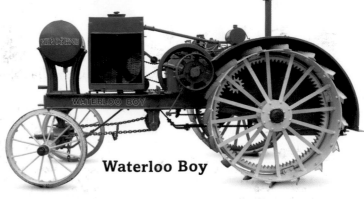

Waterloo Boy

LSER Class 395 *Javelin*

ACKNOWLEDGMENTS

THE SMITHSONIAN INSTITUTION:

Project Coordinator: Kealy Gordon

Smithsonian Enterprises:
Kealy Gordon, Product Development Manager
Ellen Nanney, Licensing Manager
Brigid Ferraro, Vice President, Consumer and Education Products
Carol LeBlanc, Senior Vice President, Consumer and Education Products
Chris Liedel, President

Reviewer:
Dr. F. Robert van der Linden, Curator of Air Transportation and Special Purpose Aircraft, National Air and Space Museum, Smithsonian

DK would like to thank:
Devika Awasthi, Siddhartha Barik, Sanjay Chauhan, Meenal Goel, Anjali Sachar, Mahua Sharma, Neha Sharma, Sukriti Sobti for design assistance; Carron Brown for proofreading; Jackie Brind for the index; Simon Mumford for photoshop work; Nic Dean for additional picture research; Charlie Galbraith for editorial assistance; Scotford Lawrence at the National Cycle Museum, Wales.

The publisher would like to thank the following for their kind permission to reproduce their photographs:

(Key: a-above; b-below/bottom; c-center; f-far; l-left; r-right; t-top)

1 **Dreamstime.com:** Swisshippo. 4 **Dorling Kindersley:** James River Equipment (br). 5 **Dorling Kindersley:** IFREMER, Paris (cl); Ukraine State Aviation Museum (br). 6 **Dorling Kindersley:** National Motor Museum, Beaulieu (tc, br); Trevor Pope Motorcycles (tl); Adrian Shooter. **New Holland Agriculture:** (tr). 7 **Dorling Kindersley:** Musee Air & Space Paris, La Bourget (tr); Mr R A Fleming, The Real Aeroplane Company (tc); James River Equipment (br). **Photo used with permission of BRP:** (bc). 8 **Alamy Images:** Trinity Mirror / Mirrorpix (cr). **Dorling Kindersley:** R. Florio (br); The National Motor Museum, Beaulieu (ca). 9 **Alamy Images:** World History Archive (cra). 10 **Dorling Kindersley:** The National Railway Museum, York / Science Museum Group (c). **Science & Society Picture Library:** National Railway Museum (bl). 10-11 **Dorling Kindersley:** The National Railway Museum, York (bc). 11 **Alamy Images:** epa european pressphoto agency b.v (br); Geoff Marshall (tl); Colin Underhill (tr). 12 **Dorling Kindersley:** The Mary Rose Trust, Portsmouth (clb); The National Maritime Museum, London (c, bc). 13 **Dorling Kindersley:** The Royal Navy Submarine Museum, Gosport (bl); The Fleet Air Arm Museum (cla). **Getty Images:** Philippe Petit / Paris Match (tr). **Science Photo Library:** Mikkel Juul Jensen (br). 14 **Dorling Kindersley:** The Shuttleworth Collection, Bedfordshire (cra); The Shuttleworth Collection (br). 15 **Alamy Images:** B Christopher (bl). **Dorling Kindersley:** Brooklands Museum (cb); Yorkshire Air Museum (tl). **ESA:** ATG medialab (br). **Getty Images:** Education Images / UIG (tr). 16-17 **Alamy Images:** Sergii Kotko. 18 **Corbis:** John Harper (cb). **Dorling Kindersley:** B&O Railroad Museum (cl). 19 **Dorling Kindersley:** The National Railway Museum, York / Science Museum Group (cr). 20-21 **Corbis:** Christophe Boisvieux / Hemis. 24 **Corbis:** Hulton-Deutsch Collection (tr). **Dorling Kindersley:** The National Cycle Collection (cra, clb). 25 **Dorling Kindersley:** The National Cycle Collection (cra, c). **Getty Images:** Science & Society Picture Library (tl, tr, cr). **Science & Society Picture Library:** (cb). 26 **Dorling Kindersley:** The National Cycle Collection (tr). **MARIN BIKES:** (clb). 27 **Dorling Kindersley:** The National Cycle Collection (tr). 28-29 **Getty Images:** AFP / Pascal Pavani. 30 **Corbis:** Ashley Cooper (tr). **Dorling Kindersley:** The National Railway Museum, York (tl); The Combined Military Services Museum (CMSM) (cl). 31 **Dorling Kindersley:** The National Cycle Collection (tl). **Dreamstime.com:** Hupeng (crb). **Getty Images:** Peter Adams (cr). **iStockphoto.com:** DNHanlon (tr). 33 **Pashley Cycles:** (cr). 34 **Dorling Kindersley:** Trek UK Ltd (clb). **First Flight Bicycles:** (tr). 35 **Alamy Images:** pzechner (clb). **Gary Sansom, owner of bmxmuseum.com:** (crb). **MARIN BIKES:** (tr). 36-37 **Getty Images:** Tommaso Boddi. 38-39 **Dorling Kindersley:** David Farnley. 40 **Dorling Kindersley:** The Motorcycle Heritage Museum, Westerville, Ohio (c). **Getty Images:** Science & Society Picture Library (tr). 41 **Dorling Kindersley:** Phil Crosby and Peter Mather (cra); The Motorcycle Heritage Museum, Westerville, Ohio (clb). 42 **Dreamstime.com:** Photo1269 (tl). 42 **Don Morley:** (cl). 42-43 **Dorling Kindersley:** The National Motorcycle Museum (crb). 43 **Dorling Kindersley:** The National Motorcycle Museum (t, ca, cr, cb); The Motorcycle Heritage Museum, Westerville, Ohio (cl). 44-45 **Dorling Kindersley:** Micheal Penn (t); Scootopia (cb). 44 **Dorling Kindersley:** Stuart Lanning (c); The Motorcycle Heritage Museum, Westerville, Ohio (cla). 45 **Dorling Kindersley:** George and Steven Harmer (clb, cr); Neil Mort, Mott Motorcycles (cb, crb). **BMW Group:** (cra). **Honda (UK):** (tr). 46 **Dorling Kindersley:** (tr); National Motor Museum, Beaulieu (tl); Micheal Penn (crb); Tony Dowden (clb). 47 **Carver Technology BV:** (tr). **Corbis:** Transtock (cl). **Dorling Kindersley:** Alan Peters (tl). **Dreamstime.com:** Amnarj2006 (crb). 48 **Dorling Kindersley:** Carl M Booth (crb); The National Motorcycle Museum (tc); Charlie Owens (c); Charlie Garratt (cr, clb); Rick Sasnett (cl). 49 **Dorling Kindersley:** George Manning (cl, cr, crb); Harley-Davidson (tr); Ian Bull (clb). 50 **Roland Brown:** Riders for Health (clb). **Dorling Kindersley:** The Deutsches Zweiradmuseum und NSU-Museum, Neckarsulm, Germany (c). **Honda (UK):** (crb). 51 **Dorling Kindersley:** Adam Atherton (cl); The Deutsches Zweiradmuseum und NSU-Museum, Neckarsulm, Germany (t); Mark Hatfield (c); Palmers Motor Company (crb/Aprilia). **Honda (UK):** (crb). 52-53 **Corbis:** Erik Tham. 54 **Dorling Kindersley:** The Motorcycle Heritage Museum, Westerville, Ohio (tl); The National Motorcycle Museum (tr); Trevor Pope Motorcycles (crb). 55 **Dorling Kindersley:** National Motor Museum, Beaulieu (cl); The Motorcycle Heritage Museum, Westerville, Ohio (t); Neil Mort, Mott Motorcycles (cr); Trevor Pope Motorcycles (clb, crb). 56 **Dorling Kindersley:** Brian Chapman and Chris Illman (c); The Motorcycle Heritage Museum, Westerville, Ohio (tl); The National Motorcycle Museum (tr); National Motorcycle Museum, Birmingham (cra). 56-57 **American Motorcyclist Association:** (b). **www.ackattackracing.com:** (crb). 57 **Dorling Kindersley:** Beaulieu National Motor Museum (tr); Pegasus Motorcycles (crb). **Marine Turbine Technologies, LLC(www.marineturbine.com):** (cr). 58 **Dorling Kindersley:** The National Motorcycle Museum (tl); The Motorcycle Heritage Museum, Westerville, Ohio (tr); Tony Dowden (b). 59 **Dorling Kindersley:** Alan Purvis (cla); Michael Delaney (tl); Wayne MacGowan (tr); Phil Davies (clb). **ECOSSE Moto Works, Inc.:** (clb/Ecosse). **Honda (UK):** (crb). **MV Agusta Motor SpA:** (cr). 60-61 **Giles Chapman Library**. 62 **Alamy Images:** Werner Dieterich (cl). 63 **Dorling Kindersley:** Colin Laybourn / P&A Wood (tr); National Motor Museum, Beaulieu (tl); Haynes International Motor Museum (b). **Getty Images:** Print Collector (cl). 64-65 **Getty Images:** ullstein bild / Robert Sennecke. 66 **Alamy Images:** pbpgalleries (crb). **Art Tech Picture Agency:** (clb). **Corbis:** Car Culture (c). **Dorling Kindersley:** Ivan Dutton (br). 67 **Dorling Kindersley:** National Motor Museum, Beaulieu (tl). **Louwman Museum-The Hague:** (crb). 68 **Dorling Kindersley:** Colin Spong (clb); The Titus & Co. Museum for Vintage & Classic Cars (c). **Louwman Museum-The Hague:** (tr). 69 **Alamy Images:** Tom Wood (c). **Art Tech Picture Agency:** (b). **Dorling Kindersley:** National Motor Museum, Beaulieu (t). 70 **Alamy Images:** Esa Hiltula (cl). **Dorling Kindersley:** The Titus & Co. Museum for Vintage & Classic Cars (cla). 70-71 **Dorling Kindersley:** The Titus & Co. Museum for Vintage & Classic Cars (t). 71 **Corbis:** Car Culture (clb). 72 **Alamy Images:** Phil Talbot (cl). 73 **Dorling Kindersley:** National Motor Museum, Beaulieu (tr). **Getty Images:** Heritage Images (crb). 74-75 **Alamy Images:** ImageGB (t). **Courtesy Mercedes-Benz Cars, Daimler AG:** (b). 74 **Alamy Images:** pbpgalleries (clb). 75 **Alamy Images:** Tribune Content Agency LLC (c). **Dreamstime.com:** Warren Rosenberg (ca). **Courtesy of Volkswagen:** (cr). 76-77 **Corbis:** Transtock. 78-79 **Dreamstime.com:** Len Green (c). 78 **Alamy Images:** Mark Scheuern (clb). **Art Tech Picture Agency:** (ca). **Suzuki Motor Corporation:** (c). 79 **Art Tech Picture Agency:** (cra, tr). 80 **Alamy Images:** Buzz Pictures (clb); ZUMA Press, Inc (cla). **Dorling Kindersley:** Chris Williams (c). **Louwman Museum-The Hague:** (tr). 80-81 **Alamy Images:** Mark Scheuern (c). **Getty Images:** Jason Kempin (crb). 81 **Dreamstime.com:** Ermess (crb). **Getty Images:** UK Press / Justin Goff (tl). **Rex Features:** Andy Willsheer (ca). **Terrafugia/www.terrafugia.com:** (c). **Toyota (GB) PLC:** (crb/Toyota FV2). 82-83 **WATERCAR**. 84-85 **Art Tech Picture Agency:** (c). 85 **Alamy Images:** Motoring Picture Library (cr). 86-87 **Alamy Images:** Mark Scheuern (c). 86 **Art Tech Picture Agency:** (crb). **LAT Photographic:** (cl). **Giles Chapman Library:** (cla, cr). **Louwman Museum-The Hague:** (tr). 87 **Corbis:** Car Culture (ca). **Volvo Car Group:** (tr). 88 **Alamy Images:** Phil Talbot (b). 89 **Alamy Images:** Motoring Picture Library (ca). **Dorling Kindersley:** Brands Hatch Morgans (crb); Gilbert and Anna East (c). 90 **Alamy Images:** West Country Images (cla). **Dorling Kindersley:** National Motor Museum, Beaulieu (tr, crb). **Louwman Museum-The Hague:** (cb). 90-91 **Alamy Images:** Shaun Finch - Coyote-Photography.co.uk (b). 91 **Giles Chapman Library:** (tl). **Malcolm McKay:** (cra). **Renault:** (crb). **Tata Limited:** (cr). 92-93 **Alamy Images:** KS_Autosport. 94 **Dorling Kindersley:** Peter Harris (tr). **www.mclaren.com:** (c). 95 **© 2015 Hennessey Performance:** (crb). **Dreamstime.com:** Swisshippo (clb). 96 **Dorling Kindersley:** The Titus & Co. Museum for Vintage & Classic Cars (t). **Dreamstime.com:** Ddcoral (cla). 97 **Art Tech Picture Agency:** (cra). **Dreamstime.com:** Olga Besnard (cr). 98 **Giles Chapman Library:** (cr). **Courtesy Mercedes-Benz Cars, Daimler AG:** (cl). 98-99 **Flock London:** (cb). 99 **Corbis:** Bettmann (tr); Reuters / Kieran Doherty (c); Car Culture (clb). **Getty Images:** Science & Society Picture Library (tl). 100-101 **Corbis:** Leo Mason. 104 **Alamy Images:** Car Collection (clb). **Corbis:** Ecoscene / John Wilkinson (crb). **Dorling Kindersley:** Milestone Museum (tr, cla). 105 **Alamy Images:** Colin Underhill (t). **Dorling Kindersley:** DAF Trucks N.V. (c); DaimlerChrysler AG (clb). 106 **Dorling Kindersley:** Yorkshire Air Museum (cla); The Tank Museum (tr). 107 **Daimler AG:** (tr). **Dorling Kindersley:** James River Equipment (c). **Max-Holder:** (crb). 108-109 **Corbis:** Reuters / Rick Fowler. 110 **Corbis:** Demotix / pqneiman (tr). **Dorling Kindersley:** Newbury Bus Rally (cl, b). **Rex Features:** Roger Viollet (tl). 110-11 **Foremost, http://foremost.ca/:** (c). 111 **Alamy Images:** Oliver Dixon (cb). **Corbis:** Reuters / Brazil / Stringer (t). 112-113 **Dorling Kindersley:** Chandlers Ltd. 114 **Dorling Kindersley:** Paul Rackham (cl, clb); Roger and Fran Desborough (cla, cr). **David Peters:** (crb). 114-115 **Dorling Kindersley:** The Shuttleworth Collection (t). 115 **AGCO Ltd:** (cra). **Dorling Kindersley:** David Wakefield (t); Doubleday Holbeach Depot (cl); Lister Wilder (cr). **John Deere:** (clb). **New Holland Agriculture:** (crb). 116 **Dorling Kindersley:** David Bowman (t); Doubleday Swineshead Depot (cl). **John Deere:** (clb). 116-117 **Dorling Kindersley:** Doubleday Swineshead Depot (b). 117 **AGCO Ltd:** (tl). **Hagie Manufacturing Company:** (crb). **New Holland Agriculture:** (cla, tr, cr). 118-119 **Action Plus**. 120-121 **Getty Images:** AFP / Viktor Drachev (c). 121 **Dorling Kindersley:** DaimlerChrysler AG (tl); James River Equipment (crb). 122 **Dorling Kindersley:** Royal Armouries, Leeds (cra); The Second Guards Rifles Division (cr); The Tank Museum (cla, cl, tr). 122-123 **Dorling Kindersley:** The Tank Museum (b). 123 **Dorling Kindersley:** Royal Armouries, Leeds (cl, cra); The Tank Museum (tl, tr, crb, crb/Leopard C2). 124-125 **Dorling Kindersley:** B&O Railroad Museum. 126 **Dorling Kindersley:** Railroad Museum of Pennsylvania (c); The Science Museum, London (tr, clb); The National Railway Museum, York (cb). **Science & Society Picture Library:** National Railway Museum (cla). 126-127 **Dorling Kindersley:** The National Railway Museum, York / Science Museum Group (c). 127 **colour-rail.com:** (cra). **Dorling Kindersley:** B&O Railroad Museum (tl, tr, br); The National Railway Museum, York (cr). 128 **Dorling Kindersley:** B&O Railroad Museum (ca); The National Railway Museum, New Dehli (cb). 128-129 **Dorling Kindersley:** Adrian Shooter (cb); The National Railway Museum, York (ca, cb/Mallard). 129 **Dorling Kindersley:** Railroad Museum of Pennsylvania (br). 130-131 **Corbis:** Milepost 92 1 / 2 / W.A. Sharman. 132-133 **Dorling Kindersley:** Ribble Steam Railway / Science Museum Group. 134 **Dorling Kindersley:** The Musee de Chemin de Fer, Mulhouse (tl). **Steam Picture Library:** (bl). 134-135 **Dorling Kindersley:** B&O Railroad Museum (bc); Harzer Schmalspurbahnen (c, tc). 135 **Corbis:** Bettmann / Philip Gendreau (tr). **Dorling Kindersley:** Virginia Museum of Transportation (cr, crb). 136 **Dorling Kindersley:** B&O Railroad Museum (cl, cb); Virginia Museum of Transportation (cla). 136-137 **Dorling Kindersley:** Ribble Steam Railway / Science Museum Group (t); Virginia Museum of Transportation (ca). **Keith Fender:** (c). 137 **colour-rail.com:** (crb). **Dorling Kindersley:** The DB Museum, Nurnburg, Germany (tr). **Keith Fender:** (clb). 138 **Dorling Kindersley:** Didcot

Acknowledgments

Railway Centre (tl); The National Railway Museum, York / Science Museum Group (cl); Railroad Museum of Pennsylvania (clb); The Verkehrshaus der Schweiz, Luzern, Switzerland (c). 138-139 **Dorling Kindersley:** Ffestiniog & Welsh Highland Railways (tr). 139 **Dorling Kindersley:** B&O Railroad Museum (c); Didcot Railway Centre (cr); Eisenbahnfreunde Traditionsbahnbetriebswerk Stassfurt (clb). **Keith Fender:** (crb). 140 **Dorling Kindersley:** B&O Railroad Museum (tl); Eisenbahnfreunde Traditionsbahnbetriebswerk Stassfurt (crb); Railroad Museum of Pennsylvania (clb); The National Railway Museum, York (ca). 140-141 **Dorling Kindersley:** The National Railway Museum, India (t). 141 **Dorling Kindersley:** DB Schenker (b); The Musee de Chemin de Fer, Mulhouse (tr); Railroad Museum of Pennsylvania (cra); Eisenbahnfreunde Traditionsbahnbetriebswerk Stassfurt (cb). 142 **Alamy Images:** Kevin Foy (cr); Colin Underhill (tl). **colour-rail.com:** (cl). **Keith Fender:** (cra). **Brian Stephenson/RAS:** (b). 143 **Alamy Images:** epa european pressphoto agency b.v (crb); Iain Masterton (tr). **Dorling Kindersley:** Hitachi Rail Europe (cra). **Dreamstime.com:** Tan Kian Yong (cl). **Keith Fender:** (cr, clb). 144-145 **Alamy Images:** Stock Connection Blue. 146 **Alamy Images:** Danita Delimont (ca); Alan Moore (clb). **Brian Stephenson/RAS:** (clb/berlin u-bahn). 146-147 **Dreamstime.com:** Alarico (cb). **Siemens AG:** (t). 147 **Alamy Images:** dpict (cl); Iain Masterton (tr). **Bombardier Transportation, Bombardier Inc.:** (cr). **WSW mobil GmbH:** büro+staubach (crb). 148 **Alamy Images:** Jon Sparks (clb). **Dreamstime.com:** Yulia Belousova (crb). 149 **Alamy Images:** RIA Novosti (br). **CAF, CONSTRUCCIONES Y AUXILIAR DE FERROCARRILES, S.A.:** (cra). **Image supplied by Transport for Greater Manchester and taken by Lesley Chalmers.:** (tl). 150-151 **Corbis:** Stringer / India / Reuters. 152-153 **Alamy Images:** Tracey Whitefoot. 154 **Dorling Kindersley:** Exeter Maritime Museum, The National Maritime Museum, London (cl); National Maritime Museum, London (b). **National Maritime Museum, Greenwich, London:** (cra). 155 **Dorling Kindersley:** Exeter Maritime Museum, The National Maritime Museum, London (ca, clb); National Maritime Museum, London (t). **National Maritime Museum, Greenwich, London:** (c, b). 156 **Dorling Kindersley:** National Maritime Museum, London (cla, bl, cr, crb). 156-157 **Dorling Kindersley:** Exeter Maritime Museum, The National Maritime Museum, London (ca). 157 **Alamy Images:** Eye Ubiquitous (cr). **Dorling Kindersley:** Maidstone Museum and Bentliff Art Gallery (t); National Maritime Museum, London (crb). **National Maritime Museum, Greenwich, London:** (clb). 158-159 **Lane Jacobs**. 160-161 **Dorling Kindersley:** National Maritime Museum, London. 162 **Dorling Kindersley:** National Maritime Museum, London (clb); The Science Museum, London (cla). **Getty Images:** DEA / G. Nimatalah (crb). **Science & Society Picture Library:** (cr). 162-163 **Dorling Kindersley:** National Maritime Museum, London (t). 163 **Dorling Kindersley:** Pitt Rivers Museum, University of Oxford (cb). **National Maritime Museum, Greenwich, London:** (crb). 164 **Dorling Kindersley:** The National Maritime Museum, London (cla, c); Virginia Museum of Transportation (clb). **Rex Features:** Ilpo Musto (crb). 164-165 **Dorling Kindersley:** National Maritime Museum, London (c). 165 **Dorling Kindersley:** National Maritime Museum, London (cb); National Maritime Museum, London (cr). **The Fram Museum, http://www.frammuseum.no/:** (tr); **Michael Czytko, www.modelships.de:** (tl). 166-167 **Dorling Kindersley:** National Maritime Museum, London (ca). 166 **John Hamill:** (tl). **National Maritime Museum, Greenwich, London:** (bl). **www.modelshipmaster.com:** (crb). 167 **Dorling Kindersley:** Fleet Air Arm Museum (c). **National Maritime Museum, Greenwich, London:** (tl, br). **www.modelshipmaster.com:** (clb). 168-169 **Gilles Martin-Raget / www.martin-raget.com**. 170-171 **National Maritime Museum, Greenwich, London**. 172 **Dorling Kindersley:** National Maritime Museum, London (cla, cb). **Getty Images:** Science & Society Picture Library (t). 172-173 **Getty Images:** Science & Society Picture Library (c). **National Maritime Museum, Greenwich, London:** (cb). 173 **National Maritime Museum, Greenwich, London:** (t, cr, cb, crb). 174 **Dorling Kindersley:** National Maritime Museum, London (clb); RNLI - Royal National Lifeboat Institution (cr). **National Maritime Museum, Greenwich, London:** (cla, cl). 174-175 **National Maritime Museum, Greenwich, London:** (cb). 175 **Dorling Kindersley:** National Maritime Museum, London (c, cb). **National Maritime Museum, Greenwich, London:** (t). 176 **Dorling Kindersley:** National Maritime Museum, London (t). **National Maritime Museum, Greenwich, London:** (ca, clb). 176-177 **Dreamstime.com:** Jhamlin (crb). 177 **National Maritime Museum, Greenwich, London:** (t). **Used with permission of Royal Çaribbean Cruises Ltd.:** (c). 178-179 **Corbis:** Joe Skipper / Reuters. 180 **Dorling Kindersley:** Fleet Air Arm Museum (cb); The Fleet Air Arm Museum (cla). **National Maritime Museum, Greenwich, London:** (cl). 180-181 **National Maritime Museum, Greenwich, London:** (c, cb). **SD Model Makers:** (t, ca). 181 **Dorling Kindersley:** Scale Model World (cb). **SD Model Makers:** (cr, tr). 182 **SD Model Makers:** (cla, ca, clb). 182-183 **Dorling Kindersley:** Model Exhibition, Telford (c, crb); Fleet Air Arm Museum (t); USS George Washington and the US Navy (ca). 183 **Alamy Images:** David Acsota Allely (cb). 184 **Alamy Images:** Joel Douillet (cr). **Dorling Kindersley:** Fleet Air Arm Museum (ca, cl). **SD Model Makers:** (cb). 184-185 **Dorling Kindersley:** Fleet Air Arm Museum (t). 185 **Alamy Images:** Jim Gibson (cr); Stocktrek Images, Inc. (cl). **Dorling Kindersley:** Scale Model World (cb). **Press Association Images:** (clb). **SD Model Makers:** (cla). 188 **Dorling Kindersley:** Fleet Air Arm Museum (cb); The Royal Navy Submarine Museum, Gosport (cla); Scale Model World (c). **National Maritime Museum, Greenwich, London:** (tr). **SD Model Makers:** (cra). 188-189 **Dorling Kindersley:** The Fleet Air Arm Museum (b). 189 **Dorling Kindersley:** IFREMER, Paris (cl); Scale Model World (t); The Science Museum, London (cla); Fleet Air Arm Museum (cb). **TurboSquid:** wdc600 (cr). 190-191 **Alamy Images:** Glyn Genin (t). 190 **British Hovercraft Company Ltd.:** (b). **Dorling Kindersley:** Search and Rescue Hovercraft, Richmond, British Columbia (ca). **LenaTourFlot LLC.:** (cl). 191 **123RF.com:** Suttipon Thanarakpong (crb). **Getty Images:** Science & Society Picture Library (cr). **Kawasaki Motors Europe N.V.:** (clb). **Photo used with permission of BRP:** (tr). 192 **123RF.com:** Richard Pross (cr). **Alpacka Raft LLC:** (tr). **Chris-Craft:** (tl). **Dreamstime.com:** Georgesixth (cb). 193 **Hamant Airboats, LLC:** (tl). **National Maritime Museum, Greenwich, London:** (tr, cl). 194-195 **Corbis:** Chen Shaojin / Xinhua Press. 196-197 **Dreamstime.com:** Bigknell. 198-199 **Dorling Kindersley:** Roy Palmer. 200 **Dorling Kindersley:** Musee Air & Space Paris, La Bourget (cl, c, cr); The Real Aeroplane Company (clb). 200-201 **Dorling Kindersley:** The Shuttleworth Collection (b). 201 **Dorling Kindersley:** Musee Air & Space Paris, La Bourget (cra, cl, c); The Planes of Fame Air Museum, Chino, California (t); Nationaal Luchtvaart Themapark Aviodome (cb). 202 **Dorling Kindersley:** Brooklands Museum (cla); The Shuttleworth Collection, Bedfordshire (t); Flugausstellung (cr); The Shuttleworth Collection (b). 203 **Dorling Kindersley:** Fleet Air Arm Museum (t); Nationaal Luchtvaart Themapark Aviodome (c); The Shuttleworth Collection (crb, crb/Avro Triplane). **U.S. Air Force:** (clb). 204-205 **Corbis:** Minnesota Historical Society. 206-207 **Dorling Kindersley:** Brooklands Museum (c); Planes of Fame Air Museum, Chino, California (cb). 206 **Dorling Kindersley:** Musee Air & Space Paris, La Bourget (cl); Flugausstellung (clb). **Richard Bungay(https://www.flickr.com/photos/98961263@N00/):** (tc). 207 **Dorling Kindersley:** Royal Airforce Museum, London (Hendon) (c); Yorkshire Air Museum (t); Planes of Fame Air Museum, Chino, California (crb); The Shuttleworth Collection (b). 208 **Dorling Kindersley:** Royal Airforce Museum, London (Hendon) (ca); The Real Aeroplane Company (tr); B17 Preservation (cl); RAF Museum, Cosford (clb). 208-209 **Alamy Images:** Anthony Kay / Flight (c). **Dorling Kindersley:** Gatwick Aviation Museum (cb). 209 **Dorling Kindersley:** Gatwick Aviation Museum (cra); Ukraine State Aviation Museum (cr, crb). **Getty Images:** Max Mumby / Indigo (t). 210-211 **Dorling Kindersley:** Royal Airforce Museum, London (Hendon) (c). 210 **©2015 National Air and Space Museum Archives, Smithsonian:** (crb). **Alamy Images:** B Christopher (clb). **Dorling Kindersley:** Musee Air & Space Paris, La Bourget (cla, cra, cl). 211 **Alamy Images:** Susan & Allan Parker (cr). **Dorling Kindersley:** Musee Air & Space Paris, La Bourget (tl, tr); Mr R A Fleming, The Real Aeroplane Company (clb); RAF Museum, Cosford (crb). 212 **Dorling Kindersley:** Royal Airforce Museum, London (Hendon) (t, ca); March Field Air Museum, California (cr); Flugausstellung (crb). **Dreamstime.com:** Gary Blakeley (clb). 212-213 **123RF.com.** **Dorling Kindersley:** Golden Apple Operations Ltd (cb). 213 **Dorling Kindersley:** RAF Coningsby (clb); Yorkshire Air Museum (t); City of Norwich Aviation Museum (cr); Flugausstellung (cl); Midlands Air Museum (ca). **Dreamstime.com:** Eugene Berman (crb). 214-215 **Alamy Images:** A. T. Willett. 216 **Dorling Kindersley:** Flugausstellung (cl); Fleet Air Arm Museum (cla); Brooklands Museum Trust Ltd, Weybridge, Surrey (tr); Gary Wenko (cr); Gatwick Aviation Museum (crb). **Dreamstime.com:** I4lcocl2 (clb). 217 **Alamy Images:** NielsVK (c). **Dorling Kindersley:** Musee Air & Space Paris, La Bourget (crb); Fleet Air Arm Museum (t); Ukraine State Aviation Museum (clb). 218 **Dorling Kindersley:** Planes of Fame Air Museum, Valle, Arizona (tl). 218-219 **Alamy Images:** Steven May (b). 219 **Alamy Images:** Susan & Allan Parker (br). **Dorling Kindersley:** Pima Air and Space Museum, Tuscon, Arizona (tl); The Real Aeroplane Company (tr). 220-221 **Dreamstime.com:** Songallery (cb). 220 **AirTeamImages.com:** (clb/Sud). **Dorling Kindersley:** Flugausstellung (b); Nationaal Luchtvaart Themapark Aviodome (cla, cra). 221 **Dorling Kindersley:** Ukraine State Aviation Museum (t). 222-223 **Alamy Images:** Jim Kidd. 224 **Dorling Kindersley:** Midlands Air Museum (clb, b); RAF Museum, Cosford (c). **Science Photo Library:** Detlev Van Ravenswaay (cla). 224-225 **NASA:** (b). 225 **Alamy Images:** NASA Archive (tr). **Dorling Kindersley:** Flugausstellung (tl); Ukraine State Aviation Museum (c); Yorkshire Air Museum (cb). 226 **Alamy Images:** Thierry GRUN - Aero (t). **Dorling Kindersley:** The Shuttleworth Collection, Bedfordshire (c); The Shuttleworth Collection (crb). **U.S. Air Force:** (clb, b). 226-227 **Alamy Images:** aviafoto (ca); Kevin Maskell (cr). 227 **NASA:** Tony Landis (tr). 228-229 **Dorling Kindersley:** RAF Boulmer, Northumberland. 230 **Dorling Kindersley:** De Havilland Aircraft Heritage Centre (tl); The Museum of Army Flying (crb). 230-231 **aviation-images.com:** (cra). 231 **aviation-images.com:** (cla). **Dorling Kindersley:** Musee Air & Space Paris, La Bourget (tr, crb); RAF Museum, Cosford (ca); Ukraine State Aviation Museum (cb, cr). 232 **Dorling Kindersley:** Norfolk and Suffolk Aviation Museum (tl). 233 **Dorling Kindersley:** Musee Air & Space Paris, La Bourget (cla). **Dreamstime.com:** Patrick Allen (cra). 234 **Dorling Kindersley:** Ukraine State Aviation Museum (cla, cb). 234-235 **Dorling Kindersley:** Ukraine State Aviation Museum. 238 **Corbis:** Imaginechina (r). **Dorling Kindersley:** Bob Gathany (l). **Getty Images:** Bloomberg / David Paul Morris (crb). **NASA:** (cl, c). 239 **Alamy Images:** Konstantin Shaklein (l). **NASA:** (cl, cb); Kim Shiflett (c). **Science Photo Library:** Detlev Van Ravenswaay (r). 240 **Corbis:** Model of the nuclear powered interplanetary probe sent to Jupiter (cla). **NASA:** JPL-Caltech / University of Arizona (c); JPL-Caltech (cr); KSC (crb). **Science Photo Library:** Ria Novosti (tr). 241 **Corbis:** JPL-Caltech (cb). **ESA:** ATG medialab (tr, cra). **Getty Images:** AFP / Akihiro Ikeshita (tl). **NASA:** JPL (cla); The Johns Hopkins University Applied Physics Laboratory LLC (c). 242 **Corbis:** Richard Cummins (c). **Dorling Kindersley:** Bob Gathany (cl). **NASA:** (crb, clb); (tr). 243 **Dorling Kindersley:** ESA (t). **NASA:** (c, crb). 244-245 **NASA:** Sandra Joseph, Kevin O'Connell. 246 **John Deere:** (bl). 247 **Dorling Kindersley:** Beaulieu National Motor Museum (br). 248-249 **Dorling Kindersley:** Adrian Shooter (b). 249 **Dorling Kindersley:** National Maritime Museum, London (tl). 250 **Dorling Kindersley:** The Tank Museum (br). 251 **Dorling Kindersley:** National Maritime Museum, London (tl). 252 **Dorling Kindersley:** National Maritime Museum, London (tl). 253 **Dorling Kindersley:** The Shuttleworth Collection (tl). 254 **Dorling Kindersley:** Hitachi Rail Europe (bl); Paul Rackham

All other images © Dorling Kindersley
For further information see: www.dkimages.com